P9-DVH-299

undergraduate

LELAND STANFORD JUNIOR UNIVERSITY

ORGANIZED 1891

book fund

contributed by
friends of Stanford

Authors on Film

Authors on Film

edited by Harry M. Geduld

INDIANA UNIVERSITY PRESS
Bloomington and London

COPYRIGHT © 1972 BY INDIANA UNIVERSITY PRESS

ALL RIGHTS RESERVED
No part of this book may be reproduced or utilized
in any form or by any means, electronic or mechanical,
including photocopying and recording, or by any information storage
and retrieval system, without permission in writing from the publisher.
The Association of American University Presses Resolution on
Permissions constitutes the only exception to this prohibition.

Published in Canada by Fitzhenry & Whiteside Limited,
Don Mills, Ontario

Library of Congress catalog card number: 72–75390
ISBN: 0–253–31080–6

Manufactured in the United States of America

For Ron Gottesman

Contents

From Silence to Sound

The Medium and Its Messages

Authors on Screenwriting

The Hollywood Experience

Of Mice and Movie Stars

Foreword

THE INVOLVEMENT OF Author and Film began virtually with the inception of cinema in the 1890s. It is a story of wonderment that gradually becomes disenchantment. The earliest writings in this book chronicle the delight of writers witnessing the birth of a new muse, rejoicing in her magic and her vigor, and heralding her promise for the artists of the twentieth century. But in the later writings we hear, increasingly, the voices of disillusion—disillusion with the medium and what it does to the work of writers, disillusion with the film industry as a willing tool of capitalism, disillusion with the industry's pusillanimous standards, its internal decadence and external puritanism, its prostitution of talent, disillusion with public taste, and ultimately—by implication—with the integrity and value of anything that smacks of mass culture.

To the movie buff and perhaps to the average moviegoer, much of this may sound like sour grapes: the writer's resentment at seeing his art eclipsed in popularity by the new mass media. In fact, there is much evidence to indicate that the creative film-maker has suffered more than the creative writer. Von Stroheim's *Greed*, Eisenstein's *Que Viva Mexico!*, John Huston's *The Red Badge of Courage* exist only in incomplete, mangled states, while writers' works that have been butchered in film adaptations remain inviolate in their original form. For all their complaints about Hollywood's prostitution of the writer, few if any writers have actually been forced onto the Hollywood treadmill, and many of those who damned it have been pleased to pocket the profits without in any way exerting themselves to change the system. Moreover, the Hollywood experience has actually inspired numerous novels (aside from a considerable number of movies). If film adaptations have often violated the letter and spirit of their literary sources, it should not be forgotten that, by way of recompense, countless writers, from Joyce and Virginia Woolf onward, have borrowed and adapted film techniques for use in their own works of fiction. Also, if film has frequently contributed to the debasement of public taste, the fact should not be overlooked that it has sometimes shown itself capable of high art. Curiously, some of the writers represented in this book, among the most sensitive spokesmen for their times, have been most insensitive where film is concerned. Their insensitivity has extended all the way from ignorant intolerance of film techniques to wholesale rejection of the medium on the basis of personal or political prejudices. Yet, repeatedly, one detects an irresistible fascination with what is being attacked, one senses that in spite of his indictments the writer has often cherished a subtle love-hate attitude toward film.

This book will, it is hoped, reveal many aspects of writers' attitudes. Its material is divided into five sections. These simply indicate broad similarities or relationships of subject matter. Some of the pieces will, however, be seen to belong appropriately to more than one section. The first part of the book contains articles, essays and reviews pertaining to the silent cinema and the transition to sound. The second section provides a selection of general statements on the film medium or film-makers and their messages. This is followed by several pieces dealing with the problems, involvements and reflections of the writer as screenwriter. A fourth section is concerned with the Hollywood experience as seen by four American novelists. The book concludes with several pieces, mostly of a lighter nature, about a small galaxy of Hollywood stars.

It must be emphasized that the book is a miscellany. The editor has, quite deliberately, endeavored *not* to select and shape the material in it so as to express some preconceived themes that will satisfy his own rather dubious prejudices. Instead, he has cast his net widely in order to expose as many different aspects as possible of the writer's interest in or involvement with film. He has also ranged from the searching to the superficial, with the conviction—for better or worse—that it is often as revealing to show an author being superficial about one serious subject as to present him being thoughtful and sober about another. Thus the reader must expect to find himself at times more interested in and surprised by who is making a particular statement and what attitudes and level of sophistication are being expressed than in what is actually being commented on.

At this point the editor must stand aside and allow the curtain to be rung up. Any attempt on his part to introduce the reader to the most distinguished array of contributors to any film book yet published would be either superfluous or unpardonably presumptuous.

Harry M. Geduld

ACKNOWLEDGMENTS

My sincere thanks are due to Royal Brown, Judy Turner, and Ulrich Weisstein for their translations; to Larry Schultz for his assistance with copyright problems; to Dorothy Wikelund for her invaluable editorial work on the ms.; to Linda for her prompt and expert typing; to Ron Gottesman and Emily Schenkman for suggesting pieces that I would certainly have overlooked; and to Carolyn whose encouragement was unfailing when it was most needed.

H.M.G.

Part One

From Silence to Sound

Maxim Gorky

The Kingdom of Shadows

A review of the Lumière programme at the Nizhni-Novgorod Fair, as printed in the *Nizhegorodski listok*, newspaper, July 4, 1896, and signed 'I. M. Pacatus' Translated by Leda Swan.

Last night I was in the Kingdom of Shadows.

If you only knew how strange it is to be there. It is a world without sound, without colour. Everything there—the earth, the trees, the people, the water and the air—is dipped in monotonous grey. Grey rays of the sun across the grey sky, grey eyes in grey faces, and the leaves of the trees are ashen grey. It is not life but its shadow, it is not motion but its soundless spectre.

Here I shall try to explain myself, lest I be suspected of madness or indulgence in symbolism. I was at Aumont's and saw Lumière's cinematograph[1]—moving photography. The extraordinary impression it creates is so unique and complex that I doubt my ability to describe it with all its nuances. However, I shall try to convey its fundamentals.

From Jay Leyda, *Kino: A History of the Russian and Soviet Film,* Allen and Unwin, London, 1960, pp. 407–409. Copyright: George Allen and Unwin; reprinted by permission of the copyright-holders. Title supplied.

1. Louis and Auguste Lumière were pioneers of the motion picture. Their Cinématographe was first presented commercially in the Salle au Grand-Café at 14 Boulevard des Capucines, Paris, on December 28th, 1895. It was the first public film show. The Russian première of the Cinématographe occurred on July 7, 1896, at the Peterhof Imperial Palace in St. Petersburg, before Empress Alexandra.

When the lights go out in the room in which Lumière's invention is shown, there suddenly appears on the screen a large grey picture, *A Street in Paris*—shadows of a bad engraving. As you gaze at it, you see carriages, buildings and people in various poses, all frozen into immobility. All this is in grey, and the sky above is also grey—you anticipate nothing new in this all too familiar scene, for you have seen pictures of Paris streets more than once. But suddenly a strange flicker passes through the screen and the picture stirs to life. Carriages coming from somewhere in the perspective of the picture are moving straight at you, into the darkness in which you sit; somewhere from afar people appear and loom larger as they come closer to you; in the foreground children are playing with a dog, bicyclists tear along, and pedestrians cross the street picking their way among the carriages. All this moves, teems with life and, upon approaching the edge of the screen, vanishes somewhere beyond it.

And all this in strange silence where no rumble of the wheels is heard, no sound of footsteps or of speech. Nothing. Not a single note of the intricate symphony that always accompanies the movements of people. Noiselessly, the ashen-grey foliage of the trees sways in the wind, and the grey silhouettes of the people, as though condemned to eternal silence and cruelly punished by being deprived of all the colours of life, glide noiselessly along the grey ground.

Their smiles are lifeless, even though their movements are full of living energy and are so swift as to be almost imperceptible. Their laughter is soundless, although you see the muscles contracting in their grey faces. Before you a life is surging, a life deprived of words and shorn of the living spectrum of colours—the grey, the soundless, the bleak and dismal life.

It is terrifying to see, but it is the movement of shadows, only of shadows. Curses and ghosts, the evil spirits that have cast entire cities into eternal sleep, come to mind and you feel as though Merlin's vicious trick is being enacted before you. As though he had bewitched the entire street, he compressed its many-storied buildings from roof-tops to foundations to yard-like size. He dwarfed the people in corresponding proportion, robbing them of the power of speech and scraping together all the pigment of earth and sky into a monotonous grey colour.

Under this guise he shoved his grotesque creation into a niche in the dark room of a restaurant. Suddenly something clicks, everything vanishes and a train appears on the screen. It speeds straight at you—watch out! It seems as though it will plunge into the darkness in which you sit, turning you into a ripped sack full of lacerated flesh and splintered bones, and crushing into dust and into broken fragments this hall and this building, so full of women, wine, music and vice.

But this, too, is but a train of shadows.

Noiselessly, the locomotive disappears beyond the edge of the screen. The train comes to a stop, and grey figures silently emerge from the cars, soundlessly greet their friends, laugh, walk, run, bustle, and . . . are gone. And here is another picture. Three men seated at the table, playing cards. Their faces are tense, their hands move swiftly. The cupidity of the players is betrayed by the trembling fingers and by the twitching of their facial muscles. They play. . . . Suddenly, they break into laughter, and the waiter who has stopped at their table with beer, laughs too. They laugh until their sides split but not a sound is heard. It seems as if these people have died and their shadows have been condemned to play cards in silence unto eternity. Another picture. A gardener watering flowers. The light grey stream of water, issuing from a hose, breaks into a fine spray. It falls upon the flowerbeds and upon the grass blades weighted down by the water. A boy enters, steps on the hose, and stops the stream, The gardener stares into the nozzle of the hose, whereupon the boy steps back and a stream of water hits the gardener in the face. You imagine the spray will reach you, and you want to shield yourself. But on the screen the gardener has already begun to chase the rascal all over the garden and having caught him, gives him a beating. But the beating is soundless, nor can you hear the gurgle of the water as it gushes from the hose left lying on the ground.

This mute, grey life finally begins to disturb and depress you. It seems as though it carries a warning, fraught with a vague but sinister meaning that makes your heart grow faint. You are forgetting where you are. Strange imaginings invade your mind and your consciousness begins to wane and grow dim. . . .

But suddenly, alongside of you, a gay chatter and a provoking laughter of a woman is heard . . . and you remember that you are at Aumont's, Charles Aumont's. . . . But why of all places should this remarkable invention of Lumière find its way and be demonstrated here, this invention which affirms once again the energy and the curiosity of the human mind, forever striving to solve and grasp all, and . . . while on the way to the solution of the mystery of life, incidentally builds Aumont's fortune? I do not yet see the scientific importance of Lumière's invention but, no doubt, it is there, and it could probably be applied to the general ends of science, that is, of bettering man's life and the developing of his mind. This is not to be found at Aumont's where vice alone is being encouraged and popularized. Why then at Aumont's, among the 'victims of social needs' and among the loafers who here buy their kisses? Why here, of all places, are they showing this latest achievement of science? And soon probably Lumière's invention will be perfected, but in the spirit of Aumont-Toulon and Company.

Besides those pictures I have already mentioned, is featured *The Family Breakfast,* an idyll of three. A young couple with its chubby first-born is seated at the breakfast table. The two are so much in love, and are so charming, gay and happy, and the baby is so amusing. The picture creates a fine, felicitous impression. Has this family scene a place at Aumont's?

And here is still another. Women workers, in a thick, gay and laughing crowd, rush out of the factory gates into the street. This too is out of place at Aumont's. Why remind here of the possibility of a clean, toiling life? This reminder is useless. Under the best of circumstances this picture will only painfully sting the woman who sells her kisses.

I am convinced that these pictures will soon be replaced by others of a genre more suited to the general tone of the *Concert Parisien*. For example, they will show a picture titled: *As She Undresses,* or *Madam at Her Bath,* or *A Woman in Stockings.* They could also depict a sordid squabble between a husband and wife and serve it to the public under the heading of *The Blessings of Family Life.*

Yes, no doubt, this is how it will be done. The bucolic and the idyll could not possibly find their place in Russia's markets thirsting for the piquant and the extravagant. I also could suggest a few themes for development by means of a cinematograph and for the amusement of the market place. For instance: to impale a fashionable parasite upon a picket fence, as is the way of the Turks, photograph him, then show it.

It is not exactly piquant but quite edifying.

Frank Norris

McTeague at the Movies

The party entered and took their places. . . . While waiting they studied their programs. First was an overture by the orchestra, after which came "The Gleasons, in their mirth-moving farce, entitled 'McMonnigal's Courtship.' " . . . After this came a great array of other artists and speciality performers, musical wonders, acrobats, lightning artists, ventriloquists, and last of all, "The feature of the evening, the crowning scientific achievement of the nineteenth century, the kinetoscope." McTeague was excited, dazzled. In five years he had not been twice to the theater. Now he beheld himself inviting his girl and her mother to accompany him. . . .

The kinetoscope fairly took their breaths away.

"What will they do next?" observed Trina in amazement. "Ain't that wonderful, Mac?"

McTeague was awestruck.

"Look at that horse move his head," he cried excitedly, quite carried away. "Look at the cable car coming—and the man going across the street. See, here comes a truck. Well, I never in all my life! What would Marcus say to this?"

"It's a drick!" exclaimed Mrs. Sieppe with sudden conviction. "I ain't no fool; dot's nothun but a drick."

From Frank Norris, *McTeague: A Story of San Francisco,* 1899. Title supplied. McTeague presumably saw the Vitagraph or the Lumière Cinématographe—not the Kinetoscope. The Kinetoscope was a peep-show machine—which could be viewed by only one person at a time.

"Well, of course, Mamma," exclaimed Trina; "it's—"

But Mrs. Sieppe put her head in the air. "I'm too old to be fooled," she persisted. "It's a drick." Nothing more could be got out of her than this. . . .

On their way home they discussed the performance. . . .

"Wasn't—wasn't that magic lantern wonderful, where the figures moved? Wonderful—ah, wonderful!"

Leo Tolstoy

It May Turn Out To Be a Powerful Thing*

"You will see that this little clicking contraption with the revolving handle will make a revolution in our life—in the life of writers. It is a direct attack on the old methods of literary art. We shall have to adapt ourselves to the shadowy screen and to the cold machine. A new form of writing will be necessary. I have thought of that and I can feel what is coming.

"But I rather like it. This swift change of scene, this blending of emotion and experience—it is much better than the heavy, long-drawn-out kind of writing to which we are accustomed. It is closer to life. In life, too, changes and transitions flash by before our eyes, and emotions of the soul are like a hurricane. The cinema has divined the mystery of motion. And that is greatness.

"When I was writing *The Living Corpse,* I tore my hair and chewed my fingers because I could not give enough scenes, enough pictures, because I could not pass rapidly enough from one event to another. The accursed stage was like a halter choking the throat of the dramatist; and I had to cut the life and swing of the work according to the dimensions and requirements of the stage. I remember when I was told that some clever person had devised a scheme for a revolving stage, on which a

From Jay Leyda, *Kino: A History of the Russian and Soviet Film,* Allen and Unwin, London, 1960, pp. 410–411. Translated by David Bernstein. Title supplied. Copyright: George Allen and Unwin; reprinted by permission of the copyright-holders.

number of scenes could be prepared in advance. I rejoiced like a child, and allowed myself to write ten scenes into my play. Even then I was afraid the play would be killed.

"But the films! They are wonderful! Drr! and a scene is ready! Drr! and we have another! We have the sea, the coast, the city, the palace—and in the palace there is tragedy (there is always tragedy in palaces, as we see in Shakespeare).

"I am seriously thinking of writing a play for the screen. I have a subject for it. It is a terrible and bloody theme. I am not afraid of bloody themes. Take Homer or the Bible, for instance. How many bloodthirsty passages there are in them— murders, wars. And yet these are the sacred books, and they ennoble and uplift the people. It is not the subject itself that is so terrible. It is the propagation of bloodshed, and the justification for it, that is really terrible! Some friends of mine returned from Kursk recently and told me a shocking incident. It is a story for the films. You couldn't write it in fiction or for the stage. But on the screen it would be good. Listen—it may turn out to be a powerful thing!"

And Lev Tolstoy related the story in detail. He was deeply agitated as he spoke. But he never developed the theme in writing. Tolstoy was always like that. When he was inspired by a story he had been thinking of, he would become excited by its possibilities. If some one happened to be near by, he would unfold the plot in all its details. Then he would forget all about it. Once the gestation was over and his brain-child born, Tolstoy would seldom bother to write about it.

Some one spoke of the domination of the films by business men interested only in profits. "Yes, I know, I've been told about that before," Tolstoy replied. "The films have fallen into the clutches of business men and art is weeping! But where aren't there business men?" And he proceeded to relate one of those delightful little parables for which he is famous.

"A little while ago I was standing on the banks of our pond.

It was noon of a hot day, and butterflies of all colours and sizes were circling around, bathing and darting in the sunlight, fluttering among the flowers through their short—their very short—lives, for with the setting of the sun they would die.

"But there on the shore near the reeds I saw an insect with little lavender spots on its wings. It, too, was circling around. It would flutter about, obstinately, and its circles became smaller and smaller. I glanced over there. In among the reeds sat a great green toad with staring eyes on each side of his flat head, breathing quickly with his greenish-white, glistening throat. The toad did not look at the butterfly, but the butterfly kept flying over him as though she wished to be seen. What happened? The toad looked up, opened his mouth wide and—remarkable!—the butterfly flew in of her own accord! The toad snapped his jaws shut quickly, and the butterfly disappeared.

"Then I remembered that thus the insect reaches the stomach of the toad, leaves its seed there to develop and again appear on God's earth, become a larva, a chrysalis. The chrysalis becomes a caterpillar, and out of the caterpillar springs a new butterfly. And then the playing in the sun, the bathing in the light, and the creating of new life, begin all over again.

"Thus it is with the cinema. In the reeds of film art sits the toad—the business man. Above him hovers the insect—the artist. A glance, and the jaws of the business man devour the artist. But that doesn't mean destruction. It is only one of the methods of procreation, or propagating the race; in the belly of the business man is carried on the process of impregnation and the development of the seeds of the future. These seeds will come out on God's earth and will begin their beautiful, brilliant lives all over again."[1]

1. Madame Alexandra Tolstaya warns me that there are several aspects of this record that make it suspect as a record, but that it incorporates remarks that Tolstoy may have made, either to Teneromo or others—but not on his eightieth birthday. [Jay Leyda's note.]

Upton Sinclair

Nickelodeons and Common Shows

In 1894 Thomas Edison had invented a device which he called a "kinetoscope." Out at his place in East Orange he had spent the enormous sum of $25,000 upon experiments, and had built a shanty covered with tar paper and known to his friends as "the Black Maria." Inside this Black Maria was a huge device weighing more than a ton, a camera with a rapidly moving shutter by which you could take a series of pictures of something in motion—provided that its motion didn't carry it away from the front of the camera. To this place came pugilists and acrobats and dancers, and they performed in front of the camera, and so there began to spring up in the cities places called nickelodeons, a sort of arcade with a row of machines having eye-pieces. You dropped a nickel into the slot and gazed into the eye-pieces, and you saw as real as life the pugilists boxing and the acrobats turning somersaults and the dancers kicking up their skirts.

Then several years later appeared another device generally called the "vitagraph" or the "bioscope," which threw these same images upon a screen. The camera weighed somewhat less than a ton now, and it could be taken on a truck and placed, say by a railroad track, and so you could see the Twentieth Century Limited emerging from a tunnel and rushing down upon you. I well remember seeing the first pictures in a place called the

Excerpted from *Upton Sinclair Presents William Fox* (1933). By permission of Mr. David Sinclair.

Eden Musee on Twenty-third Street in New York. There were waxworks and all sorts of horrors—President Garfield being shot, and the Chicago anarchists making bombs, and a policeman who looked so lifelike that you went up and asked him the way to the labyrinth of mirrors or whatever delightful thrill you were seeking. Then you went into a little court with palm and rubber trees, and sat in rows of chairs, and there was the image of the Twentieth Century Limited. It trembled and jumped so that it almost put your eyes out, but nevertheless it was so real that you could hardly keep from ducking out of the way as it bore down upon you. A tremendous adventure!

It happened that on Fourteenth Street there was a place called the "Automat," with phonographs, punching bags, weighing machines, chewing-gum machines and, of course, kinetoscopes. The Automat was one of the sights of the town, because no employees were needed, only a watchman. You dropped your nickels into the machines, and down in the basement there was a track running under the machines and a little car running on the track, and as it passed, the machines spilled their nickels into it, and then the car ran around to the other side of the room and dumped the nickels into a funnel, from the other end of which they emerged, all counted and wrapped and ready for deposit in the bank. It was almost as marvelous as the Chicago stock-yards, where a hog was dropped into the machine at one end, and sausages and buttons and hair-combs came out at the other end.

The Automat pleased W[illiam] F[ox][1] and he made it known that he was in the market to buy an establishment of that sort. Soon there came an agent suggesting that there was one at 700 Broadway, Brooklyn, owned by a man named J. Stewart Blackton, then president of the Vitagraph Company of America, and destined to become one of the big moving picture million-

1. William Fox (1879–1952), founding father of the American film industry: the "Fox" in 20th Century-Fox.

aires. W. F. made an appointment to inspect the property, and he tells this story:

"When I went there, by appointment, there was a large crowd. When I went again a little later in the week, also by appointment, there was an even larger crowd. I thought it was a good thing, and after certain negotiations, I bought the establishment. I took charge of it on the following Monday, and only about two persons dropped in all day. I realized that someone had supplied the crowd on the two former occasions when I had gone to see the place. This was somewhere around in May, and I was told that business was always bad in summer."

I asked W. F. to describe the agent who had sold him that "salted" gold mine. The answer was: "He was the handsomest man you ever saw; well built, well dressed and always immaculate." Sometime afterwards, it appears, he came to W. F. and said he was broke, and borrowed $50 to go out West. Twenty years later, in a brokers' board-room, he recognized his old-time victim, and came up and introduced himself, and repaid the $50. The story he told was that he had discovered land containing sulphur, and had come back and sold it to New York capitalists, and was now worth $7,000,000. He offered his old-time victim a tip, to buy the stock of the Texas Gulf and Sulphur Company; in a year or two the buyer would make millions. W. F., having bought a "salted" gold-mine from this man, declined to buy a "salted" sulphur-mine. The joke of the story is that the tip was a real one, for the stock went from $40 a share to $240.

But let us return to No. 700 Broadway, Brooklyn, in the year 1903. . . . How was the crowd to be induced to enter the Fox Automat? Quite recently he had attended a showing of the new "moving pictures"; he had seen a picture of a tree, and the leaves of the tree had moved, and the man behind him had said that it was a trick, someone was shaking the curtain. But W. F., with his inquiring mind, had talked to the operator after the performance was over, and asked to have the trick explained. No, the screen had not been shaken; the pictures actually did move of themselves. The operator showed the film, which was nearly three times as wide as it is now, and did not run on sprockets, but merely through a groove. The length of the film was then 100 feet.

W. F. investigated further. He saw the pictures of the Twentieth Century Limited, and a still more marvelous production, a little story told in front of the camera, called *The Life of an American Fireman*[2]; then another one, still more thrilling, *The Great Train Robbery*.[3] He saw the public pouring in to witness these spectacles, and he examined the premises he had rented and noted that there were rooms upstairs used as a dwelling. It occurred to him that he might rent these premises also, and put out the tenants and turn it into a showroom for the new picture stories. If he took the people up by the front stairway, and after the show sent them down by the rear stairway, they would enter the nickelodeon at the rear and have to walk past all the machines, and very probably they would drop some nickels on the way.

With W. F. a thing is done almost as soon as he thinks of it. There was a show room with a screen, and 146 chairs, and some display posters outside informing the public that moving pictures were to be seen. But alas, the Brooklyn public didn't know what moving pictures were, and nobody went upstairs. W. F. stood outside for a whole day, gazing anxiously at the public, and regretting that he had no personal charms to lure them into his establishment.

But then came a man who had the necessary charms. W. F. describes him as a fellow with a great big Western hat. He said: "What are you worrying about?" and W. F. told his troubles. He had the greater part of his fortune in the place, and it wasn't

2. Directed by Edwin S. Porter, 1902.
3. Directed by Edwin S. Porter, 1903.

so much the fortune as that he hated to fail. The fellow offered to take charge of it and run it, and told him to shut up the place that day and come back the next.

The next day he came, and had with him a coin-manipulator, a sword-swallower and a fire-eater—which did W. F. prefer? W. F. carried no fire insurance, so fire-eaters were ruled out; also swallowing swords might possibly be dangerous—there might be employers' liability laws. But there could be no harm in a coin-manipulator. He was a little fellow, dressed in black satin breeches and a black satin coat, wearing a black mustache and a little black goatee, neither of which belonged to him. All this was in imitation of "Hermann the Great." He set up his table and started to work in the doorway of the establishment; and when the crowd gathered, he told them that he would finish the performance upstairs, and show them yet more wonderful tricks, and that admission was free for the present. The crowd came trooping up, and there they found out what moving pictures were, and in a week there was such a crowd that the police had to be called in to control them.

So at last W. F. had found a real gold mine! Here was the way of fortune plain before him, and his one task was to get there ahead of the others. He got two friends to join him, and began renting stores on the crowded avenues of Brooklyn, and in each one of them they set up a screen and a projection machine and rows of chairs—of which the total must not exceed 299. Up to that limit you could have a "common show" license; but if you had 300 chairs or more, you were a theatre, and the fire laws took strict charge of you.

So presently here was William Fox with fifteen show places in Brooklyn and New York. I made him search his memory for all the details about those old-time pictures. There was one called *The Automobile Thieves*. Automobiles were then just coming into fashion, and some producer had conceived the idea of a new way of stealing. Soon after this someone did actually steal an automobile, and was arrested, and there was a great clamor in the newspapers—this new device of moving pictures was corrupting public morals and stimulating crime! The New York *World,* which built up its circulation by carrying on crusades, started a crusade against moving pictures.

Also there was one called *The Runaway Wagon.* This was a trick picture. It wasn't an automobile, merely a wagon, yet it went running up and down hill all by itself. The trick was that the photographer had blotted out the horse. A still trickier one was a man putting on a pair of shoes and the shoes lacing themselves.

The names of the companies that made the pictures were Vitagraph, Biograph, Lubin, Pathé, and Essanay.

The clamor against these pictures continued in the newspapers. In court the lawyer would say: "Your Honor, this child never stole before. He saw stealing in a moving picture and that suggested it to him." This clamor disturbed the associates of W. F., whose wives thought they were in a disreputable business. So W. F. bought them out, and added more places until he had twenty-five. He had his own ideas about the moral effect of pictures, for he noticed that wherever the shows were going well, the business of saloons began to dwindle.

"My conclusion was that the workingman's wage was not large enough to buy tickets to the theatre for himself and family, so he found his recreation in drinking his glass of beer against the bar. But when the motion picture theatre came, he could buy a ticket for 10 cents, and for his wife the same, and if he had a child he could buy a ticket for 5 cents. They could be entertained anywhere from two and a half to three hours, and the man found he was getting a much bigger kick holding his kid's hand, or the hand of his wife, than he would be getting from his drink at the bar. I have always contended that if we had never had prohibition, the motion pictures would have wiped out the saloon. We then opened a theatre at 110th and

Broadway. On the corner of this property was a saloon and we tried to buy the lease of the owner but he wouldn't sell. Within a year after that theatre opened, he could not get enough business to pay his rent."

W. F. went on to tell me of a later experience when he leased the Star Theatre, on Lexington Avenue near 107th Street, which had been used for melodrama. They were then called "ten-twenty-thirts." On the four corners of 107th Street there were four saloons, frequently called "gin-mills," but after this theater was converted into a moving picture theatre, one after another the gin-mills closed up, and within two or three months were occupied by other tenants.

Not since the days of the forty-niners had there been such a way for the little fellow to get rich as in this new business. Everything depended upon a location where the crowds were passing. W. F. found that in order to get the right location, it would often pay him to lease the whole building—even though the fire laws required that the upstairs tenants be turned out before moving pictures were shown in the building.

He conceived the idea of combining motion pictures and vaudeville, with the admission price of 10 cents to any seat in the house. He tried in each case to find a manager who had a good voice, and this manager would sing what were called illustrated songs. It was easy to get new songs, because the song writers wanted them popularized before the sheet music was offered to the public. The manager would sing the song and there would be lantern slides with pictures illustrating the songs. The audience would be invited to join the singing—the more the merrier. There was always a line of people waiting to get into these shows. The problem was to rent new places ahead of the other fellow. Here is the story of the first Fox theatre:

"It was located at 194 Grand Street, Brooklyn, and had been devoted to burlesque. When I went to visit the premises, it was winter and the agent told me to bring along rubber boots. I did, and we walked in snow and water up to the knees; the roof was practically gone and it was the most dilapidated structure I ever saw. When I inquired as to how the building came to be in such a deplorable condition, the agent explained that the building was fifty years old and had been unoccupied for two years. He told me that the man who owned the mortgage had it now. It was known as the Bum Theatre and I changed the name to Comedy. I think I paid about $20,000 for the land and building.

"While making extensive repairs, there arose the necessity of a campaign to acquaint the people of the neighborhood that this was to be a theatre for nice people. We made a list of 10,000 names of people living in that vicinity, and for ten weeks we sent them a weekly letter, telling them how this building was progressing. The tenth letter quoted someone as saying that the theatre had been called the 'Bum' because the people around there were bums. I suggested that perhaps those who resented this reference would like to form a parade in the main street of town the night my theatre opened. That night there were 10,000 people in that parade. The theatre did a terrific business, and in a short space of time we paid off the mortgage and declared hundreds of thousands of dollars of dividends."

The next theatre was the Folly, a place which had been showing melodramas and not doing so well. W. F. went to see a member of the firm, Richard Hyde, who offered the theatre on a ten-year lease for $35,000 a year, and required a deposit of half a year's rent to apply to the last half year. He said he would give W. F. twenty-four hours in which to make a decision. He offered to put this option into writing, but W. F. said he would take his word. The option was to expire at noon, and W. F. was on hand at 10 o'clock with a certified check in his pocket. But meanwhile, it happened some other motion picture concern had got wind of the matter, and had made Hyde an offer of $10,000 more for the lease. Apparently it was Hyde's idea that if he could keep Fox pre-occupied until after 12 o'clock, the deal would be off. So he started telling stories, and he told one after another without stopping until 11:15. Then W. F. broke in:

"Just a minute. I wish to give you an answer. I accept your terms and here is the check."

Hyde seemed troubled, and became solicitous concerning the welfare of his would-be tenant. "You had better not be hasty," he said, "but listen to a man who has been in the business for half a century."

Hyde called his bookkeeper and ordered him to tell W. F. the exact truth about the property. Said the bookkeeper: "Last year we took a loss of $7,500."

Said W. F.: "I am not interested in all that, because the policy I am going to use in the theatre is not the same as yours, and I think I can make a go of it."

Said Hyde: "Darn your soul, I dislike you! You are the first man who has taken my word in the last twenty-five years. I am known as a man who never keeps his word." So Hyde told him about the offer of $10,000 more. In closing the deal, he made only one request: "Wherever you get a chance to talk, be sure to tell people I kept my word with you."

This theatre held about 2,000 chairs, and the performance lasted two hours, with five performances a day. It was a tremendous success, and during the first ten years of the lease, it earned from five to six hundred thousand dollars in profit. At the expiration of this lease, Hyde was dead, and the sons renewed the lease to W. F., because they said: "If father were alive, he would want you to have that theatre."

W. F. realized that the people who were leasing the films to him were making more money than he was. So he began to buy films, and became president of a concern called "The Greater New York Film Rental Company." Two years later the manufacturers decided to form a trust, and set up a company known as "The Motion Picture Patents Company," and claimed that they owned all the patents used in motion pictures. All the manufacturers had to have licenses, and nobody could get films anywhere but from them. It was like the old days of the Beef Trust and the butcher stores. They set out to get possession of the business from top to bottom. They would offer to buy you out, and if you refused to sell, they would cancel your license. They had 120 licensees in America, and in a short time, 119 of them had been either bought out or forced out. The only one left was William Fox, by this time thirty years of age.

This was the greatest battle of his life so far, and he is proud of the service he rendered to the motion picture industry. At that time it was completely throttled. The trust fixed all the prices everywhere. The highest price paid for a scenario was $62.50. No writer's name ever appeared upon the screen, because they did not want anyone to become popular, and so have a chance to raise his price. Of course no writer of talent was going to work on that basis. The salaries of the actors were correspondingly low, and no actor's name ever appeared upon the screen. So long as these conditions continued, motion pictures could make no progress whatever.

The representatives of the trust sent for W. F., and I will let him tell the story of what happened:

"They said: 'We have been very kind to you. We have allowed you to make a large profit for the last two years by leaving you to the last. Now we have to get you out of the way—how much do you want for your plant?' I told them I wanted $750,000. They asked me if I thought that that was what I was going to get, and I told them yes. They told me to think it over and come back later. I came back the next day and still quoted $750,000. Then they told me they had decided to cancel my license. The next day there came a cancellation of my license in the mail."

They had a charge against W. F., whereby they justified their decision to cancel his license. They charged that he had permitted their motion pictures to be shown in a house of prostitution in Hoboken. W. F. tells a curious story about this which illustrates the method of monopolies, not merely in the moving picture industry, but in all others that I have investigated. It appears that W. F.'s concern was supplying pictures to an exhibitor in Paterson, New Jersey, and after the show the operator would bring the films back to New York and get the material for the next day's show. It appeared that the trust had bribed this operator to take the films each night after the show to a house of prostitution in Hoboken, and the trust had caused a projection machine to be set up in this place and had run the films.

Under the terms of his contract with the trust, they had been obliged to give him fourteen days' notice before stopping the supplies of films, and he used that period to play a shrewd trick upon them. He says:

"I went back and suggested that they tell me how much they would give me for my establishment. They said $75,000. I sold it. Then I said, 'Now you have cancelled my license. I think you ought to reinstate the license, so that you have an active business when you take it over and not a pile of junk.' They thought that was a good idea, and the next day I got a letter reinstating the license. A couple days after that I said I did not want to sell out, and I got another cancellation. I then had grounds, and began a legal action under the Sherman Antitrust Act."

This controversy began in 1908 and was carried to the Court of Appeals of New York State, and was not settled until 1912.

"If successful, we were to get triple damages. We were suing for $600,000 dollars and if successful, it meant $1,800,000. One evening about 8 o'clock a man called and said that the other people were offering to settle out of court. While the decision was due soon, my lawyer thought we should settle out of court, as there was no assurance that the decision would be in our favor. We drew the settlement papers that night, working until 6 o'clock the next morning, and they paid me $350,000. The next day it was announced that the case had been settled. The judge told my lawyer that we should have waited, because they were in unanimous agreement that the judgment was to be in my favor."

This was a suit for damages, not selling. W. F. got his money, and he still had his company and the right to do business. The manufacturers were not permitted to cancel the license, and were compelled to market their films to William Fox at the same prices as to their own company.

The result of this campaign was to put the film trust out of business. Anyone could make pictures, and many began to do so. Under competitive conditions, writers and actors could ask higher prices for their work, and could demand that their names be advertised; so reputations could be built up and talent developed. An odd circumstance is that the men who had organized the trust were unable to meet this new competition, and within five years none of those who had fought William Fox were any longer in the business.

All these four years W. F. had been going ahead with the leasing, buying and building of theatres, and turning them into motion picture "palaces." When you were running a regular theatrical production, you had as a rule only one company, and drew your audience from all over the city. But for these 10-cent theatres, you drew the people of the neighborhood, and since you could make hundreds of prints of the film, you could have a theatre in every neighborhood; you could have a chain of theatres all over New York and Brooklyn and the suburbs—it was a series of gold mines, and the deeper you dug into these mines, the richer became the vein. The quality of the films became better, and a better class of people would come to see them. It became possible to have real "palaces"; to spend money on theatre decorations, and charge 15 cents, 25 cents, even 50 cents admission.

In the case of the City Theatre, Fourteenth Street between Third and Fourth avenues, W. F. put in one-fourth of the money; two-fourths of the remaining interest were taken by the two Timothy Sullivans, prominent leaders of Tammany Hall, known as "Big Tim" and "Little Tim." The total amount invested was $100,000, and the building was to cost $300,000. Big Tim produced a contractor who offered to do the rest of the financing, taking 50 per cent of his money in cash each month, and taking a six months' note for the other 50 per cent, agreeing to renew these notes for an additional six months. In this way the theatre would be making money before the first of the notes became due.

The work proceeded, and at the end of the first six months there was a note for $10,000 falling due at the Colonial Bank. W. F. received a notice from the bank, and set out to find Mahoney, the contractor, and take him to the bank to renew the note. For days W. F. hunted for Mahoney but Mahoney could not be found. Then W. F. went to Big Tim, who saw no reason to worry; it was Mahoney's problem, not Tim's. W. F. couldn't understand this attitude, but realized after a while that Big Tim was accustomed to signing notes quite freely; it meant no more to him than slapping somebody on the back; it was part of his stock in trade as a politician. Nobody who wanted to go on doing business in New York City would ever dream of suing Big Tim Sullivan on a note.

But it was different with a little fellow like William Fox. He had never had a note go to protest, and it seemed to him the most terrible thing in his whole life. For a week before the note was due, he worried Big Tim, but in vain. Then he went to the Colonial Bank and presented himself to the president, Mr. Walker. W. F. laid $2,500 upon the banker's desk and asked the banker to release him from his share of the obligation. But Walker couldn't see it that way. Under the law, each of the signers was responsible for the full amount. As for W. F.'s statement that Mahoney had agreed to renew the note, Walker said he didn't want to know anything about that. Probably he thought it was just a bluff. Anyhow, he refused to take the $2,500, and when W. F. insisted, he brushed it onto the floor, and when W. F. went on insisting, he pressed a button, and a man in a gray uniform appeared and gently escorted the protestor to the door.

W. F. had until 3 o'clock that afternoon to save his good name, and he was in a terrible state. He called Walker on the telephone and heard him hang up the receiver. Then he waited outside the building, hoping that Walker would come out to lunch, but 1 o'clock came, and W. F. saw a tray carried in, and, peering through a window of the bank, he saw Walker seated at his desk eating his lunch.

"Then I noticed him light his pipe. I have always known that a man with a full stomach is in a better humor than with an empty. Back to Walker's office I went, and my presence caused the man to go into a convulsion. He yelled, 'Get out!' and this time two men came in and just threw me out. Mr. Walker could see me from the window standing outside, because from time to time I would rap on the window to let him know I was there. Finally I saw the clock hands turn to three. I had endorsed this note in good faith and it was to be protested. I knew of no humiliation in my whole career greater than at 3 o'clock that day."

But it turned out all right, as Mahoney appeared the next day, and the note was renewed, and the City Theatre was completed, and opened with the *Zeigfeld Follies of 1910*. It was a loss from the beginning, and presently the theatre was closed, and W. F. leased it from his associates for $75,000 a year, and put moving pictures into it, and it has been making a profit of $45,000 a year ever since.

There is another story having to do with this president of the Colonial Bank; and W. F. laid stress upon this story, saying: "I want you to see that there is a difference in bankers."

W. F. thinks that a banker is all right when he is really a banker, and the trouble only begins when he ceases to be a banker, and becomes a speculator and promoter, or a conspirator and bandit. Throughout this period of his career, W. F. dealt with bankers, who looked into his business affairs, judged his character, and loaned him money with which to buy and rent new theatres, or to put up new buildings. If the buildings cost a little more than was expected, or if it took a little longer to finish them, they cheerfully renewed his notes, and in due course he opened his theatres, and the public came pouring into them, and he paid off his notes at the banks with the agreed amount of interest. That is W. F.'s conception of what banking should be, and if all the bankers had been like that, he would never have come to Upton Sinclair to write the story of his career.

Late in 1912 and early in 1913, W. F. conceived the idea of larger and more beautiful houses for the new motion picture art. One was to be the Audubon, on Broadway near 165th Street, and the other was to be on Tremont Avenue in the Bronx. He had at this time half a million dollars in cash, and this was to be the largest venture of his career. There were to be stores in connection with the theatres, and when the construction was half completed, it was found that the cost would be nearly twice as much as had been expected. Money was very tight at this time, and W. F. found himself chasing about the city trying to borrow some. It was the story of the sandwiches and pretzels and buffalo pans all over again—if he couldn't find the money, he would lose the buildings. Let him tell the story himself:

"One day while I was in this quandary, trying to see or find a way out, the man who had the plaster contract of these buildings called on me. He told me he was in trouble and that I could help him out. You can imagine my feelings as I realized that he must have come for his money. He said: 'I know I haven't any right to ask you to pay me in advance, but if you could give me a note for four months instead of paying me on the fifteenth, I would be very grateful.' What a load fell from my shoulders at his words! Of course I gave him the note and he gave me the receipted bill. It seemed that he must have spread the word around because one by one the contractors called and asked for notes. The same thing occurred every month until the buildings were completed and opened, which was inside of four months, and before the first payment came due on these notes.

"One day one of the contractors asked if I knew Mr. Walker, the president of the Colonial Bank, and if I had ever done any business with him. I told him I was sorry to admit I had not been successful in my attempt to do business with him. He suggested that I go around to the bank and see him, and he would say no more. I was mystified. I called on Mr. Walker. He remembered me and asked how I was getting along. I told him the whole story. He said, 'Then you have no worries.' I said, 'Yes, I have, as the first notes are soon due, and I am no better off now than the day I gave them as the theatres are only just opened.' He rang the bell (not the same bell he rang on the previous occasion to have me thrown out) and a young man brought in an envelope. He said: 'Here are $250,000 worth of those notes. The other $150,000 worth are with the Nassau Bank. I knew you were in trouble and sent those contractors to you.' When I asked him why he had done that, he replied: 'I became interested in you that day three years ago when you put up such a battle to keep your name from going to protest. Now it happens that I live across the street from the Audubon

Theatre and early every morning during its construction I could see you from my window watching the work in progress, and it made me dizzy to see you climbing around on the scaffolding. And many nights I saw your white roadster circling the property. I felt that a man so zealous of his good name and so untiring and conscientious in his endeavors was a good risk and a good investment. Take your time and pay it back when convenient.'

"Within a year after that I had paid that debt all off. One of those places opened Thanksgiving Eve and the other a few days before Christmas in 1913."

UPTON SINCLAIR
Over the Hill

I asked W[illiam] F[ox] about the authors he had dealt with in those early days, but he couldn't remember that he had ever met one; he rarely met them at any time. The purchases were made through agents. For *Life's Shop Window* $100 was paid. Later on prices rose. After some effort W. F. remembered an author—"Oh, yes, I met Zane Grey. We bought half a dozen of his stories. I don't remember that he made any impression on me. He seemed to be a nice sort of a man."

You can see how little the author was needed by one curious tale which W. F. tells me. "Some other film concern made a motion picture, using a musical comedy star by the name of

Excerpted from *Upton Sinclair Presents William Fox* (1933). By permission of Mr. David Sinclair.

Josie Collins. When the picture was completed, it was terrible, and there was no possible market for it. It so happened that just at this time Fox Film was behind on its schedule and in great need of a picture. Here was a chance to buy one at a bargain, so they bought it and cut it to pieces, and reconstructed it, making an entirely different story without an additional scene being shot. The aunts became grandmothers, the grandmothers became friends, and if anything was missing, we filled in the gaps with titles. It was previewed, and the trade papers all agreed that it was a fine picture. It was a success."

I asked about the movie stars and how they were made, which brought a very interesting story to mind:

"Before making *A Fool There Was*,[1] I consulted Robert Hilliard, who had produced it on the stage and played the leading role for years. He said, 'In my experience, I have had to change my leading lady six times. As soon as one scored a tremendous hit in the part, she believed herself to be a Sarah Bernhardt and became unmanageable, and I had to let her go. My advice would be to put the girl you choose under contract, as the part will make her.' We made a test of a girl called Theodosia Goodman, who had no theatrical experience, and decided she would do. She was the daughter of a tailor in Cincinnati. Miss Goodman gave a very remarkable performance in this picture; and then came our problem. If we were going to continue her services, the name didn't have quite the theatrical feeling, and we must find a stage name for her.

"One day it was conceived in our publicity department that we had had every type of woman on the screen except an Arabian; our publicity director felt that the public would like an Arabian. He conceived the story that this Miss Goodman was born in Arabia—her father was an Arab and her mother

1. *A Fool There Was* (1915) directed by Frank Powell; based on the play by Porter Emerson Browne which was originally suggested by Rudyard Kipling's poem, "The Vampire." The term "Vamp" originated with this movie.

a French woman who had played the theatres in Paris. So we took 'Arab,' and spelling it backwards, made it 'Bara,' and shortened the first name 'Theodosia' to 'Theda' and thus the name 'Theda Bara.' Then the director said, 'Now let's not settle on this until we see if it will go over. Let me invite the newspapers to an interview and see if they will swallow this.'"

"He dressed her in the regular Arabian costume, and surrounded her with the proper atmosphere, and then the newspaper boys all came in. He said, 'I want you to meet Miss Bara,' and gave them her history. He said she didn't speak a word of English. The newspaper men left that day and said that the Fox Film Corporation had discovered the greatest living actress in the world. At first when we would want to attract the attention of Miss Goodman, we would call her 'Miss Bara,' and she would not pay any attention. But after a short time she became used to it, and took to the name perfectly, and she still retains it. Miss Bara got $75 a week for her first picture, and when her contract expired, we were paying her $4,000 a week."

And here is a story of genius and temperament. There was a Broadway favorite by the name of Valeska Suratt. She had the reputation that whenever she got angry, she walked out and wouldn't appear at the studio to finish her picture; so W. F., as a precaution, took the last part of the picture first. There was a scene in a gambling house, and then a scene in which the leading lady fell downstairs. Next she was required to go up to Sing Sing and there encounter a prisoner who had once stabbed her. (They lived a varied and exciting career, the movie stars of that early decade.) Miss Suratt was supposed to be happy at the idea that the prisoner in Sing Sing prison was chopping stones into small pieces. She was supposed to sneer at him, but she said to the director, "I can do anything but sneer at a prisoner. I will laugh at him, but I will not sneer." There was an argument, and in the end Miss Suratt said that she would go home from Sing Sing, and home she went.

They heard no more from her, so W. F. decided that they would put out the picture as it was, and it was so announced. Then Miss Suratt came to his office.

"What is this rubbish about this picture being released?"

W. F. assured her that it was a very good picture indeed.

"But there is no ending to the picture!"

"Oh, yes," said W. F., "don't you remember where you rolled down the flight of stairs from the gambling house? The camera photographed you as you lay on the ground, and we have now put in the title, 'And poor Suratt died from this fall.' "

Then W. F. told her that the director had written in some more scenes. The next scene showed a hearse in front of an old house. There were four dirty bums carrying a coffin, and the hearse proceeded down Broadway with the director running ahead with a megaphone yelling, "In this hearse lies Miss Suratt." He went on to describe a scene in the cemetery, where-upon the actress burst out laughing and gave up. She came back, and from that time on never failed to appear on time at the studio.

In the early days the studio was out on Staten Island, and the "rushes" were brought in every day. Later the studio was moved into New York, and in 1916 the production part of the enterprise was moved to Hollywood. On W. F.'s first visit to the studio at the coast, he noticed a man leaning up against a lamp post in front of the door, wearing a very loud cowboy costume.

He says: "Every morning for a week this same figure was waiting, always in a different costume, each one louder than the last, until my curiosity was aroused. One day he approached me and said: 'My name is Tom Mix. I made up my mind I wouldn't work for any other company until I saw you, Mr. Fox.'

"He was a very picturesque figure and I interviewed him and decided to engage him. When the subject of salary was broached, he said that the thing he was interested in was the provision for the care and feeding of his horses. We agreed on $350 a week, including feed and stables for his horses. When his last contract expired, we were paying him $7,500 a week. His first pictures were two-reelers and the audience liked them. And though Tom became the hero to the youth of the nation, the interesting thing about him is that he never changed. He was with our company for ten years or more, and to me he was no different when he got $7,500 a week than when he was getting $350."

I think the production of which W. F. is proudest is the picture called *Over the Hill,* produced about 1920.[2] This picture had no stars. It cost $100,000 to make, and netted over $3,000,000—which is very high praise for a picture. The story was W. F.'s own idea, and started when he heard a young man recite Will Carleton's poem "Over the Hill to the Poor House." The poem made a sensation, and W. F. was led to read this volume. He was always on the lookout for plots, and this poem brought to mind all the old people left in institutions through the neglect of thoughtless and selfish children.

A short time after, Mrs. Fox asked him to do her a favor. An old man had appealed to her to get him into a home. He was seventy-five years old, in broken health and great need and without a friend or relative in the world. W. F. went to see Jacob Schiff about it, and told him the sad story. A few days later Schiff sent for W. F. and, to the latter's great embarrassment, reported the result of an investigation: the old man had six children, several of them well-to-do. W. F. brought the report back to his wife, and naturally was much annoyed.

2. *Over the Hill to the Poor House* (1920) directed by Harry Millarde; starred Mary Carr, William Welch, and John Walker. *The New York Times* reviewer commented (Sept. 18, 1920): "Seldom has a motion picture been so deliberately sentimental as this one. Its assault upon the emotions is undisguised and sweeping. It is ruthless in its mass attack. . . . It does a wholesale business in the theatrical commodities of mother-love, filial nobility, the ungratefulness of children . . . and so on."

A month passed, and Mrs. Fox told her husband the sequel to the story. She had written to each of those six sons and daughters, inviting them to her home on a certain evening. They all came. There were six brothers and sisters meeting one another after long separation, and naturally they wondered what it was about. Said Mrs. Fox:

"I am confronted with a grave problem concerning a worthy old man seventy-five years of age, who appealed to me for help and begged that I provide a home for him, as he hadn't a soul to turn to. In my efforts to have him admitted to a home, I find he has four sons and two daughters." At this point one of the girls was crying with embarrassment and said she knew Mrs. Fox was referring to their father. This daughter had lost her husband and the others agreed to contribute money so that the old man could live with her. They all agreed to send their remittances to Mrs. Fox, so that she could be sure the plan would be carried out.

So the story started in the mind of W. F. He worked it out himself. He says:

"We used no script for this picture. The director came to me every morning and I recited the scenes that he would photograph that day. Many times while the story was in progress, he insisted that the material he had finished could not possibly make a motion picture."

When it was finished, it was very sad and sentimental. It was in ten reels, and nobody liked it as it "preached a sermon." W. F. determined at least to give it a trial. It so happened that he had a lease on the Astor Theatre in New York; the lease was to expire in five days, and the picture that was showing there was not very good. W. F. decided that since he had to pay for the theatre anyway, he would put in *Over the Hill* for that five days and see what happened. He continues:

"The next night this picture went in, and we gave free passes to fill the theatre. I remember standing in the lobby after the show, asking this one and that one how they liked the picture. One of the last persons to come out was a man whom I wouldn't want to meet on a dark night alone; he had the hardest face of any man I had ever seen. He was smoking his pipe, and I asked him for a light. While we smoked, I asked him how he liked the picture. He spoke with a Scotch accent and said: 'I liked it very much, lad, but it's had a terrible effect on me. You see, I'm a seaman—I am only fifty, but I have been out to sea forty out of those fifty years. I ran away from home when I was a lad and never returned or wrote me mither a line. Ah, but tomorrow I buy me a ticket to go home to Scotland—I am going to see me mither again.' I suggested he had better cable first, because he had been away a long time and his mother might be dead. He said, 'I will go home to Scotland, and if she be dead, I am going to kneel at her grave and ask her to forgive me.' "

Says W. F.: "When I realized that this man was so affected that he would travel 3,500 miles to kneel at his mother's grave, I knew I had created a story that would do much good. Men and women by the millions poured into the theatres all over the world and came out thinking about their old parents and whether they were doing their duty. My publicity people communicated with homes for the aged to find out whether there were any old people being reclaimed from these homes; they found that in the eighteen months following the production of *Over the Hill,* more than 5,000 old men and women had been taken back to live with their children! When the picture was sent to England, the government revised its regulations, and for the first time permitted a moving picture to be shown in the prisons."

Such is the power of the "movies," and that of the "talkies" is even greater. W. F. had a full realization of this power; and in common with every other producer, he used it to uphold the established social order. The "talkies" will tell all children to be kind to their parents, and all parents to be kind to their children; but they will never tell anyone that there is anything fundamentally wrong with our social system. . . .

For the moment we have come to the war time and W. F.'s attitude to that. He tells:

"I left instructions here in California that we must do all things that would help our cause, regardless of profit and gain; that sequences should be written into our pictures that would arouse patriotism. . . . We sold Liberty bonds from the stage of every theatre we had, many times much to the annoyance of our patrons, who came there to be entertained, and not to be reminded that there was a war. They came to forget there was a war, which we never allowed them to do."

Also he gave the greater part of his time to the raising of Red Cross funds. He was "captain" of several teams which raised millions, and would have come out ahead of all the other teams with their millionaire captains—except that courtesy required him to permit John D. Rockefeller, Jr.'s team to come out No. 1. . . .

All through the war the Fox Film Corporation prospered; it prospered even in the panic year of 1920. It broke all records in that year, and never had a loss so long as its founder was in charge. In 1925 it became a public corporation, and then it purchased the West Coast chain of theatres. Also the Fox Theatres Corporation was established, to take over all the theatres in which William Fox was interested. Ultimately he had 800 as an outlet for his productions, and his profits were growing at a rate which astounded Wall Street.

The radio had come in 1921, and had brought sharp competition to the moving picture business. W. F. first noticed it on rainy nights. "Prior to this, on a rainy night our business would be larger than it would be on a clear night. When the radio came in, I made a careful observation and found that on rainy nights we were doing little or no business." So he began to watch the experiments being tried with talking pictures. The first efforts in America were made by means of a synchronization of a moving picture film with a phonograph disc. The film was run through a projection machine, and the disc was played by a phonograph, and the enlarged sound thrown into the theatre. But W. F. insisted from the beginning that this method was hopeless; real success would begin only when the sound track was put on the film with the pictures. He tells the basis of this conviction:

"I went to the Warner Theatre one day, to hear a man sing the introductory number of *Pagliacci*. Of course, I went expecting to be thrilled. This was the first person from grand opera who consented to sing for talkies. The picture started, and he was making all the gestures he used on the stage, and the sound I heard was a banjo playing, accompanied by a colored man singing 'I Wish I Was in Dixie.' Of course the operator had put on the wrong record! And later they ran into this difficulty— they had the problem of shipping the reels to the exhibitor, and if one record was broken, no show could be given. When film gets old you must cut out the brittle part; and of course when this was done, the record and the film did not synchronize. At one time I wrote a paper with 101 definite reasons why it was not possible to have the industry adopt records and film and make them synchronize."

W. F. stood out for "sound on film," and tells the very interesting story of how he got it:

"In the winter of 1925 I was in California, and in the spring I returned to New York. The first day I arrived at my office I was greeted by my brother-in-law, Jack Leo, who said he would like to show me something in the projection room. I went to the room, and to my amazement, in this projection room that I had visited for many years and that had always been silent, the machine went into operation, and there was a little canary bird in a cage and it was singing. It sang beautifully from the lowest to the highest note it was possible to sing. It sang for several minutes, and then following that came a Chinaman who had a ukelele and he sang an English song. He sang terribly and played none too well, but to me it was a marvel. At the conclusion of that the lights went up, and they said, 'What do you think of it?' I said it was marvelous. Leo said, 'It is all right if you think it is marvelous, because I have incurred an expense of about $12,000 without your consent while you were away. Upstairs I have built a temporary sound-proof stage and we have been photographing sound-proof pictures. If you didn't like it, I was prepared to pay the $12,000 out of my own pocket.' I said, 'Like it? This is revolutionary!' This bird sang just as though it were in a tree, and I found that the sound had been recorded on film and that it was reproduced by light from the film to the screen. All mechanical sound was eliminated.

"I went up on this temporary stage floor and saw the temporary sound-proof room, where everything had to be done. I said that couldn't be right. If the photographing had to be done in a sound-proof room, then you are going to rob this camera of seeing nature. They said there was only one way to record sound, and that was in sound-proof rooms. I said, 'That can't be so—you must be in error.' But they were sure of their position, and it was necessary to build a perfected sound-proof room. We let a contract to build our first sound-proof stages on 54th Street and Tenth Avenue. The contractors said it would take four months to build this studio.

"I called for the inventor, Mr. Case, and said, 'I am going to give you a million dollars, and you can spend this million dollars in the next four months, any way you like, in experimenting how to make this camera photograph on the outside without a sound-proof room.' Shortly thereafter they brought the various things they had photographed outside. One was a rooster crowing and it sounded exactly like a pig squealing. Another was a dog barking which sounded like a cow. They recognized that they didn't have it, because of the confusion of sound. About thirty or forty days later they said, 'Here, this time we have it.' On the screen there came rushing before me a train photographed on the Jersey Central tracks, and I heard the whistles blowing and the wheels turning just as though the train were with me in that room. I said, 'Now you have it.' . . ."

For the moment I am dealing with the cultural aspects of W. F.'s activities, and the benefits which the public got from his work. One of these was the Fox Movietone News. For the first time it was possible for the public not merely to see the crowned heads and generals of Europe marching in parades and reviewing their soldiers, but to hear the cheers of the crowds and the playing of the bands. The dwellers in remote cattle and lumber towns of the West could now leap magically over the world, and they came every week for this thrilling ten or fifteen minutes. Sound newsreels became the rage.

Also there was W. F.'s dream of educational, religious, and scientific pictures. He had been making silent pictures for schools, and was proud of them. The American Telephone and Telegraph Company claimed all the patent rights for sound pictures, and W. F. made a tie-up with them, and took Walter S. Gifford, president of the Telephone Company, to see some of his pictures in a school somewhere on the East Side of New York.

"We showed some of our silent educational pictures we had made to a classroom of boys and girls, and Mr. Gifford came and brought his little son with him. Of course, Gifford was delighted with it and thought it was wonderful. I said, 'If you think this is wonderful, wait until you see them when we make them in sound,' and he concurred. . . ."

He had been caught napping by the radio, which had taken

away his audiences on rainy nights, and in 1928 he saw television on the way, and didn't want to be caught napping again. "I reached a conclusion that the one thing that would make it possible to compete with television was to use a screen ten times larger than the present screen, a camera whose eye could see ten times as much as at present. For example, Roxy's picture screen is eighteen feet wide, and the screen I proposed was about ninety feet. I believed this 'Grandeur' would come closer to the third dimension we hear scientists talking about."

W. F. proceeded to form the Fox Grandeur Corporation, and ordered the making of a "Grandeur" projecting machine at his own expense. "This was an experiment William Fox was making—it was not an experiment of the Fox companies, because there was a great hazard about it, and I always took the hazards myself."

The other motion picture producers were greatly disturbed by the development of "Fox Grandeur." Zukor, president of Paramount, and Sarnoff, representing RKO, the all-powerful Radio Corporation of America, came to call on W. F. "They said I was about to make a great mistake: the industry had just changed from silent to sound; a great inventory had to be wiped down, and we were just about catching our breath, and here I was trying to upset it again. I was calling it progress, and they called it destruction. They said that enlarging the pictures could be done at another time, when all the companies would agree on a uniform size. Each company was claiming they had a much finer development at that time, and their purpose was to persuade me not to give the premiere performance. I described to them the necessity of it, that we could not see television destroy us. Of course, I was firm in my position, that my duty was to further the motion picture business—I hoped it would hurt no one. I was going to give my premiere, and if the public decided it was no good, that would be the end of it. Shortly thereafter, we gave the premiere of *Sunny Side Up*,[3] and it was hailed as a great success. I ordered more pictures made."

So here again we see William Fox, the stubborn and egotistical person, making powerful enemies. We shall see him [in later chapters of Upton Sinclair's book] thus making one enemy after another; playing a lone hand, insisting on having his own way, regardless of how much trouble he makes for his competitors, and for the great monopolies of manufacturing and finance. We shall see exactly how they stopped him. For the moment suffice it to say that with his "ousting," the "Grandeur" movement died, and has never been heard of since. A second picture, *The Big Trail*,[4] which he had in production, was the last the public ever saw.

And the same thing has happened to the elaborate schemes for the making of sound pictures for churches, schools, scientific institutions and homes. W. F. had this all figured out, and had begun production. He had plans for the making of school and church equipment, at very low prices. He is still cherishing this dream.

3. *Sunny Side Up* (1929) directed by David Butler; starred Janet Gaynor and Charles Farrell.
4. *The Big Trail* (1930) directed by Raoul Walsh; starred John Wayne, Marguerite Churchill, Tully Marshall, Tyrone Power, and Ward Bond.

Jean-Paul Sartre

Childhood Memories

On rainy days, Anne Marie would ask me what I felt like doing. We would hesitate for a long time between the circus, the Châtelet, the Electric House, and the Grévin Museum. At the last moment, with calculated casualness, we would decide to go to the movies. Once, as we were about to leave, my grandfather appeared at the door of his study and asked: "Where are you going, children?"—"To the movies," my mother answered. He frowned and she quickly added, "To the Panthéon Cinema. It's nearby. We just have to cross the Rue Soufflot." He let us leave, shrugging his shoulders. The following Thursday, he said to M. Simonnot: "Look here, Simonnot, you who are a serious man, do you understand it? My daughter takes my grandson to the cinema!" And M. Simonnot replied, in a conciliatory tone: "I've never been, but my wife sometimes goes."

The show had begun. We would stumblingly follow the usherette. I would feel I was doing something clandestine. Above our heads, a shaft of light crossed the hall; one could see dust and vapor dancing in it. A piano whinnied away. Violet pears shone on the walls. The varnish-like smell of a disinfectant would bring a lump to my throat. The smell and the fruit of that living darkness blended within me: I ate the lamps of the emergency exit, I filled up on their acid taste. I would scrape my back

From *The Words* by Jean-Paul Sartre; reprinted with the permission of the publisher. Copyright © 1964 George Braziller, Inc. Title supplied.

against knees and take my place on a creaky seat. My mother would slide a folded blanket under my behind to raise me. Finally, I would look at the screen. I would see a fluorescent chalk and blinking landscapes streaked with showers; it always rained, even when the sun shone brightly, even in apartments. At times, an asteroid in flames would shoot across the drawing-room of a baroness without her seeming to be surprised. I liked that rain, that restless anxiety which played on the wall. The pianist would attack the overture to *Fingal's Cave* and everyone understood that the criminal was about to appear: the baroness would be frightened out of her wits. But her beautiful, sooty face would make way for a purple show-card: "End of Part I." The lights would go on, it was a sudden awakening. Where was I? In a school? In an official building? Not the slightest ornament: rows of flap-seats beneath which could be seen their springs, walls smeared with ochre, a floor strewn with cigarette stubs and gobs of spit. Confused murmurs filled the hall, language was reinvented, the usherette would walk up and down selling hard candies. My mother would buy me some, I would put them into my mouth, I would suck the emergency lamps. The people would rub their eyes, everyone discovered his neighbors. Soldiers, maids from the neighborhood; a bony old man would be chewing tobacco; bare-headed working girls would laugh loudly. That world wasn't ours. Fortunately, here and there on that sea of heads were big fluttering hats which were reassuring.

The social hierachy of the theatre had given my grandfather and late father, who were accustomed to second balconies, a taste for ceremonial. When many people are together, they must be separated by rites; otherwise, they slaughter each other. The movies proved the opposite. This mingled audience seemed united by a catastrophe rather than a festivity. Etiquette, now dead, revealed the true bond among men: adhesion. I developed a dislike for ceremonies, I loved crowds. I have seen crowds of all kinds, but the only other time I have witnessed that naked-

ness, that sense of everyone's direct relationship to everyone
else, that waking dream, that dim consciousness of the danger of
being a man, was in 1940, in Stalag XII D.

My mother grew bolder, to the point of taking me to the
boulevard houses: the Kinérama, the Folies Dramatiques, the
Vaudeville, the Gaumont Palace, which was then called the
Hippodrome. I saw *Zigomar* and *Fantômas, The Exploits of
Maciste, The Mysteries of New York.*[1] The gilding spoiled my
pleasure. The Vaudeville, a former legitimate theatre, was unwilling to give up its former grandeur: until the very last minute,
the screen was hidden by a red tassled curtain; three raps were
given to announce the beginning of the performance; the orchestra would play an overture; the curtain would go up; the lights
would go down. I was irritated by that incongruous ceremonial,
by that dusty pomp, the only result of which was to move the
characters further away. In the balcony, in the gallery, our
fathers, impressed by the chandelier and the paintings on the
ceiling, neither could nor would believe that the theatre belonged to them: they were received there. As for me, I wanted
to see the film *as close up as possible.* I had learned in the
equalitarian discomfort of the neighborhood houses that this
new art was mine, just as it was everyone else's. We had the
same mental age: I was seven and knew how to read; it was
twelve and did not know how to talk. People said that it was in
its early stages, that it had progress to make; I thought that we
would grow up together. I have not forgotten our common childhood: whenever I am offered a hard candy, whenever a woman
varnishes her nails near me, whenever I inhale a certain smell of
disinfectant in the toilet of a provincial hotel, whenever I
see the violet bulb on the ceiling of a night-train, my eyes,
nostrils, and tongue recapture the lights and odors of those

1. These were immensely popular serials, c. 1913–1920. *Fantomas* was one
of the serials of Louis Feuillade; *The Mysteries of New York* was the French
name for one of Pearl White's serials.

bygone halls; four years ago, in rough weather off the coast of Fingal's Cave, I heard a piano in the wind.

Though impervious to the sacred, I loved magic. The cinema was a suspect appearance that I loved perversely for what it still lacked. That streaming was everything, it was nothing, it was everything reduced to nothing. I was witnessing the delirium of a wall; solids had been freed from a massiveness that weighed on me, that weighed even on my body, and my young idealism was delighted with that infinite contraction. At a later time, the transpositions and rotations of triangles reminded me of the gliding figures on the screen. I loved the cinema even in plane geometry. To me, black and white were the supercolors that contained all the others and revealed them only to the initiate; I was thrilled at seeing the invisible. Above all, I liked the incurable muteness of my heroes. But no, they weren't mute, since they knew how to make themselves understood. We communicated by means of music; it was the sound of their inner life. Persecuted innocence did better than merely show or speak of suffering: it permeated me with its pain by means of the melody that issued from it. I would read the conversations, but I heard the hope and bitterness; I would perceive by ear the proud grief that remains silent. I was compromised; the young widow who wept on the screen *was not I*, and yet she and I had only one soul: Chopin's funeral march; no more was needed for her tears to wet my eyes. I felt I was a prophet without being able to foresee anything: even before the traitor betrayed, his crime entered me; when all seemed peaceful in the castle, sinister chords exposed the murderer's presence. How happy were those cowboys, those musketeers, those detectives: their future was there, in that premonitory music, and governed the present. An unbroken song blended with their lives, led them on to victory or death by moving toward its own end. They were expected: by the girl in danger, by the general, by the traitor lurking in the forest, by the friend who was tied up near a powder-keg and who sadly watched the flame run along the fuse. The course of that flame, the virgin's desperate struggle against her abductor, the hero's gallop across the plain, the interlacing of all those images, of all those speeds, and, beneath it all, the demonic movement of the "Race to the Abyss," an orchestral selection taken from *The Damnation of Faust* and adapted for the piano, all of this was one and the same: it was Destiny. The hero dismounted, put out the fuse, the traitor sprang at him, a duel with knives began: but the accidents of the duel likewise partook of the rigor of the musical development; they were fake accidents which ill concealed the universal order. What joy when the last knife stroke coincided with the last chord! I was utterly content, I had found the world in which I wanted to live, I touched the absolute. What an uneasy feeling when the lights went on: I had been wracked with love for the characters and they had disappeared, carrying their world with them. I had felt their victory in my bones; yet it was theirs and not mine. In the street I found myself superfluous.

Carl Sandburg

The Cabinet of Dr. Caligari

The most important and the most original photoplay that has come to this city of Chicago the last year is being presented at the Ziegfeld theater this week in *The Cabinet of Dr. Caligari*. That is exactly the way some people say it. The craziest, wildest, shivery movie that has come wriggling across the silver sheet of a cinema house. That is the way other people look at it. It looks like a collaboration of Rube Goldberg, Ben Hecht, Charlie Chaplin and Edgar Allan Poe—a melting pot of the styles and techniques of all four.

Are you tired of the same old things done the same old way? Do you wish to see murder and retribution, insanity, somnambulism, grotesque puppetry, scenery solemn and stormy, wild as the wildest melodrama and yet as restrained as comic and well manipulated marionettes? Then it is for you this Caligari and his cabinet. However, if your sense of humor and your instinct of wonder and your reverence of human mystery is not working well this week then you should stay away from the Ziegfeld because you would go away saying Caligari and his cabinet are sick, morbid, loony.

Recall to yourself before going that Mark Twain is only one of numerous mortal philosophers who has declared some one streak of insanity runs in each of us.

Title supplied. Originally published in *The Daily News*, Chicago, May 12, 1921. Reprinted by permission of *The Chicago Daily News*.

Only two American motion picture artists have approached the bold handling, the smash and the getaway, the stride and rapidity of this foreign made film. Those two artists are Charlie Chaplin and D. W. Griffith.

It is a healthy thing for Hollywood, Culver City, Universal City, and all other places where movie film is being produced, that this photoplay has come along at this time. It is sure to have healthy hunches and show new possibilities in style and method to our American Producers.

This film, *The Cabinet of Dr. Caligari,* is so bold a work of independent artists going it footloose, that one can well understand it might affect audiences just as a sea voyage affects a ship-load of passengers. Some have to leave the top decks, unable to stand sight or smell of the sea. Others take the air and the spray, the salt and the chill, and call the trip an exhilaration.

There are two murders [in the film]. They are the creepiest murders this observer has thus far noted in photoplays. Yet the killings are only suggested. They are not told and acted out fully. (No censor could complain in this respect.) As murders they remind one of the darker pages of Shakespeare, of *Hamlet, Macbeth,* and again of the De Quincey essay "On Murder as one of the Fine Arts." Then a sleepwalker is about to kill a woman. He drops the dagger instead, and carries her away across house roofs, down a street. Oh, this sad sleepwalker and how and why he couldn't help it!

This is one of the few motion picture productions that might make one say, "Here is one Shakespeare would enjoy coming back to have a look at." However, be cheerful when you go to see this. Or else terribly sad. Its terrors and grotesques will match any sadness you may have and so comfort you. But if you go feeling real cheerful and expecting to be more cheerful, you may find yourself slipping.

The music is worked out well. The orchestral passages run

their tallies of chord and rhythm and silence—they growl or they are elated—with the story running on the silversheet.

When it's a crackerjack of a production and the observer feels good about it he mentions the screen as a silversheet. Whereas if it's otherwise he says celluloid. Personally, in this instance one says silversheet.

In a range of three blocks on Michigan boulevard this week one may see Ben Ami in legitimate [theater], the exhibition of the "introspectives" at the Arts Club, and *The Cabinet of Dr Caligari* at the Ziegfeld. It is quite a week.

Yes, we heard what a couple of people said going out. One said, "It's the craziest movie I ever went to." The other one said, "I don't know whether I want this for a steady diet but it's the best picture I've seen in a long while."

Cubist, futurist, post-impressionist, characterize it by any name denoting a certain style, it has its elements of power, knowledge, technic, passion, that make it sure to have an influence toward more easy flowing, joyous, original American movies.

André Gide

Nosferatu

Monday, 27 February [1928][1]

Yesterday, *Nosferatu, the Vampire.*[2]

A rather nondescript German film, but of a nondescript quality that forces one to reflect and to imagine something better. Terror, just like pity, can be excited in the mind of the spectator (at least of *this* spectator) only if he is not too much aware of the author's concern to move to terror or pity; furthermore, I doubt whether the classic precept *If you wish me to weep, you yourself must grieve first*[3] is a very good recipe.

In *Nosferatu* the hero's terror checks, gets in the way of, mine. The hero, who is depicted as dashing, venturesome, and even very pleasingly bold, undergoes a dreadful change and passes from excessive joy to the expression of an excessive terror. I should myself be more frightened if I were less aware of his being afraid.

If I were to make over the film, I should depict Nosferatu— whom we know to be *the vampire* from the start—not as

From *The Journals of Andre Gide,* Vol. III, 1928–1939, by André Gide, translated by Justin O'Brien. Copyright 1949 by Alfred A. Knopf, Inc. Reprinted by permission of the publisher. Title supplied.

1. Dictated
2. A German film adapted from Bram Stoker's *Dracula,* directed by F. W. Murnau and featuring Max Schreck, produced by Prana-Film in 1922.
3. Horace: *Epistolae,* II, iii. 102–3.

terrible and fantastic, but on the contrary in the guise of an inoffensive young man, charming and most obliging. I should like it to be only on the basis of very mild indications, in the beginning, that any anxiety should be aroused, and in the spectator's mind before being aroused in the hero's. Likewise, wouldn't it be much more frightening if he were first presented to the woman in such a charming aspect? It is a kiss that is to be transformed into a bite. If he shows his teeth at the outset, it becomes nothing but a childish nightmare.

How much cleverer it would be, instead of constantly emphasizing that concern with terror, to pretend on the contrary a desire to reassure the spectator: "No, not at all, there is nothing terrible there at all, nothing that is not quite natural; at most something a bit *too* charming"; even though one might have to let Nosferatu be more open about it on the boat with the sailors.

Likewise for the pseudo-scientific part, presented here with a truly German heavy hand; absurd. How much cleverer it would have been, beside the fantastic explanation, to provide the spectator with a perfectly rational and plausible explanation based on this little precise fact that we all know: that a plague can be transmitted by rats!

In a well-constructed fantastic tale the mind must be able to be satisfied with the natural explanation. It must *almost* be able to suffice; but the narrator will go about it in such a way that the skeptic is he who does *not* happen to be satisfied with it. It is the materialistic and positivistic mind that must appear as naive in this case.

The wonderful thing in Goethe's *Erlkönig,* for instance, is that the child is not so much terrified as charmed, that he surrenders to the mysterious blandishments the father does not see. At first all the fright is on the father's part. I should have wished that, likewise, the young woman of *Nosferatu,* though conscious of her sacrifice in the beginning, had lost that consciousness, so to speak, yielding to the vampire's charms, and that he had not been horrible in her eyes. It might be rather startling, further-more, for the vampire to yield to the woman's charms, to forget the hour. . . . I can easily see him appearing a hideous monster to everyone, and charming only in the eyes of the young woman, a voluntary, fascinated victim; but that, fascinated in turn, he should become less and less horrible until he really *becomes* the delightful person whose mere appearance he only took on at first. And it is this delightful person that the cock's crow must kill, that the spectator must see suddenly disappear with relief and, at the same time, *regret.*

In short, a film that was completely spoiled.

Jack Kerouac

Nosferatu

Nosferatu is an evil name suggesting the red letters of hell—the sinister pieces of it like "fer" and "eratu" and "nos" have a red and heinous quality like the picture itself (which throbs with gloom), a masterpiece of nightmare horror photographed fantastically well in the old grainy tones of brown-and-black-and-white.

It's not so much that the woods are "misty" but that they are bright shining Bavarian woods in the morning as the young jerk hero hurries in a Transylvanian coach to the castle of the Count. Though the woods be bright you feel evil lurking behind every tree. You just know the inner sides of dead trees among the shining living pines have bats hanging upsidedown in torpid sated sleep. There's a castle right ahead. The hero has just had a drink in a Transylvanian tavern and it would be my opinion to suggest "Don't drink too deep in Transylvanian taverns!" The maids in the Inn are as completely innocent as NOSFERATU is completely evil. The horses drawing the coach cavort, the youth stretches in the daytime woods, glad . . . but! . . . *the little traveled road!* The castle coach transfers him at Charlie Chaplin speed to the hungry cardinal of vampires. The horses are hooded! They know that vampire bats will clamp against their withers by nightfall!

From *The New Yorker Film Society Notes,* January 9, 1960, pp. 1–4. Copyright © 1960 by *The New Yorker Film Society Notes.* Reprinted by permission of The Sterling Lord Agency, Inc.

They rush hysterically through a milky dimming forest of mountain dusk, you suddenly see the castle with bats like flies round the parapet. The kid rushes out looking for to go find his gory loss. In a strange wool cap a thin hawknosed man opens the big oaken door. He announces his servants are all gone. The audience realizes this is Count Nosferatu himself! Ugh! The castle has tile floors:—somehow there's more evil in those tile floors than in the dripping dust of later Bela Lugosi castles where women with spiders on their shoulders dragged dead muslin gowns across the stone. They are the tile floors of a Byzantine Alexandrian Transylvanian throat-ogre.

The Count Nosferatu has the long hook nose of a Javelin vampire bat, the large eyes of the Rhinolophidae vampire bat, long horsey mouth looking like it's full of W-shaped cusps with muggly pectinated teeth and molars and incisors like Desmondontae vampire bats with a front tooth missing the better to suck the blood, maybe with the long brush-tipped tongue of the *sanguisuga* so sanguine. He looks in his hunched swift walk like he probably also has his intestinal tract specially modified in accordance with his nocturnal habits . . . the general horrid harelipped look of the Noctilio . . . small guillotines in his mouth . . . the exceeding thinness of his gullet. His hands are like the enormous claws of the Leporinus bat and keep growing longer and longer fingernails throughout the picture.

Meanwhile the kid rushes around enjoying the scenery:—little dusty paths of the castle by day, but by twilight?

The Count plunges to sign his deeds with that thirsty eagerness of the Vampire.

The kid escapes over the wall just in time . . .

The scene shifts to Doktor Van Hellsing in sunny classroom Germany nevertheless photographed as dark as Wolfbane or the claws that eat a fly. Then it goes to a gorgeously filmed dune where women's Victorian dresses flutter in the fresh sea wind. Then finally the haunted ship sails down the navigable canal or river and out to sea; aboard is the Count in pursuit of his boy. When they open his coffin a dozen rats plop out of the dirt and slink and bite the seamen on the ankles (how they ever filmed this I'll never know: great big rats) . . . The whole scene on the ship testifies to the grandeur of the horror of Coleridge's Ancient Mariner. Of itself the schooner glides into the port of Bremen with all the crew dead. The sucked-out Captain is tied to his wheel. A disciple of the Count imprisoned in a Bremen cell sees the schooner glide right by like a ghost and says: "The master is here!" Down cobbles deserted at dusk suddenly, like an insane delivery boy here comes Count Nosferatu carrying his own coffin of burial earth under his arm. He goes straight to establish residence in an eerie awful warehouse or armory which made me think: "I shall never go to Bremen if they have things like that! Armories with empty windows! Ow!"

The old Bremen lamplighter is aware of the foolish hallucinations of Bremen folk but he also looks scared as he lights the evening lamp, naturally, as the next day processions carry the coffined victims of the vampire down the gloomy street. People close their shutters. There is real evil swarming all over the screen by now. Nosferatu looks worse and worse: by now his teeth are stained, his fingernails are like rats' tails, his eyes are on fire. He stares from his warehouse window like someone in an old dream. He rises from his coffin at eve like a plank. His disciple who escapes from the prison looks like Mr. Pickwick on a rampage in a chase that has everybody breathing furiously (a masterpiece of breathing), ends in a field, with torches.

At night, by moonlight there he is, the Great Lover, staring across that awful plaza or canal into the heroine's window and into her eye. She waits for him. She wants to save the hero and has read in the "Book of Vampires" that if a victim stays with the vampire till cock's crow he will be destroyed. He comes to her swiftly with that awful quickfooted walk, fingernails dripping. The shadow of the hand crawls like ink across her snowy bedspreads. The last scene shows him kneeling at her bedside kissing into her neck in a horribly perverted love scene unequalled for its pathetic sudden revelation of the vampire's essential helplessness. The sun comes up, you see its rays light the top of his warehouse, the cock crows, he can't get away. He vanishes in a puff of smoke like the Agony of the West. Right there on the floor as the puffing hero arrives too late to save his love.

The creator of this picture, F. W. Murnau, may have drawn a lot of information from the great vampire dissertations of Ranft and Calmet written in the 18th century. Vampire is a word of Serbian origin (Wampir),—meaning blood-sucking ghosts. They were supposed to be the souls of dead wizards and witches and suicides and victims of homicide and the Banished! (those banished from family or church). But vampires were also thought to be the souls of ordinary living people which leave the body in sleep and come upon other sleepers in the form of down-fluff! . . . so don't sleep in your duck-down sleepingbag in Transylvania! (or even in California, they say).

Actually, don't worry . . . scientifically speaking, the only blood-sucking bats in the world are located in South America from Oaxaca on down.

Bertolt Brecht

On *The Gold Rush:* "Less Security" (1926)

I took my time about going to see Charlie Chaplin's film *The Gold Rush* because the music played in the theater where it is shown is so horrible. But finally the despondency over it which seems to have gripped all the theater people of my acquaintance prodded me to take that step. I find their despondency justified.

I do not hold the view that what is done in the film cannot be done in the contemporary theater due to the latter's inherent shortcomings. I think that, without Charlie Chaplin, it cannot be done in the theater nor in the cabaret nor in the movies. This artist is a document which already qualifies as a historical event. From the point of view of thought content, however, *The Gold Rush* would be hopelessly inadequate for the stage and insufficient to satisfy a theatrical audience. To be sure, there is a certain charm in seeing how in such young art media as the film the indulgence in certain personal experiences has not yet been replaced by a dramaturgy with the experience of a seasoned whore.

Suffering from amnesia, Big Jim, unable to find his gold mine, meets Charlie, the only man who could show it to him, and each passes the other indifferently; here we have an occurrence which, on the stage, would permanently destroy an audience's faith in the author's ability to manipulate events.

From Bertolt Brecht, *Schriften zum Theater* (Frankfurt: Suhrkamp-Verlag, 1963), II, by permission of the publisher. Translated by Ulrich Weisstein. Translation copyright 1972 by Stefan Brecht.

The film has no responsibility; it does not have to strain itself. Its dramaturgy remains uncomplicated simply because the product is nothing but a few thousand yards of celluloid in a tin box. Don't expect a fugue from a saw which a man is bending between his knees.

Today, the film no longer offers technical problems. The techniques it has developed cover up these problems successfully. It is rather the theater which is presently facing technical difficulties. . . .

H. G. Wells

The Silliest Film: Will Machinery Make Robots of Men?

I have recently seen the silliest film. I do not believe it would be possible to make one sillier. And as this film sets out to display the way the world is going, I think [my book] *The Way the World Is Going* may very well concern itself with this film. It is called *Metropolis*,[1] it comes from the great Ufa studios in Germany, and the public is given to understand that it has been produced at enormous cost. It gives in one eddying concentration almost every possible foolishness, *cliché,* platitude, and muddlement about mechanical progress and progress in general served up with a sauce of sentimentality that is all its own.

It is a German film and there have been some amazingly good German films. Before they began to cultivate bad work under cover of a protective quota. And this film has been adapted to the Anglo-Saxon taste, and quite possibly it has suffered in the process, but even when every allowance has been made for that, there remains enough to convince the intelligent observer that most of its silliness must be fundamental. Possibly I dislike this soupy whirlpool none the less because I find decaying fragments

From H. G. Wells, *The Way the World is Going,* 1929. Copyright: Geo. P. Wells and Francis R. Wells; published here by permission of Geo. P. Wells & Messrs A. P. Watt & Son, London.

1. *Metropolis* (1926) directed by Fritz Lang; screenplay by Fritz Lang and Thea Von Harbou. With Brigitte Helm (in the dual role of the heroine and a robot), Rudolf Klein-Rogge, and Alfred Abel.

of my own juvenile work of thirty years ago, *The Sleeper Awakes,* floating about in it. Čapek's Robots have been lifted without apology, and that soulless mechanical monster of Mary Shelley's, who has fathered so many German inventions, breeds once more in this confusion. Originality there is none. Independent thought, none. Where nobody has imagined for them the authors have simply fallen back on contemporary things. The aeroplanes that wander about above the great city show no advance on contemporary types, though all that stuff could have been livened up immensely with a few helicopters and vertical and unexpected movements. The motor cars are 1926 models or earlier. I do not think there is a single new idea, a single instance of artistic creation or even of intelligent anticipation, from first to last in the whole pretentious stew; I may have missed some point of novelty, but I doubt it; and this, though it must bore the intelligent man in the audience, makes the film all the more convenient as a gauge of the circle of ideas, the mentality, from which it has proceeded.

The word "Metropolis," says the advertisement in English, "is in itself symbolical of greatness"—which only shows us how wise it is to consult a dictionary before making assertions about the meaning of words. Probably it was the adapter who made that shot. The German "Neubabelsburg" was better, and could have been rendered "New Babel." It is a city, we are told, of "about one hundred years hence." It is represented as being enormously high; and all the air and happiness are above and the workers live, as the servile toilers in the blue uniform in *The Sleeper Awakes* lived, down, down, down below.

Now far away in dear old 1897 it may have been excusable to symbolize social relations in this way, but that was thirty years ago, and a lot of thinking and some experience intervene. That vertical city of the future we know now is, to put it mildly, highly improbable. Even in New York and Chicago, where the pressure upon the central sites is exceptionally great, it is only the central office and entertainment region that soars and exca-vates. And the same centripetal pressure that leads to the utmost exploitation of site values at the centre leads also to the driving out of industrialism and labour from the population center to cheaper areas, and of residential life to more open and airy surroundings. That was all discussed and written about before 1900. Somewhere about 1930 the geniuses of the Ufa studios will come up to a book of *Anticipations* which was written more than a quarter of a century ago.[2] The British census returns of 1901 proved clearly that city populations were becoming centrif-ugal, and that every increase in horizontal traffic facilities pro-duced a further distribution. This vertical social stratification is stale old stuff. So far from being "a hundred years hence," *Metropolis,* in its forms and shapes, is already, as a possibility, a third of a century out of date.

But its form is the least part of its staleness. This great city is supposed to be evoked by a single dominating personality. The English version calls him John Masterman, so that there may be no mistake about his quality. Very unwisely he has called his son Eric, instead of sticking to good hard John, and so relaxed the strain. He works with an inventor, one Rotwang, and they make machines. There are a certain number of other rich people, and the "sons of the rich" are seen disporting them-selves, with underclad ladies in a sort of joy conservatory, rather like the "winter garden" of an enterprising 1890 hotel during an orgy. The rest of the population is in a state of abject slavery, working in "shifts" of ten hours in some mysteriously divided twenty-four hours, and with no money to spend or property or freedom. The machines make wealth. *How,* is not stated. We are shown rows of motor cars all exactly alike; but the workers cannot own these, and no "sons of the rich" would. Even the middle classes nowadays want a car with personality.

2. Title of a collection of prophetic essays by H. G. Wells, published in 1900.

Probably Masterman makes these cars in endless series to amuse himself.

One is asked to believe that these machines are engaged quite furiously in the mass production of nothing that is ever used, and that Masterman grows richer and richer in the process. This is the essential nonsense of it all. Unless the mass of the population has spending power there is no possibility of wealth in a mechanical civilization. A vast, penniless slave population may be necessary for wealth where there are no mass production machines, but it is preposterous with mass production machines. You find such a real proletariat in China still; it existed in the great cities of the ancient world; but you do not find it in America, which has gone furthest in the direction of mechanical industry, and there is no grain of reason for supposing it will exist in the future. Masterman's watchword is "Efficiency," and you are given to understand it is a very dreadful word, and the contrivers of this idiotic spectacle are so hopelessly ignorant of all the work that has been done upon industrial efficiency that they represent him as working his machine-minders to the point of exhaustion, so that they faint and machines explode and people are scalded to death. You get machine-minders in torment turning levers in response to signals—work that could be done far more effectively by automata. Much stress is laid on the fact that the workers are spiritless, hopeless drudges, working reluctantly and mechanically. But a mechanical civilization has no use for mere drudges; the more efficient its machinery the less need there is for the quasimechanical minder. It is the inefficient factory that needs slaves; the ill-organized mine that kills men. The hopeless drudge stage of human labour lies behind us. With a sort of malignant stupidity this film contradicts these facts.

The current tendency of economic life is to oust the mere drudge altogether, to replace much highly skilled manual work by exquisite machinery in skilled hands, and to increase the relative proportion of semi-skilled, moderately versatile and fairly comfortable workers. It may indeed create temporary masses of unemployed, and in *The Sleeper Awakes* there was a mass of unemployed people under hatches. That was written in 1897, when the possibility of restraining the growth of large masses of population had scarcely dawned on the world. It was reasonable then to anticipate an embarrassing underworld of under-productive people. We did not know what to do with the abyss. But there is no excuse for that to-day. And what this film anticipates is not unemployment, but drudge employment, which is precisely what is passing away. Its fabricators have not even realized that the machine ousts the drudge.

"Efficiency" means large-scale productions, machinery as fully developed as possible, and *high wages*. The British Government delegation sent to study success in America has reported unanimously to that effect. The increasingly efficient industrialism of America has so little need of drudges that it has set up the severest barriers against the flooding of the United States by drudge immigration. "Ufa" knows nothing of such facts.

A young woman appears from nowhere in particular to "help" these drudges; she impinges upon Masterman's son Eric, and they go to the "Catacombs," which, in spite of the gas mains, steam mains, cables, and drainage, have somehow contrived to get over from Rome, skeletons and all, and burrow under this city of Metropolis. She conducts a sort of Christian worship in these unaccountable caverns, and the drudges love and trust her. With a nice sense of fitness she lights herself about the Catacombs with a torch instead of the electric lamps that are now so common.

That reversion to torches is quite typical of the spirit of this show. Torches are Christian, we are asked to suppose; torches are human. Torches have hearts. But electric hand-lamps are wicked, mechanical, heartless things. The bad, bad inventor uses quite a big one. Mary's services are unsectarian, rather like afternoon Sunday-school, and in her special catacomb she has not so much an altar as a kind of umbrella-stand full of crosses. The leading idea of her religion seems to be a disapproval of machinery and efficiency. She enforces the great moral lesson that the bolder and stouter human effort becomes, the more spiteful Heaven grows, by reciting the story of Babel. The story of Babel, as we know, is a lesson against "Pride." It teaches the human soul to grovel. It inculcates the duty of incompetence. The Tower of Babel was built, it seems, by bald-headed men. I said there was no original touch in the film, but this last seems to be a real invention. You see the bald-headed men building Babel. Myriads of them. Why they are bald is inexplicable. It is not even meant to be funny, and it isn't funny; it is just another touch of silliness. The workers in *Metropolis* are not to rebel or do anything for themselves, she teaches, because they may rely on the vindictiveness of Heaven.

But Rotwang, the inventor, is making a Robot, apparently without any licence from Čapek, the original patentee. It is to look and work like a human being, but it is to have no "soul." It is to be a substitute for drudge labour. Masterman very properly suggests that it should never have a soul, and for the life of me I cannot see why it should. The whole aim of mechanical civilization is to eliminate the drudge and the drudge soul. But this is evidently regarded as very dreadful and impressive by the producers, who are all on the side of soul and love and suchlike. I am surprised they do not pine for souls in the alarm clocks and runabouts. Masterman, still unwilling to leave bad alone, persuades Rotwang to make this Robot in the likeness of Mary, so that it may raise an insurrection among the workers to destroy the machines by which they live, and so learn that it is necessary to work. Rather intricate that, but Masterman, you understand, is a rare devil of a man. Full of pride and efficiency and modernity, and all those horrid things.

Then comes the crowning imbecility of the film, the conversion of the Robot into the likeness of Mary. Rotwang, you must understand, occupies a small old house, embedded in the modern city, richly adorned with pentagrams and other reminders of the antiquated German romances out of which its owner has been taken. A quaint smell of Mephistopheles is perceptible for a time. So even at Ufa, Germany can still be dear old magic-loving Germany. Perhaps Germans will never get right away from the Brocken. Walpurgis Night is the name-day of the German poetic imagination, and the national fantasy capers insecurely for ever with a broomstick between its legs. By some no doubt abominable means Rotwang has squeezed a vast and well-equipped modern laboratory into this little house. It is ever so much bigger than the house, but no doubt he has fallen back on Einstein and other modern bedevilments. Mary has to be trapped, put into a machine like a translucent cocktail shaker, and undergo all sorts of pyrotechnic treatment in order that her likeness may be transferred to the Robot. The possibility of Rotwang just simply making a Robot like her, evidently never entered the gifted producer's head. The Robot is enveloped in wavering haloes, the premises seem to be struck by lightning repeatedly, the contents of a number of flasks and carboys are violently agitated, there are minor explosions and discharges. Rotwang conducts the operations with a manifest lack of assurance, and finally, to his evident relief, the likeness is taken and things calm down. The false Mary then winks darkly at the audience and sails off to raise the workers. And so forth and so on. There is some rather good swishing about in water, after the best film traditions, some violent and unconvincing machine-breaking and rioting and wreckage, and then, rather confusedly, one gathers that Masterman has learnt a lesson, and that workers and employers are now to be reconciled by "Love."

Never for a moment does one believe any of this foolish story; never for a moment is there anything amusing or convincing in its dreary series of strained events. It is immensely and strangely dull. It is not even to be laughed at. There is not one good-looking nor sympathetic nor funny personality in the cast; there is, indeed, no scope at all for looking well or acting like a rational creature amid these mindless, imitative absurdities. The film's air of having something grave and wonderful to say is transparent pretence. It has nothing to do with any social or moral issue before the world or with any that can ever conceivably arise. It is bunkum and poor and thin even as bunkum. I am astonished at the toleration shown it by quite a number of film critics on both sides of the Atlantic. And it cost, says the London *Times*, six million marks! How they spent all that upon it I cannot imagine. Most of the effects could have been got with models at no great expense.

The pity of it is that this unimaginative, incoherent, sentimentalizing, and make-believe film, wastes some very fine possibilities. My belief in German enterprise has had a shock. I am dismayed by the intellectual laziness it betrays. I thought Germans even at the worst could toil. I thought they had resolved to be industriously modern. It is profoundly interesting to speculate upon the present trend of mechanical invention and of the real reactions of invention upon labour conditions. Instead of plagiarizing from a book thirty years old and resuscitating the banal moralizing of the early Victorian period, it would have been almost as easy, no more costly, and far more interesting to have taken some pains to gather the opinions of a few bright young research students and ambitious, modernizing architects and engineers about the trend of modern invention, and develop these artistically. Any technical school would have been delighted to supply sketches and suggestions for the aviation and transport of A.D. 2027. There are now masses of literature upon the organization of labour for efficiency that could have been boiled down at a very small cost. The question of the development of industrial control, the relation of industrial to political direction, the way all that is going, is of the liveliest current interest. Apparently the Ufa people did not know of these things and did not want to know about them. They were too dense to see how these things could be brought into touch with the life of to-day and made interesting to the man in the street. After the worst traditions of the cinema world, monstrously self-satisfied and self-sufficient, convinced of the power of loud advertisement to put things over with the public, and with no fear of searching criticism in their minds, no consciousness of thought and knowledge beyond their ken, they set to work in their huge studio to produce furlong after furlong of this ignorant, old-fashioned balderdash, and ruin the market for any better film along these lines.

Six million marks! The waste of it!

The theatre when I visited it was crowded. All but the highest-priced seats were full, and the gaps in these filled up reluctantly but completely before the great film began. I suppose every one had come to see what the city of a hundred years hence would be like. I suppose there are multitudes of people to be "drawn" by promising to show them what the city of a hundred years hence will be like. It was, I thought, an unresponsive audience, and I heard no comments. I could not tell from their bearing whether they believed that *Metropolis* was really a possible forecast or no. I do not know whether they thought that the film was hopelessly silly or the future of mankind hopelessly silly. But it must have been one thing or the other.[3]

17 April, 1927.

3. This critique of *Metropolis* provoked notable responses from Paul Rotha, *Film Till Now,* London, 1967, pp. 274–276, and Herman G. Weinberg in *Jewish Times* (Baltimore) 34:10, July 10, 1936.

Aldous Huxley

Silence is Golden

I have just been, for the first time, to see and hear a picture talk.
"A little late in the day," my up-to-date readers will remark,
with a patronizing and contemptuous smile. "This is 1929; there
isn't much news in talkies now. But better late than never."

Better late than never? Ah, no! There, my friends, you're
wrong. This is one of those cases where it is most decidedly
better never than late, better never than early, better never
than on the stroke of time. One of the numerous cases, I may
add; and the older I grow, the more numerous I find them. There
was a time when I should have felt terribly ashamed of not
being up-to-date. I lived in a chronic apprehension lest I might,
so to speak, miss the last bus, and so find myself stranded and
benighted, in a desert of demodedness, while others, more
nimble than myself, had already climbed on board, taken their
tickets and set out toward those bright but, alas, ever receding
goals of Modernity and Sophistication. Now, however, I have
grown shameless, I have lost my fears. I can watch unmoved
the departure of the last social-cultural bus—the innumerable
last buses, which are starting at every instant in all the world's
capitals. I make no effort to board them, and when the noise of
each departure has died down, "Thank goodness!" is what I say
to myself in the solitude. I find nowadays that I simply don't

From *Do What You Will* by Aldous Huxley. Copyright 1929, 1956 by
Aldous Huxley. Reprinted by permission of Harper & Row, Publishers, Inc.

want to be up-to-date. I have lost all desire to see and do the things, the seeing and doing of which entitle a man to regard himself as superiorly knowing, sophisticated, unprovincial; I have lost all desire to frequent the places and people that a man simply *must* frequent, if he is not to be regarded as a poor creature hopelessly out of the swim. "Be up-to-date!" is the categorical imperative of those who scramble for the last bus. But it is an imperative whose cogency I refuse to admit. When it is a question of doing something which I regard as a duty I am as ready as anyone else to put up with discomfort. But being up-to-date and in the swim has ceased, so far as I am concerned, to be a duty. Why should I have my feelings outraged, why should I submit to being bored and disgusted for the sake of somebody else's categorical imperative? Why? There is no reason. So I simply avoid most of the manifestations of that so-called "life" which my contemporaries seem to be so unaccountably anxious to "see"; I keep out of range of the "art" they think is so vitally necessary to "keep up with"; I flee from those "good times" in the "having" of which they are prepared to spend so lavishly of their energy and cash.

Such, then, are the reasons for my very tardy introduction to the talkies. The explanation of my firm resolve never, if I can help it, to be reintroduced will be found in the following simple narrative of what I saw and heard in that fetid hall on the Boulevard des Italiens, where the latest and most frightful creation-saving device for the production of standardized amusement had been installed.

We entered the hall halfway through the performance of a series of music-hall turns—not substantial ones, of course, but the two-dimensional images of turns with artificial voices. There were no travel films, nothing in the Natural History line, none of those fascinating Events of the Week—lady mayoresses launching battleships, Japanese earthquakes, hundred-to-one outsiders winning races, revolutionaries on the march in Nicaragua—which are always the greatest and often the sole attractions in the programmes of our cinemas. Nothing but disembodied entertainers, gesticulating flatly on the screen and making gramophone-like noises as they did so. Some sort of comedian was performing as we entered. But he soon vanished to give place to somebody's celebrated jazz band—not merely audible in all its loud vulgarity of brassy guffaw and caterwauling sentiment, but also visible in a series of apocalyptic close-ups of the individual performers. A beneficent Providence has dimmed my powers of sight so that at a distance of more than four or five yards I am blissfully unaware of the full horror of the average human countenance. At the cinema, however, there is no escape. Magnified up to Brobdingnagian proportions, the human countenance smiles its six-foot smiles, opens and shuts its thirty-two-inch eyes, registers soulfulness or grief, libido or whimsicality, with every square centimetre of its several roods of pallid mooniness. Nothing short of total blindness can preserve one from the spectacle. The jazz players were forced upon me; I regarded them with a fascinated horror. It was the first time, I suddenly realized, that I had ever clearly *seen* a jazz band. The spectacle was positively terrifying.

The performers belonged to two contrasted races. There were the dark and polished young Hebrews, whose souls were in those mournfully sagging, seasickishly undulating melodies of mother love and nostalgia and yammering amorousness and clotted sensuality which have been the characteristically Jewish contributions to modern popular music. And there were the chubby young Nordics, with Aryan faces transformed by the strange plastic forces of the North American environment into the likeness of very large uncooked muffins or the unveiled posteriors of babes. (The more sympathetic Red Indian type of Nordic-American face was completely absent from this particular assemblage of jazz players.) Gigantically enlarged, these personages appeared one after another on the screen, each singing or playing his instrument, and at the same time registering the emotions appropriate to the musical circumstances. The spectacle, I repeat, was really terrifying. For the first time I felt grateful for the defect of vision which had preserved me from an earlier acquaintance with such aspects of modern life. And at the same time I wished that I could become, for the occasion, a little hard of hearing. For if good music has charms to soothe the savage breast, bad music has no less powerful spells for filling the mildest breast with rage, the happiest with horror and disgust. Oh, those mammy songs, those love longings, those loud hilarities! How was it possible that human emotions intrinsically decent could be so ignobly parodied? I felt like a man who, having asked for wine, is offered a brimming bowl of hogwash. And not even fresh hogwash. Rancid hogwash, decaying hogwash. For there was a horrible tang of putrefaction in all that music. Those yearnings for Mammy of Mine and My Baby, for Dixie and the Land Where Skies Are Blue and Dreams Come True, for Granny and Tennessee and You—they were all a necrophily. The Mammy after whom the black young Hebrews and the blond young muffinfaces so retchingly yearned was an ancient Gorgonzola cheese; the Baby of their tremulously gargled desire was a leg of mutton after a month in warm storage; Granny had been dead for weeks; and as for Dixie and Tennessee and Dream Land—they were odoriferous with the least artificial of manures.

When, after what seemed hours, the jazz band concluded its dreadful performance, I sighed in thankfulness. But the thankfulness was premature. For the film which followed was hardly less distressing. It was the story of the child of a cantor in a synagogue, afflicted, to his father's justifiable fury, with an itch for jazz.[1] This itch, assisted by the cantor's boot, sends him out

1. The reference is to *The Jazz Singer* (1927) directed by Alan Crosland; starring Al Jolson (as the jazz singer), Warner Oland (as the cantor), and May McAvoy (as the jazz singer's girl).

into the world, where, in due course and thanks to My Baby, his dreams come tree-ue, and he is employed as a jazz singer on the music-hall stage. Promoted from the provinces to Broadway, the jazz singer takes the opportunity to revisit the home of his childhood. But the cantor will have nothing to do with him, absolutely nothing, in spite of his success, in spite, too, of his moving eloquence. "You yourself always taught me," says the son pathetically, "that the voice of music was the voice of God." *Vox jazzi vox Dei*—the truth is new and beautiful. But stern old Poppa's heart refuses to be melted. Even Mammy of Mine is unable to patch up a reconciliation. The singer is reduced to going out once more into the night—and from the night back to his music hall, where, amid a forest of waving legs, he resumes his interrupted devotions to that remarkable god whose voice is the music of Mr. Irving Berlin as interpreted by Mr. Paul Whiteman's orchestra.

The crisis of the drama arrives when, the cantor being mortally sick and unable to fulfil his functions at the synagogue, Mammy of Mine and the Friends of his Childhood implore the young man to come and sing the atonement service in his father's place. Unhappily, this religious function is booked to take place at the same hour as that other act of worship vulgarly known as the First Night. There ensues a terrific struggle, worthy of the pen of a Racine or a Dryden, between love and honour. Love for Mammy of Mine draws the jazz singer toward the synagogue; but love for My Baby draws the cantor's son toward the theatre, where she, as principal Star, is serving the deity no less acceptably with her legs and smile than he with his voice. Honour also calls from either side; for honour demands that he should serve the God of his fathers at the synagogue, but it also demands that he should serve the jazz-voiced god of his adoption at the theatre. Some very eloquent captions appear at this point. With the air of a Seventeenth Century hero, the jazz singer protests that he must put his career before even his love. The nature of the dilemma has changed, it will be seen, since Dryden's day. In the old dramas it was love that had to be sacrificed to painful duty. In the modern instance the sacrifice is at the shrine of what William James called "the Bitch Goddess, Success." Love is to be abandoned for the stern pursuit of newspaper notoriety and dollars. The change is significant of the *weltanschauung,* if not of the youngest generation, at any rate of that which has passed and is in process of passing. The youngest generation seems to be as little interested in careers and money as in anything else, outside its own psychology. But this is by the way.

In the end the singer makes the best of both worlds—satisfies Mammy of Mine and even Poor Poppa by singing at the synagogue and, on the following evening, scores a terrific success at the postponed first night of My Baby's revue. The film concludes with a scene in the theatre, with Mammy of Mine in the stalls (Poor Poppa is by this time safely under ground), and the son, with My Baby in the background, warbling down at her the most nauseatingly luscious, the most penetratingly vulgar mammy song that it has ever been my lot to hear. My flesh crept as the loud speaker poured out those sodden words, that greasy, sagging melody. I felt ashamed of myself for listening to such things, for even being a member of the species to which such things are addressed. But I derived a little comfort from the reflection that a species which has allowed all its instincts and emotions to degenerate and putrefy in such a way must be pretty near either its violent conclusion or else its radical transformation and reform.

To what length this process of decay has gone was very strikingly demonstrated by the next item on the programme, which was the first of that series of music-hall turns of which the dreadful jazz band had been the last. For no sooner had the singer and My Baby and Mammy of Mine disappeared into the limbo of inter-cinematographic darkness, than a very large and classically profiled personage, dressed in the uniform of a clown, appeared on the screen, opened his mouth very wide indeed and poured out, in a terrific Italian tenor voice, the famous soliloquy of Pagliacci from Leoncavallo's opera. Rum, tum, ti-tum, tum; Rum-ti-ti, tum, ti-tum, tum—it is the bawling-ground of every Southern virtuoso, and a piece which, at ordinary times, I would go out of my way to avoid hearing. But in comparison with the jazz band's Hebrew melodies and the singer's jovialities and mammy yearnings, Leoncavallo's throaty vulgarity seemed not only refined and sincere, but even beautiful, positively noble. Yes, noble; for after all, the composer, whatever his native second-rateness, had stood in some sort of organic relationship, through a tradition of taste and of feeling, with the men who built Santa Maria del Fiore and the Malatestan temple, who painted the frescoes at Arezzo and Padua, who composed the Mass of Pope Marcellus and wrote the *Divine Comedy* and the *Orlando Furioso*. Whereas the Hebrew melodists and the muffin-faced young Nordics, with their Swanee whistles and their saxophones, the mammy songsters, the vocal yearners for Dixie and My Baby are in no kind of relationship with any of the immemorial decencies of human life, but only with their own inward decay. It is a corruption as novel as the régime under which they and all the rest of us now live—as novel as Protestantism and capitalism; as novel as urbanization and democracy and the apotheosis of the Average Man; as novel as Benjamin-Franklinism and the no less repulsive philosophy and ethic of the young Good Timer; as novel as creation-saving machinery and the thought-saving, time-killing press; as novel as Taylorized work and mechanized amusement. Ours is a spiritual climate in which the immemorial decencies find it hard to flourish. Another generation or so should see them definitely dead. Is there a resurrection?

Part Two

The Medium and Its Messages

W. D. Howells

Editor's Easy Chair

It is perhaps the main characteristic, the ruling principle of this judgment-seat to regard nothing human as alien to it. In the unbounded range of its interests, its amenities, all that concerns mankind is included, but from time to time it is able to afford its votaries a refreshing and invigorating surprise by something especially recondite in its inquiries.

With the Easy Chair there is no high, no low; or if not quite that, there is nothing too high or too low. It is not long, as years count in the age of nations, since it looked carefully into the nature of something so far beneath the regard of most philosophers as vaudeville, and found much to praise in that variegated form of dramatic performance. Now it is moved by the course of events to invite its familiar circle of two or three million associate casuists to the consideration of that younger sister of vaudeville, the cinematographic show, its essence, its potentiality for good and evil, and its actual influence on the manners and morals of the community as one of the most novel of the social forces. We are the more eager to enter upon the question because it seems to us that the feeling against this sort of show, though most respectable in its origin, has been too exaggerated in its expression. What to our experience (founded on a tolerant taste in such matters which we could not commend too highly

Originally published in *Harper's Magazine*, September 1912.

to other observers) has appeared far more innocently tedious as well as innocently entertaining than the ordinary musical comedy or the problem play of commerce has been found by some experts in ethics deleterious in high degree. The pictures thrown upon the luminous curtain of the stage have been declared extremely corrupting to the idle young people lurking in the darkness before it. The darkness itself has been held a condition of inexpressible depravity and a means of allurement to evil by birds of prey hovering in the standing-room and the foyers of the theaters.

Just how these predacious fowl operate, the censors of the moving-picture show have not felt it necessary to say; the lurid imagination of the public has been invoked without the specifications, and the moving-picture show has dropped to zero in the esteem of most self-respecting persons. It is possibly the showmen themselves who have therefore seen that something must be done, and who have sought for government approval of their films, quite unaware that this was a renunciation of individuality verging hard upon socialism. At any rate, the pictures shown are now proclaimed as bearing the warrant of censorship; and still another and more surprising step has been taken toward safeguarding the public morals. The pictures are sometimes shown in a theater lighted as broad as day, where not the silliest young girl or the wickedest young fellow can plot fully unseen, or even the most doting and purblind grandams and grandsires, who seem always to form a large part of the audience.

This ought, one would think, to be enough. But apparently it is not, if we may take in proof the case of a Massachusetts village where the moving-picture show prevails. The moving-picture show prevails everywhere, in Europe as well as America, and doubtless Asia, Africa, South America, and Oceanica. It has become the most universally accepted of modern amusements; the circus compared with it is partial and provincial. But in this particular New England village it is of an evolution which peculiarly threatens the spiritual peace and the intellectual growth of the place unless its forces can be turned to the promise of ultimate good. It began there in a simple town hall which three hundred people of every age and sex filled afternoon and evening at ten cents each, and so prospered the proprietor that now, after two years, he has built a much roomier theater, which the villagers continue to throng. He gives them, it seems, a very acceptable amusement, and they in turn give him some fifteen thousand dollars a year, or about twice the sum they pay in school taxes.

One would say this was very well, supposing the money of the villagers and their neighbors was not tainted money, and if they liked to spend it in that way. But it has been discovered in Massachusetts, if not in Europe, Asia, Africa, Oceanica, and the rest of North and South America, that the moving-picture habit tends in both old and young to lethargy of mind and inertness of body, and that especially the school-children, when they have become accustomed to looking at the scenes and incidents thrown upon the white curtain, acquire a fixed indifference to the claims of orthography, mathematics, history, and geography. This is said to be undeniably the case, and we could readily imagine it, just as we could imagine that a very fatuous type of fiction such as most of our people read might disgust them with every sort of edifying literature.

The question in Massachusetts, as elsewhere, is what shall be done about it. The moving-picture show, like some other things, "has come to stay"; it cannot be mocked or scolded away, but, as it has already shown itself capable of uplift, we may fitly ask ourselves not only what it esthetically is, but what it ethically may be.

> Oh, to what uses shall we put
> The wild-weed flower that simply blows
> And is there any moral shut
> Within the bosom of the rose?

But we need not decide at once that the moving-picture show is either a wild-weed flower or a rose, and poetically despair of its capacity to do nothing more than impart a "giddy pleasure of the eye." If the authorities wish to share in delighting as well as instructing youth, why should not they make this enemy their ally?

The moving-picture show is in a mechanical way not only the latest of "the fairy dreams of science," but it is the most novel of all the forms of dramatic entertainment. Yet if pantomime is one of the oldest forms of drama, the moving-picture show is of an almost Saturnian antiquity, for pantomime is what the moving picture is, whether representing a veritable incident or a fanciful invention. As even the frequenter of it may not realize, its scenes have been photographically studied from the action of performers more rather than less skilled than the average, who have given the camera a dress-rehearsal of the story thrown upon the white curtain for his pleasure or improvement. The stage direction flashed on the same space between the acts or scenes offers the spectator the needed clue, and in the vivid action of the dumb-show he scarcely misses the text which would be spoken in the theater. In fact, as most plays in most theaters are done, he is the gainer by the silent demonstration, which in the dress-rehearsal may well have included spoken dialogue. Of course, the stuff itself is crude enough, oftenest; yet sometimes it is not crude, and the pantomime has its fine moments, when one quite loses one's self in the artistic pleasure of the drama. Where a veritable incident is portrayed, one has the delight of perceiving how dramatic life is, and how full of tragedy and comedy.

It is a convention of the moving picture that life is mostly full of farce, but that is an error which it shares with the whole modern stage, and it is probable that when the moving-picture show is asked to be serious, as we propose it shall be, it will purge itself of this error. Meanwhile our proposition is that the school committee of that dismayed Massachusetts town, who find their pupils and their pupils' money going to the moving-picture theater, shall make friends with its manager. They will possibly not find him a mammon of unrighteousness, but a fellow-man willing to cooperate with them to a good end if they can show him that it will pay. To this end they can contribute by actually paying him out of the school fund on condition that he will make his theater a part of the school system during certain hours of the day.

The educators now find that the children would rather give ten cents of their parents' money to go and look idly on at a succession of fictitious and largely impossible events as portrayed on the white curtain of the theater than come to school for nothing, or for nothing more than their fathers and mothers must now pay in taxes, and pass the day in studying and reciting from text-books which do not offer the allure of the picture show. But there is no reason why their studies, many of them, should not offer that allure. It is difficult, of course, and very likely it is impossible, say, for English spelling to be made pictorially charming, but it might very easily be made amusing by throwing on the white curtain an illustrated series of the more preposterous instances in which our orthography insults the reason and sins against common sense. Arithmetic would not lend itself much more readily to the processes of the moving pictures, and yet the mathematical ambition of the children might be stimulated by the vision, say, of a lightning-calculator working his miracles at a quivering blackboard. Every other branch of learning might be turned from the dry stock which now revolts the youthful mind, though it no longer threatens the youthful body so much as formerly, and set it before the charmed sense in all the bloom and sweetness of a living plant. We do not know just what sciences are studied in our public schools, but we will suppose geology may be one of them, and we believe that nothing more attractive to the young is now set forth on the theater curtain than some scene of Eocene life would be. No imaginative boy could fail of high joy in the presentation of

> dragons of the prime
> That tear each other in the slime,

or even a peaceful moment when the ichthyosaurus and the plesiosaur amphibiously sported together on the shores of time and the pterodactyl floated in the warm air above them. A flower-loving little maid might usefully lose herself in the vision of a forest of tree-ferns, and in thinking of the specimens she could gather for her herbarium from them she might feel through the association of geology with botany the unity of all science.

We are trying, perhaps too playfully, to commend to the reader the possibility which we have seriously in mind. We would really like to convince our educators of the immense helpfulness which they might find in the managers of the moving-picture shows if it came to their joint instruction in geography, history, and the various branches of biology. Fancy the appeal which ethnology alone, presented in pictured studies of the different races and civilizations, would have! Realize the immense advantage of presenting human events in pictures which the most careless eye could not refuse to seize, over the actual method of teaching history by names and dates meaningless to most of the young minds which now reject them! Consider the charm which visual knowledge of the discoverers and explorers, conquerors, heroes of all sorts, reformers of every type, martyrs, inventors, authors—even authors—would have if the student could know them in their persons as well as their experiences and performances!

We would not trifle with the case as the authorities of that Massachusetts town conceive it. They have reason to be anxious, if the moving pictures beguile once studious youth from the desire of learning; and wherever the moving-picture show prevails the custodians of childhood have the same reason to be anxious. But we would by no means have them vex the managers of such shows by vain opposition. Failing their co-operation, we would have the authorities take counsel with themselves whether moving pictures may not be introduced into the school curriculum. We are too little acquainted with the machinery and its working to suggest what steps should be taken to this end, but doubtless there are those who know. What we confidently look to is the excellent result. The children will no longer waste their money on the private picture show when they can have the public one for nothing, and the school will not be so hateful when learning is to be acquired with no more labor than lolling in the seats of the cinematographic theater now costs them. The lessons will be largely object-lessons. The wretched little boy or hapless little girl will not be obliged to try and guess what the different races of men are like; he or she will be shown the fact in photographs snapshotted from the originals in the streets of their cities or the depths of their jungles. At the mention of Columbus, the great admiral's best portrait will be reproduced on the white curtain, and Napoleon, Washington, Lincoln, and George the Third will be likewise visualized as they looked in life. The children can be shown a volcano in full blast, and its liquid rival, the waterspout, moving rapidly over the sea in pursuit of the nearest liner. A group of icebergs and a chain of mountains can be contrasted with equal advantage. An earthquake will not perhaps exceed the powers of the all-comprehending camera, and a modern battle with smokeless powder may be taught to rage before their eyes, with every detail of heads and legs blown off that they may realize how glorious war is at close range; towns burning in the background and women and children flying for their lives will fill the perspective. A sea-flight, with armored battle-ships sinking one another, could be as easily rendered if the films were recovered from the body of some witness representing an enterprising metropolitan journal in the engagement.

No economic or social fact need transcend the scope of the public-school picture show. The operations of some giant industry, such as coal-mining or iron-smelting, or some vast cotton-mill, with children younger than themselves tending the machinery, and the directors in their oriental-rugged and mahogany arm-chaired parlors, could be illustrated for the entertainment and instruction of the school boys and girls. Strikers and strike-breakers in a street fight, or the spectacle of policemen clubbing mothers from a train in which they are trying to send their little ones out of town beyond the struggling and starving, would impart an idea of our civilization which no amount of study could without it.

Of course, the more pleasing branches of study can be taught as easily as those we have glanced at. Agriculture, for instance, which is becoming more and more a science with every year; forestry, which vitally concerns our deforested continent; dynamitic culture, by which the fertility of the earth, sick of having its mere surface scratched, is restored a hundredfold; fruit-growing, cattle-grazing, can all be taught best with the help of illustrations. It is only a summer or two ago since the Central Park authorities thought it advisable to show the poor, ignorant East Side children where milk came from, and by having a cow milked in their presence convince all that would come to see the process. But the ignorance of such a simple primary fact could be universally dispersed by a moving picture far less cumbrously and at incalculably less cost to the community.

We have said enough, we hope, to persuade the public-school committees everywhere to try first what may be done with the moving-picture managers. They may be assured that in any conflict with these managers they will be beaten; for the managers will have all the children on their side; clandestinely, we fear, they will have the parents, too. But by inviting the managers to co-operate with them, they will have a fair chance of winning them over and at the same time sugar-coating the pill of learning so that the youth of this fair land of ours will eagerly swallow it. But if the managers hold out against the committees, and selfishly refuse to help them in their present strait, then we hope the committees will set up moving-picture shows of their own and make them an integral part of the public-school system. This, however, should be their final resort. It would savor of socialism, and socialism is the last thing we would advise, though as our whole public-school system is a phase of socialism, it might not be immediately anarchistic to try it.

Virginia Woolf

The Movies and Reality

People say that the savage no longer exists in us, that we are at the fag-end of civilization, that everything has been said already, and that it is too late to be ambitious. But these philosophers have presumably forgotten the movies. They have never seen the savages of the twentieth century watching the pictures. They have never sat themselves in front of the screen and thought how, for all the clothes on their backs and the carpets at their feet, no great distance separates them from those bright-eyed, naked men who knocked two bars of iron together and heard in that clangor a foretaste of the music of Mozart.

The bars in this case, of course, are so highly wrought and so covered over with accretions of alien matter that it is extremely difficult to hear anything distinctly. All is hubble-bubble, swarm and chaos. We are peering over the edge of a cauldron in which fragments of all shapes and savors seem to simmer; now and again some vast form heaves itself up, and seems about to haul itself out of chaos. Yet, at first sight, the art of the cinema seems simple, even stupid. There is the King shaking hands with a football team; there is Sir Thomas Lipton's yacht; there is Jack Horner winning the Grand National. The eye licks it all up instantaneously, and the brain, agreeably titillated, settles down to watch things happening without bestirring itself to think. For the ordinary eye, the English unaesthetic eye, is a simple mecha-

Originally published in *The New Republic,* August 4, 1926, pp. 308–310.

nism, which takes care that the body does not fall down coal-holes, provides the brain with toys and sweetmeats to keep it quiet, and can be trusted to go on behaving like a competent nursemaid until the brain comes to the conclusion that it is time to wake up. What is its surprise, then, to be roused suddenly in the midst of its agreeable somnolence and asked for help? The eye is in difficulties. The eye wants help. The eye says to the brain, "Something is happening which I do not in the least understand. You are needed." Together they look at the King, the boat, the horse, and the brain sees at once that they have taken on a quality which does not belong to the simple photograph of real life. They have become not more beautiful, in the sense in which pictures are beautiful, but shall we call it (our vocabulary is miserably insufficient) more real, or real with a different reality from that which we perceive in daily life? We behold them as they are when we are not there. We see life as it is when we have no part in it. As we gaze we seem to be removed from the pettiness of actual existence. The horse will not knock us down. The King will not grasp our hands. The wave will not wet our feet. From this point of vantage, as we watch the antics of our kind, we have time to feel pity and amusement, to generalize, to endow one man with the attributes of the race. Watching the boat sail and the wave break, we have time to open our minds to beauty and register on top of it the queer sensation—this beauty will continue, and this beauty will flourish whether we behold it or not. Further, all this happened ten years ago, we are told. We are beholding a world which has gone beneath the waves. Brides are emerging from the Abbey—they are now mothers; ushers are ardent—they are now silent; mothers are tearful; guests are joyful; this has been won and that has been lost, and it is over and done with. The War sprung its chasm at the feet of all this innocence and ignorance, but it was thus that we danced and pirouetted, toiled and desired, thus that the sun shone and the clouds scudded up to the very end.

But the picture-makers seem dissatisfied with such obvious sources of interest as the passage of time and the suggestiveness of reality. They despise the flight of gulls, ships on the Thames, the Prince of Wales, the Mile End Road, Piccadilly Circus. They want to be improving, altering, making an art of their own—naturally, for so much seems to be within their scope. So many arts seemed to stand by ready to offer their help. For example, there was literature. All the famous novels of the world, with their well known characters, and their famous scenes, only asked, it seemed, to be put on the films. What could be easier and simpler? The cinema fell upon its prey with immense rapacity, and to this moment largely subsists upon the body of its unfortunate victim. But the results are disastrous to both. The alliance is unnatural. Eye and brain are torn asunder ruthlessly as they try vainly to work in couples. The eye says: "Here is Anna Karenina." A voluptuous lady in black velvet wearing pearls comes before us. But the brain says: "That is no more Anna Karenina than it is Queen Victoria." For the brain knows Anna almost entirely by the inside of her mind—her charm, her passion, her despair. All the emphasis is laid by the cinema upon her teeth, her pearls, and her velvet. Then "Anna falls in love with Vronsky"—that is to say, the lady in black velvet falls into the arms of a gentleman in uniform, and they kiss with enormous succulence, great deliberation, and infinite gesticulation on a sofa in an extremely well appointed library, while a gardener incidentally mows the lawn. So we lurch and lumber through the most famous novels of the world. So we spell them out in words of one syllable written, too, in the scrawl of an illiterate schoolboy. A kiss is love. A broken cup is jealousy. A grin is happiness. Death is a hearse. None of these things has the least connection with the novel that Tolstoy wrote, and it is only when we give up trying to connect the pictures with the book that we guess from some accidental scene—like the gardener mowing the lawn—what the cinema might do if it were left to its own devices.

But what, then, are its devices? If it ceased to be a parasite, how would it walk erect? At present it is only from hints that one can frame any conjecture. For instance, at a performance of *Dr. Caligari* the other day, a shadow shaped like a tadpole suddenly appeared at one corner of the screen. It swelled to an immense size, quivered, bulged, and sank back again into nonentity. For a moment it seemed to embody some monstrous, diseased imagination of the lunatic's brain. For a moment, it seemed as if thought could be conveyed by shape more effectively than by words. The monstrous, quivering tadpole seemed to be fear itself, and not the statement, "I am afraid." In fact, the shadow was accidental, and the effect unintentional. But if a shadow at a certain moment can suggest so much more than the actual gestures and words of men and women in a state of fear, it seems plain that the cinema has within its grasp innumerable symbols for emotions that have so far failed to find expression. Terror has, besides its ordinary forms, the shape of a tadpole; it burgeons, bulges, quivers, disappears. Anger is not merely rant and rhetoric, red faces and clenched fists. It is perhaps a black line wriggling upon a white sheet. Anna and Vronsky need no longer scowl and grimace. They have at their command—but what? Is there, we ask, some secret language which we feel and see, but never speak, and, if so, could this be made visible to the eye? Is there any characteristic which thought possesses that can be rendered visible without the help of words? It has speed and slowness; dartlike directness and vaporous circumlocution. But it has also, especially in moments of emotion, the picture-making power, the need to lift its burden to another bearer; to let an image run side by side along with it. The likeness of the thought is, for some reason, more beautiful, more comprehensible, more available than the thought itself. As everybody knows, in Shakespeare the most complex ideas form chains of images through which we mount, changing and turning, until we reach the light of day. But, obviously, the images of a poet are not to be cast in bronze, or traced by pencil. They are compact of a thousand suggestions of which the visual is only the most obvious or the uppermost. Even the simplest image: "My luve's like a red, red rose, that's newly sprung in June," presents us with impressions of moisture and warmth and the glow of crimson and the softness of petals inextricably mixed and strung upon the lilt of a rhythm which is itself the voice of the passion and hesitation of the lover. All this, which is accessible to words, and to words alone, the cinema must avoid.

Yet if so much of our thinking and feeling is connected with seeing, some residue of visual emotion which is of no use either to painter or to poet may still await the cinema. That such symbols will be quite unlike the real objects which we see before us seems highly probable. Something abstract, something which moves with controlled and conscious art, something which calls for the very slightest help from words or music to make itself intelligible, yet justly uses them subserviently—of such movements and abstractions the films may, in time to come, be composed. Then, indeed, when some new symbol for expressing thought is found, the film-maker has enormous riches at his command. The exactitude of reality and its surprising power of suggestion are to be had for the asking. Annas and Vronskys— there they are in the flesh. If into this reality he could breathe emotion, could animate the perfect form with thought, then his booty could be hauled in hand over hand. Then, as smoke pours from Vesuvius, we should be able to see thought in its wildness, in its beauty, in its oddity, pouring from men with their elbows on a table; from women with their little handbags slipping to the floor. We should see these emotions mingling together and affecting each other.

We should see violent changes of emotion produced by their collision. The most fantastic contrasts could be flashed before us with a speed which the writer can only toil in vain; the dream architecture of arches and battlements, of cascades falling and fountains rising, which sometimes visits us in sleep or shapes itself in half-darkened rooms, could be realized before our waking eyes. No fantasy could be too farfetched or insubstantial. The past could be unrolled, distances annihilated, and the gulfs which dislocate novels (when, for instance, Tolstoy has to pass from Levin to Anna, and in so doing jars his story and wrenches and arrests our sympathies) could, by the sameness of the background, by the repetition of some scene, be smoothed away.

How all this is to be attempted, much less achieved, no one at the moment can tell us. We get intimations only in the chaos of the streets, perhaps, when some momentary assembly of color, sound, movement suggests that here is a scene awaiting a new art to be transfixed. And sometimes at the cinema in the midst of its immense dexterity and enormous technical proficiency, the curtain parts and we behold, far off, some unknown and unexpected beauty. But it is for a moment only. For a strange thing has happened—while all the other arts were born naked, this, the youngest, has been born fully clothed. It can say everything before it has anything to say. It is as if the savage tribe, instead of finding two bars of iron to play with, had found, scattering the seashore, fiddles, flutes, saxophones, trumpets, grand pianos by Erard and Bechstein, and had begun with incredible energy, but without knowing a note of music, to hammer and thump upon them all at the same time.

H. L. Mencken

Appendix from Moronia

Part 1

Note on Technic

Having made of late, after a longish hiatus, two separate attempts to sit through movie shows, I can only report that the so-called art of the film still eludes me. I was not chased out either time by the low intellectual content of the pictures on display. For one thing, I am anything but intellectual in my tastes, and for another thing the films I saw were not noticeably deficient in that direction. The ideas in them were simply the common and familiar ideas of the inferior nine-tenths of mankind. They were hollow and obvious, but they were not more hollow and obvious than the ideas one encounters in the theater every day, or in the ordinary run of popular novels, or, for that matter, in the discourses of the average American statesman or divine. Rotary, hearing worse once a week, still manages to preserve its idealism and digest carbohydrates.

What afflicts the movies is not an unpalatable ideational content so much as an idiotic and irritating technic. The first moving-pictures, as I remember them thirty years ago, presented more or less continuous scenes. They were played like ordinary

From *Prejudices:* Sixth Series, by H. L. Mencken. Copyright 1927 by Alfred A. Knopf, Inc. and renewed 1955 by H. L. Mencken. Reprinted by permission of the publisher.

plays, and so one could follow them lazily and at ease. But the modern movie is no such organic whole; it is simply a maddening chaos of discrete fragments. The average scene, if the two shows I attempted were typical, cannot run for more than six or seven seconds. Many are far shorter, and very few are appreciably longer. The result is confusion horribly confounded. How can one work up any rational interest in a fable that changes its locale and its characters ten times a minute? Worse, this dizzy jumping about is plainly unnecessary: all it shows is the professional incompetence of the gilded pants-pressers, decayed actors and other such half-wits to whom the making of movies seems to be entrusted. Unable to imagine a sequence of coherent scenes, and unprovided with a sufficiency of performers capable of playing them if they were imagined, these preposterous mountebanks are reduced to the childish device of avoiding action altogether. Instead of it they present what is at bottom nothing but a poorly articulated series of meaningless postures and grimaces. One sees a ham cutting a face, and then one sees his lady co-star squeezing a tear—and so on, endlessly. These mummers cannot be said, in any true sense, to act at all. They merely strike attitudes—and are then whisked off. If, at the first attempt upon a scene, the right attitude is not struck, then all they have to do is to keep on trying until they strike it. On those terms a chimpanzee could play Hamlet, or even Juliet.

To most of the so-called actors engaged in the movies, I daresay, no other course would be possible. They are such obvious incompetents that they could no more play a rational scene, especially one involving any subtlety, than a cow could jump over the moon. They are engaged, not for their histrionic skill, but simply for their capacity to fill the heads of romantic virgins and neglected wives with the sort of sentiments that the Christian religion tries so hard to put down. It is, no doubt, a useful office, assuming that the human race must, should and will go on, but it has no more to do with acting, as an art, than being a Federal judge has with preserving the Constitution. The worst of it is that the occasional good actor, venturing into the movies, is brought down to the common level by the devices thus invented to conceal the incompetence of his inferiors. It is quite as impossible to present a plausible impersonation in a series of unrelated (and often meaningless) postures as it would be to make a sensible speech in a series of college yells. So the good actor, appearing in the films, appears to be almost as bad as the natural movie ham. One sees him only as one sees a row of telegraph poles, riding in a train. However skillful he may be, he is always cut off before, by any intelligible use of the devices of his trade, he can make the fact evident.

In one of the pictures I saw lately a principal actor was George Bernard Shaw. The first scene showed him for fifteen or twenty seconds continuously, and it was at once plain that he had a great deal of histrionic skill—far more, indeed, than the average professional actor. He was seen engaged in a friendly argument with several other dramatists, among them Sir James M. Barrie and Sir Arthur Wing Pinero. Having admired all these notorious men for many years, and never having had the honor of meeting or even witnessing them, I naturally settled down with a grateful grunt to the pleasure of feasting my eyes upon them. But after that first scene all I saw of Shaw was a series of fifteen or twenty maddening flashes, none of them more than five seconds long. He would spring into view, leap upon Barrie or Pinero—and then disappear. Then he would spring back, his whiskers bristling—and disappear again. It was as maddening as the ring of the telephone.

There is, of course, a legitimate use for this off-again-on-again device in the movies: it may be used, at times, very effectively and even intelligently. The beautiful heroine, say, is powdering her nose, preparing to go out to her fatal dinner with her libidinous boss. Suddenly there flashes through her mind a pro-phylactic memory of the Sunday-school in her home town far away. An actress on the stage, with such a scene to play, faces serious technical difficulties: it is very hard for her—that is, it has been hard since Ibsen abolished the soliloquy—to convey the exact revolutions of her conscience to her audience. But the technic of the movies makes it very easy—in fact, so easy that it requires no skill at all. The director simply prepares a series of scenes showing what is going through the heroine's mind. There is the church on the hill, with the horde of unhappy children being driven into its basement by the town constable. There is the old maid teacher expounding the day's Golden Text, II Kings, ıı, 23–24. There is a flash of the two she-bears "taring" the "forty and two" little children. There is the heroine, in ringlets, clapping her hands in dutiful Presbyterian glee. There is a flash of the Sunday-school superintendent, his bald head shining, warning the scholars against the sins of simony, barratry and adultery. There is the collection, with the bad boy putting in the suspenders' button. There is the flash showing him, years later, as a bank president.

All this is ingenious. More, it is humane, for it prevents the star trying to act, and so saves the spectators pain. But it is manifestly a poor substitute for acting on the occasions when acting is actually demanded by the plot—that is, on the occasions when there must be cumulative action, and not merely a series of postures. Such occasions give rise to what the old-time dramatic theorists called *scènes à faire,* which is to say, scenes of action, crucial scenes, necessary scenes. In the movies they are dismembered, and so spoiled. Try to imagine the balcony scene from *Romeo and Juliet* in a string of fifty flashes—first Romeo taking his station and spitting on his hands, then Juliet with her head as big as a hay-wagon, then the two locked in a greasy kiss, then the Nurse taking a drink of gin, then Romeo rolling his eyes, and so on. If you can imagine it, then you ought to be in Hollywood, dodging bullets and amassing wealth.

If I were in a constructive mood I'd probably propose reforms, but that mood, I regret to say, is not on me. In any case, I doubt that proposing reforms would do any good. For this idiotic movie technic, as I have shown, has its origin in the incompetence of the clowns who perform in the great majority of movies, and it would probably be impossible to displace them with competent actors, for the customers of the movie-parlors appear to love them, and even to admire them. It is hard to believe, but it is obviously so. A successful movie mime is probably the most admired human being ever seen in the world. He is admired more than Napoleon, Lincoln or Beethoven; more, even, than Coolidge. The effects of this adulation, upon the mime himself and especially upon his clients, ought to be given serious study by competent psychiatrists, if any can be found. For there is nothing more corrupting to the human psyche, I believe, than the mean admiration of mean things. It produces a double demoralization, intellectual and spiritual. Its victim becomes not only a jackass, but also a bounder. The movie-parlors, I suspect, are turning out such victims by the million: they will, in the long run, so debauch the American proletariat that it will begin to put Coolidge above Washington, and Peaches Browning above Coolidge.

Meanwhile, they are ruining the ancient and noble art of the dramatist—an art that has engaged the talents of some of the greatest men the world has ever seen. And they are, at the same time, ruining the lesser but by no means contemptible art of the actor. It is no advantage to a movie ham to be a competent actor; on the contrary, it is a handicap. If he tried to act, as acting has been understood since the days of Æschylus, his director would shut him off instanter: what is wanted is simply aphrodisiacal posturing. And if, by any chance, his director were drunk and let him run on, the vast majority of movie morons would probably rush out of the house, bawling that the film was dull and cheap, and that they had been swindled.

Part 2

Interlude in Socratic Manner

Having completed your æsthetic researches at Hollywood, what is your view of the film art now?

I made no researches at Hollywood, and was within the corporate bounds of the town, in fact, only on a few occasions, and then for only a few hours. I spent my time in Los Angeles, studying the Christian pathology of that great city. When not so engaged I mainly devoted myself to quiet guzzling with Joe Hergesheimer, Jim Quirk, Johnny Hemphill, Jim Tully, Walter Wanger and other such literati.[1] For the rest, I visited friends in the adjacent deserts, some of them employed in the pictures and some not. They treated me with immense politeness. With murderers as thick in the town as evangelists, nothing would have been easier than to have had me killed, but they let me go.

Did any of them introduce you to the wild night-life of the town?

The wildest night-life I encountered was at Sister Aimée McPherson's tabernacle. I saw no wildness among the movie-folk. They seemed to me, in the main, to be very serious and even gloomy people. And no wonder, for they are worked like Pullman porters or magazine editors. When they are engaged in posturing for a film and have finished their day's labor they are far too tired for any recreation requiring stamina. I encountered but two authentic souses in three weeks. One was a cowboy and the other was an author. I heard of a lady getting tight at a party, but I was not present. The news was a sensation

1. A collection of miscellaneous talents: Hergesheimer was a novelist (author of *Java Head*), Quirk was editor of *Photoplay* magazine; Tully was an actor; Wanger a producer.

in the town. Such are the sorrows of poor mummers: their most banal peccadilloes are magnified into horrors. Regard the unfortunate Chaplin. If he were a lime and cement dealer his latest divorce case would not have got two lines in the newspapers. But, as it was, he was placarded all over the front pages because he had had a banal disagreement with one of his wives. The world hears of such wild, frenzied fellows as Tully, and puts them down as typical of Hollywood. But Tully is not an actor; he eats actors. I saw him devour half a dozen of them on the half-shell in an hour. He wears a No. 30 collar and has a colossal capacity for wine-bibbing; I had to call up my last reserves to keep up with him. But the typical actor is a slim and tender fellow. What would be a mere apéritif for Tully or me would put him under the table, yelling for his pastor.

So you caught no glimpses of immorality?

Immorality? Oh, my God! Hollywood, despite the smell of patchouli and rattle of revolver fire, seemed to me to be one of the most respectable towns in America. Even Baltimore can't beat it. The notion that actors are immoral fellows is a delusion that comes down to us from Puritan days, just as the delusion that rum is a viper will go down to posterity from our days. There is no truth in it. The typical actor, at least in America, is the most upright of men: he always marries the girl. How many actors are bachelors? Not one in a thousand. The divorce rate is high among them simply because the marriage rate is so high. An actor, encountering a worthy girl, leaps from the couch to the altar almost as fast as a Baptist leaps from the altar to the couch. It is his incurable sentimentality that fetches him: if he was not born a romantic he is not an actor. Worse, his profession supports his natural weakness. In plays and movies he always marries the girl in the end, and so it seems to him to be the decent thing to do it in his private life. Actors always copy the doings of the characters they impersonate: no Oscar was needed to point out that nature always imitates art. I heard, of course, a great deal of gossip in Los Angeles, but all save a trivial part of it was excessively romantic. Nearly every great female star, it appeared, was desperately in love, either with her husband or with some pretty and well-heeled fellow, usually not an actor. And every male star was mooning over some coy and lovely miss. I heard more sweet love stories in three weeks than I had heard in New York in the previous thirty years. The whole place stank of orange-blossoms. Is honest love conducive to vice? Then one may argue that it is conducive to delirium tremens to be a Presbyterian elder. One of the largest industries in Hollywood is that of the florists. Next comes that of the traffickers in wedding silver. One beautiful lady star told me that buying such presents cost her $11,000 last year.

But the tales go round. Is there no truth in them at all?

To the best of my knowledge and belief, none. They are believed because the great masses of the plain people, though they admire movie actors, also envy them, and hence hate them. It is the old human story. Why am I hated by theologians? It is because I am an almost unparalleled expert in all branches of theology. Whenever they tackle me, my superior knowledge and talent floor them. In precisely the same way I hate such fellows as the movie Salvini, Jack Gilbert.[2] Gilbert is an amiable and tactful young man, and treats me with the politeness properly due to my years and learning. But I heard in Culver City that no less than two thousand head of women, many of them rich, were mashed on him. Well, I can recall but fifteen or twenty women who have ever showed any sign of being flustered by me, and not one of them, at a forced sale, would have realized $200. Hence I hate Gilbert, and would rejoice unaffectedly to see him taken in some scandal that would stagger humanity. If he is ac-

2. John Gilbert (1895 1936), star of *Flesh and the Devil* (1927); several times co-starred with Garbo. Tommaso Salvini (1829–1916) was an Italian actor who specialized in tragic roles.

cused of anything less than murdering his wife and eight children I shall be disappointed.

Then why do you speak for Mr. Chaplin?

Simply because he is not a handsome dog, as Gilbert is. The people who hate him do so because he is rich. It is the thought that his trouble will bust him that gives them delight. But I have no desire for money and so his prosperity does not offend me. I always have too much money; it is easy to get in New York, provided one is not a professing Christian. Gilbert, I suppose, is rich too; he wears very natty clothes. But it is not his wealth that bothers me: it is those two thousand head of women.

So, failing researches, you continue ignorant of the film art?

Ignorant? What a question! How could any man remain ignorant of the movies after three weeks in Los Angeles? As well continue ignorant of laparotomy after three weeks in a hospital sun-parlor! No, I am full of information about them, some of it accurate, for I heard them talked day and night, and by people who actually knew something about them. There was but one refuge from that talk, and that was La McPherson's basilica. Moreover, I have hatched some ideas of my own.

As for example?

That the movie folks, in so far as they are sentient at all, are on the hooks of a distressing dilemma. They have built their business upon a foundation of morons, and now they are paying for it. They seem to be unable to make a presentable picture without pouring out tons of money, and when they have made it they must either sell it to immense audiences of half-wits, or go broke. There seems to be very little ingenuity and resourcefulness in them. They are apparently quite unable, despite their melodramatic announcements of salary cuts, to solve the problem of making movies cheaply, and yet intelligently, so that civilized persons may visit the movie-parlors without pain. But soon or late some one will have to solve it. Soon or late the movies will have to split into two halves. There will be movies for the present mob, and there will be movies for the relatively enlightened minority. The former will continue idiotic; the latter, if competent men to make them are unearthed, will show sense and beauty.

Have you caught the scent of any such men?

Not yet. There are some respectable craftsmen in Hollywood. (I judged them by their talk: I have not seen many of their actual pictures.) They tackle the problems of their business in a more or less sensible manner. They have learned a lot from the Germans. But I think it would be stretching a point to say that there are any artists among them—as yet. They are adept, but not inspired. The movies need a first-rate artist—a man of genuine competence and originality. If he is in Hollywood to-day, he is probably bootlegging, running a pants pressing parlor, or grinding a camera crank. The movie magnates seek him in literary directions. They pin their faith to novelists and playwrights. I presume to believe that this is bad medicine. The fact that a man can write a competent novel is absolutely no reason for assuming that he can write a competent film. The two things are as unlike as Pilsner and coca-cola. Even a sound dramatist is not necessarily a competent scenario-writer. What the movies need is a school of authors who will forget all dialogue and description, and try to set forth their ideas in terms of pure motion. It can be done, and it will be done. The German, Dr Murnau, showed the way in certain scenes of *The Last Laugh* [1925]. But the American magnates continue to buy bad novels and worse plays, and then put over-worked hacks to the sorry job of translating them into movies. It is like hiring men to translate college yells into riddles. Æschylus himself would have been stumped by such a task.

When do you think the Shakespeare of the movies will ap-pear? And where will he come from?

God knows. He may even be an American, as improbable as it may seem. One thing, only, I am sure of: he will not get much for his masterpieces. He will have to give them away, and the first manager who puts them on will lose money. The movies to-day are too rich to have any room for genuine artists. They produce a few passable craftsmen, but no artists. Can you imagine a Beethoven making $100,000 a year? If so, then you have a better imagination than Beethoven himself. No, the present movie folk, I fear, will never quite solve the problem, save by some act of God. They are too much under the heel of the East Side gorillas who own them. They think too much about money. They have allowed it to become too important to them, and believe they couldn't get along without it. This is an unfortunate delusion. Money is important to mountebanks, but not to artists. The first really great movie, when it comes at last, will probably cost less than $5000. A true artist is always a romantic. He doesn't ask what the job will pay; he asks if it will be interesting. In this way all the loveliest treasures of the human race have been fashioned—by careless and perhaps some-what foolish men. The late Johann Sebastian Bach, compared to a movie star with nine automobiles, was simply a damned fool. But I cherish the feeling that a scientific inquiry would also develop other differences between them.

Are you against the star system?

I am neither for it nor against it. A star is simply a performer who pleases the generality of morons better than the average. Certainly I see no reason why such a performer should not be paid a larger salary than the average. The objection to swollen salaries should come from the stars themselves—that is, assum-ing them to be artists. The system diverts them from their proper business of trying to produce charming and amusing movies, and converts them into bogus society folk. What could be more ridiculous? And pathetic? I go further: it is tragic. As I have said in another place, nothing is more tragic in this world than for otherwise worthy people to meanly admire and imitate mean things. One may have some respect for the movie lady who buys books and sets up as an intellectual, for it is a creditable thing to want to be (or even simply to want to appear) well-informed and intelligent. But I can see nothing worthy in wanting to be mistaken for the president of a bank. Artists should sniff at such dull drudges, not imitate them. The movies will leap ahead the day some star in Hollywood organizes a string quartette and begins to study Mozart.

Jack London

The Message of Motion Pictures

Pantomime and pictures—the symbols have marked every forward step in the evolution of the human race.

The vague things that flitted through the consciousness of prehistoric man made him grope for a means of expression, and the language of gutturals was born. Perhaps, in that day, the vocabulary numbered thirty or forty words relating to concrete things. Then came an unrecorded period when certain molecular changes occurred in the cerebral cells. A gibbering ancestor peered cautiously through the branches and twigs and the rustling leaves of his arboreal shelter. There was less slant to his forehead, and more bridge to his nose, in comparison with the others of his kind. He wondered greatly as the altered cells formed a glimmering nebula into an abstract idea—the beginning of thought. He wanted to tell of the strange event, but there were no sounds to convey his meaning. He invented a new sound, and the others stared and chattered in bewilderment; so he resorted to pantomime to explain the sound.

When his descendants had left the trees for the rocky dens in the cliffs, the urge to express their thoughts led to a new discovery. With a sharpened stone one could scratch a likeness of things that had no sound on the smooth walls of the cave; so

Originally published in *Paramount Magazine,* I, no. 2 (February 1915), pp. 1–2.

they produced pictures and originated sounds to represent them in vocabulary.

The language grew. Thoughts expanded through expression, and the ability to discuss them. These half-men learned to unite in a common defense against the primeval monsters.

Language bridged the chasm, thousands of centuries wide, and enabled the human race to cross over from the aboriginal wilderness to this day of newspapers and electric lights. Without pictures and pantomime there would have been no bridge. They were the helpers who built it.

The prod of gregarious instinct had impelled men to live together. Language had given expression to the adumbrations of thought which urged them to strengthen individual weakness by cooperation. The day of right by physical might commenced to wane. But human greed is insatiate. When one monster of selfishness is overthrown another is born to threaten the advancement of the human race. It is a freak of heredity—-an atavism, if you will.

Pantomime and pictures created words; words paved the way to language, and language to education. In the egotism of superior knowledge, education all but discarded the lowly workers who had helped in the making. A new abyss yawned deeply across the pathway of progress.

A dynasty of right by mental might was the outgrowth of education, and language was its Prime Minister. One must know the Prime Minister well to achieve the inner circle of the court, and the selfish few saw to it that the circle was small. The others hobbled along, sullen, dejected. They no longer feared the dangers of the forests and cliffs—they shrank from the predatory monsters of their own kind, those cold, calculating brutes that tortured with cruel slavery rather than death.

And so it went through the centuries of medievalism! The people groped for ways to express the dim and formless thoughts against oppression that grew in their consciousness. In a more developed mind, here and there, the nebulous mental picture solidified, and they went forth to explain the message. Many could not understand the new sounds; but others grasped the meaning and spread the knowledge. Men united, and the new sounds became the slogan of revolution. Education became free to all.

It is the nature of people to be inconsequential. The victory gained, some have been slow to take advantage, some lack the opportunity. The vocabulary of the average man today numbers about two hundred words. Vague, restless thoughts of injustice crowd the cerebral cells without power of expression, while the predatory few gather the fruits of industrial slavery.

Again the cycle of evolution comes with pantomime and pictures—motion pictures. It batters down the barriers of poverty and environment that obstructed the roads to education, and distributes knowledge in a language that all may understand. The workingman with the meager vocabulary is the equal of the scholar. The dynasty of right by mental might had pinned its faith to the spoken word. It is on the wane.

Universal education—that is the message.

Let the doubting Thomases remember that evolution works slowly. Compare the pictures of today with the feeble output of a short decade back. Time and distance have been annihilated by the magic film to draw the world's people closer together. We travel—the black man in his daily life on the Ganges is much like ourselves, but for the environment. The houses and villages of the yellow men appear like toys, and the people as children. Wander through the cities of our own country, and feel the primitive bonds of community drawing you nearer to the people you see in the picture. Gaze horror-struck on the war scenes, and you become an advocate of peace. No language can imprint things on your consciousness so vividly.

The greatest minds have delivered their messages through the book or play. The motion picture spreads it on the screen where all can read and understand—and enjoy. No more are the pleasures of the theater for the rich alone. The poor man's pennies spread before him and his family the best of the drama in its finest forms. World renowned actors and actresses walk, and even speak, for them upon the screen.

And so, by this magic means, are the extremes of society brought a step nearer to each other in the inevitable readjustment in the ways of men.

G. K. Chesterton

On the Movies

There is a fault in the current art of the films which is intensely typical of our time. I have hardly ever seen a motion picture in which the motion was not too rapid to give any real sense of rapidity. For just as a thing can be too small to be even seen as small, or too large to be even seen as large, so it can easily be too swift to be even seen as swift. In order that a man riding on a horse should look as if he were riding hard, it is first necessary that he should look like a man riding on a horse. It is not even an impossibly rapid ride, if he only looks like a Catherine wheel seen through a fog. It is not an impression of swiftness; because it is not an impression of anything. It is not an exaggeration of swiftness; because there is nothing to exaggerate. It would be perfectly natural that the pace of such a gallop should be exaggerated; but it is not. All art has an element of emphasis, which is really exaggeration; the exaggeration varies with the type of artistic work to be done, as whether it is tragedy, comedy, farce, or melodrama; but the exaggeration may go to the very wildest lengths without necessarily losing this vividness and actuality. But when it goes past a certain point, in a certain direction, it passes a merely material border of the powers of the eye and the conditions of time and space; and it becomes not a rapid but rather an invisible thing. This would seem to be a very

From *Generally Speaking* (1929) by G. K. Chesterton. Published by permission of Messrs. A. P. Watt & Son, London, England.

obvious piece of common sense in connexion with any artistic effect; yet these artists and producers, who talk so learnedly and work so laboriously, in connexion with artistic effects, have apparently not yet learnt even a little thing like that.

For instance, I have a simple, melodramatic mind; there is nothing lofty or peace-loving about me; and I thoroughly enjoy seeing people knocked down on the stage. I should have no objection to seeing them knocked down in real life, if the people were wisely and thoughtfully selected. In fact, I have seen them knocked down in real life; and sometimes knocked down very rapidly. It would be entirely in the right spirit of representative art if on the stage or on the film they were knocked down rather more rapidly than they can be in real life. But in nearly all those American cinema stories about "the great open spaces where men are men," my complaint is that when they begin to fight, the men are not men; but blurred and bewildering flashes of lightning. No man however slick, in no saloon however wild, in no mountains however rocky, ever moved with that degree of celerity to do anything. I therefore cease to believe in the man altogether; as much as if his body had visibly burst in two and the sawdust run out. He may be quicker on the draw than any other man in Red Dog Canyon, but I will be shot if any man ever shot or hit as quickly as all that. The principle applies to every sort of shooting. In one of Mr. Belloc's satires there is an allusion to an aristocratic infant who was "three years old and shooting up like a young lily." It is just as if the film were to take this sort of swiftness literally; and show the heroine rapidly elongating like the neck of Alice in Wonderland. It is as if the Coming of Spring were represented on the film in a series of jerks and leaps; as in that famous legendary landscape in which the hedges are shooting and the bull rushes out. In growing more rapid it would grow less realistic; and even if the bull does rush out, he must not rush ten times quicker than any bull is capable of rushing. We may well be content if he rushes about twice as quickly as the quickest bull in the world. But we, who sit watching these bloodless and blameless bull-fights, do not like to see the shattering of all conviction by mere confusion. We do like to fancy for a moment that we are looking at a real bull-fight; that we are contemplating a Spanish bull and not merely an Irish bull.

It is but part of the modern malady; the incapacity for doing things without overdoing things. It is an incapacity to understand the ancient paradox of moderation. As the drunkard is the man who does not understand the delicate and exquisite moment when he is moderately and reasonably drunk, so the motorist and the motion-picture artist are people who do not understand the divine and dizzy moment when they really feel that things are moving. Sometimes the drunkard and the motorist are blended in one perfect whole; and I disclaim all responsibility for the misuse of my jest about drunkenness, especially when it is combined with motoring. But the point is that there is probably an ultimate extreme of speed in which even a drunkard would enjoy nothing except a strangled sense of standing still. There comes a point at which speed stuns itself; and there is an unintentional truth in the exclamation of the radiant ass who declares that his new car is simply stunning. If speed can thus devour itself even in real life, it need not be said that on the accelerated cinema it swallows itself alive with all the suicidal finality of the hero who jumped down his own throat. Cars on the film often go much too fast, not for the laws of New York or London, but for the laws of space and time. For nature has written a Speed Limit in the nerves of the eye and the cells of the brain; and exceeding it, or even trying to exceed it, does not mean going to a prison but to a madhouse.

An artistic effect is something that is slightly impossible; though grammarians and logicians may both think this an impossible phrase. It is something that is mildly mad or faintly absurd. It is something that is just over the precipice of this

prosaic world; but not far out in the void of vanity and emptiness. To accelerate a machine so as to make Mr. Tom Mix or
Mr. Douglas Fairbanks run *a little* faster than a man can really
run produces a magnificent impression; a theatrical effect like a
thunderclap. To make him run a little faster than that destroys
the whole effect at a blow; it merely extinguishes the man and
exposes the machine. There is a figure in one of Michael
Angelo's frescoes, in which the legs are somewhat lengthened
so as to give an overwhelming impression of flying through the
air. But if the legs had been extended indefinitely like the two
parallel straight lines that could never meet, if they had wan-
dered away in two endless strips over the whole of the Sistine
Chapel, they would not produce any impression of rushing or of
anything else. But the modern sensationalist has no notion of
effecting anything except by extending it; by tugging its nerves
out telescopically like some form of Asiatic torture; and increasing the pleasures of man by interminably pulling his leg.
And that is why some of us feel the presence of something stupid
and even barbaric in all this progress and acceleration; because
it is but the elongation of one line and the exaggeration of one
idea.

Speed itself is a balance and a comparison, as we know when
two railway trains are moving at the same rate and both seem to
be standing still. So a whole society may seem to be standing
still, if it is only rushing unanimously in a mere routine; for
indeed the whole society which we call mankind is for ever rushing on the round orbit of the earth about the sun; but rushing
without any marked feeling of exhilaration. The extension of
speed in area, as well as in degree, is a way of neutralizing its
full artistic effect. I have seen this error also on the films; when
so many things are made to move and mix in the motion picture
that it seems to be a whirlpool rather than a river. First it is all
motion and no picture; and then it is not even motion because it
is not even aim; and in all motion there must be the outline of

motive. But I suppose that so very simple a blunder must have a rather subtle cause. Nothing is more curious, in the artistic history of mankind, than the obviousness of the things that were left out, compared with the cunning and intelligence of the things that were put in. It is a puzzle to understand how the splendid pagan poets of antiquity managed to get their effects with such few and vague ideas about colour; so that we do not always know whether they mean purple or blue or merely bright. It is equally a puzzle how the magnificent mediaeval craftsmen could not see that their figure-drawing was as bad as their colour scheme was brilliant. All ages leave out something, which to other ages seems very simple and self-evident; and it seems as if this age would make itself a laughing-stock in turn to later times, by not seeing the most obvious of all the psychological facts in æsthetics—the principle of contrast. It will have failed even to understand that you cannot see a man run fast if you cannot see him at all.

G. K. CHESTERTON

About the Films

The time has come to protest against certain very grave perils in the cinema and the popular films. I do not mean the peril of immoral films, but the peril of moral ones. I have, indeed, a definite objection to immoral films, but it is becoming more

From *As I Was Saying* (1936) by G. K. Chesterton. Published by permission of Messrs. A. P. Watt & Son, London, England.

and more difficult to discuss a definite morality with people whose very immorality is indefinite. And, for the rest, merely lowbrow films seem to me much more moral than many of the highbrow ones. Mere slapstick pantomime, farces of comic collapse and social topsy-turvydom, are, if anything, definitely good for the soul. To see a banker or broker or prosperous business man running after his hat, kicked out of his house, hurled from the top of a skyscraper, hung by one leg to an aeroplane, put into a mangle, rolled out flat by a steam-roller, or suffering any such changes of fortune, tends in itself rather to edification; to a sense of the insecurity of earthly things and the folly of that pride which is based on the accident of prosperity. But the films of which I complain are not those in which famous or fashionable persons become funny or undignified, but those in which they become far too dignified and only unintentionally funny.

In this connexion, it is especially the educational film that threatens to darken and weaken the human intelligence. I do not mean the educational film in the technical or scientific sense; the presentation of the definite details of some science or branch of study. In these innocent matters, even education can do comparatively little harm to the human brain. There are a number of really delightful films, for instance, dealing with exploration and local aspects of biology or botany. Nothing could be more charmingly fanciful than such natural history; especially when its monsters seem to emulate the Snark or the Jumblies, and become figures of unnatural history. But in that sort of unnatural history there is nothing unnatural. The Loves of the Penguins are doubtless as pure as the Loves of the Triangles; and to see a really fine film in which an elephant playfully smashes up four or five flourishing industrial towns or imperial outposts only realizes a daydream already dear to every healthy human instinct. Where the real peril begins to appear is not in natural history, but in history. It is in the story of those talkative and inventive penguins of whom M. Anatole France wrote in the tale of that terrible and incalculable creature, who is so much more ruthless and devastating than the wildest rogue elephant, since he does not destroy industrial cities, but builds them.

In short, it is in relation with the story of Man, the monster of all monsters and the mystery of all mysteries, that our natural history may become in the dangerous sense unnatural. And everybody knows that the commonest way in which history can grow crooked, or become unnatural, is through partisanship and prejudice, and the desire to draw too simple a moral from only one side of the case. Now, it is just here that the most successful films are in some danger of becoming actually anti-educational, while largely professing to be educational. In this connexion, it will be well to recall two or three determining facts of the general situation of society and the arts to-day. The first fact to realize is this: that only a little while ago the more thick-headed prejudices of provincial history were beginning to wear a little thin. Men would still take, as they were entitled to take, their own side according to their own sympathies. But they were beginning to realize that history consists of human beings, and not of heroes and villains out of an old Adelphi melodrama. Whether men were for or against Queen Elizabeth, they did begin to understand that she was something a little more complex than Good Queen Bess; and that even her unfortunate sister was in a situation not to be completely simplified by the use of a popular expletive, as in Bloody Mary.

It began to be admitted that the great seventeenth-century struggle, about whether England should be a Monarchy or an Aristocracy, could not be used merely to prove that Cromwell was never anything but a saint or Charles I never anything but a martyr. This great change for the good was very largely connected with the passing of the old Two-Party System. There had been a time when people were told to choose, not so much between Gladstone and Disraeli, as between a popular figure who was not Gladstone and another popular figure who was not Disraeli. The wary Old Parliamentary Hand, with his Tory traditions of the Oxford Movement, was represented as a wild, revolutionary idealist, everywhere demanding that the heavens should fall, that some Utopian justice might be done. The cynical cosmopolitan adventurer, with his romantic loyalty to Israel and his open contempt for the common Conservative point of view, was praised as a hearty English country gentleman, innocently interested in crops which consisted chiefly of primroses. These fatuous electioneering fictions were beginning to fade away; partly through a reaction towards the rather acid Lytton Strachey biographies, partly through a more sane and liberal historical interest in historical characters who really were very interesting human beings. And then, when the truth was beginning to pierce through in books, and even in newspapers, the whole light was blotted out by a big, fashionable film, cunningly written and brilliantly performed, in which Disraeli appeared once more as God's Englishman covered with primroses and breathing the innocent patriotism of our native fields.

The second fact to remember is a certain privilege almost analogous to monopoly, which belongs of necessity to things like the theatre and the cinema. In a sense more than the metaphorical, they fill the stage; they dominate the scene; they create the landscape. That is why one need not be Puritanical to insist on a somewhat stricter responsibility in all sorts of play-acting than in the looser and less graphic matter of literature. If a man is repelled by one book, he can shut it and open another; but he cannot shut up a theatre in which he finds a show repulsive, nor instantly order one of a thousand other theatres to suit his taste. There are a limited number of theatres; and even to cinemas there is some limit. Hence there is a real danger of historical falsehood being popularized through the film, because there is not the normal chance of one film being corrected by another film. When a book appears displaying a doubtful por-

trait of Queen Elizabeth, it will generally be found that about
six other historical students are moved to publish about six other
versions of Queen Elizabeth at the same moment. We can buy
Mr. Belloc's book on Cromwell, and then Mr. Buchan's book
on Cromwell; and pay our money and take our choice. But few
of us are in a position to pay the money required to stage a
complete and elaborately presented alternative film-version of
Disraeli. The fiction on the film, the partisan version in the
movie-play, will go uncontradicted and even uncriticized, in a
way in which few provocative books can really go uncontradicted and uncriticized. There will be no opportunity of meeting
it on its own large battlefield of expansive scenario and multitu-
dinous repetition. And most of those who are affected by it
will know or care very little about its being brought to book by
other critics and critical methods. The very phrase I have
casually used, 'brought to book', illustrates the point. A false
film might be refuted in a hundred books, without much affecting
the million dupes who had never read the books but only seen
the film. The protest is worth making, because provincial prejudice of this kind is frightfully dangerous in the present international problem of the hour. It is perfectly natural for nations to
have a patriotic art, and even within reason a patriotic education. It naturally teaches people, especially young people, to be
proud of the great heroes of their great history; and to conceive
their own past in a sort of poetic way like legends. But this is
exactly where we may test the difference between a legend and a
lie. The outlines of a real hero, like Nelson or Sarsfield, are not
altered when the figure is filled up, in maturer stages of knowledge, by the facts about failure or weakness or limitation. The
hero remains a hero; though the child, being now grown up,
knows that a hero is a man. But the figure of the fictitious
Beaconsfield will not support the intrusion of the real Disraeli.
It would be destroyed by all that was most interesting in Disraeli;
even by all that was most genuine in Disraeli. A dummy of that

sort does no good to national credit or glory; all foreigners laugh at it, knowing more about it than we do; and we ourselves can only preserve our solemnity by not going near enough to laugh. That is to make the thing a mere 'film' on the eyes of official obscurantism; and to give a new secretive meaning to the title of 'The Screen'.

G. Bernard Shaw

On Cinema

An interview by Archibald Henderson

HENDERSON: Has the enormous development of the cinema industry benefited the drama, or the reverse?

SHAW: No: the huge polynational audience makes mediocrity compulsory. Films must aim at the average of an American millionaire and a Chinese coolie, a cathedral-town governess and a mining-village barmaid, because they have to go everywhere and please everybody. They spread the drama enormously; but as they must interest a hundred per cent. of the population of the globe, barring infants in arms, they cannot afford to meddle with the upper-ten-percent. theatre of the highbrows or the lower-ten-per-cent. theatre of the blackguards. The result is that the movie play has supplanted the old-fashioned tract and Sunday School prize: it is reeking with morality but dares not touch virtue. And virtue, which is defiant and contemptuous of morality even when it has no practical quarrel with it, is the life-blood of high drama.

HENDERSON: In spite of the fame of certain artistic directors —the Griffiths, De Milles, Lubitschs, and Dwans—perhaps it is true that the film industry is, for the most part, directed and controlled by people with imperfectly developed artistic instincts

From Archibald Henderson, *Table-Talk of G.B.S.*, Chapman & Hall, London, 1925, pages 55–65. Published here by permission of the Society of Authors and the Bernard Shaw Estate. Title supplied.

and ideals who have their eyes fixed primarily on financial rewards.

SHAW: All industries are brought under the control of such people by Capitalism. If the capitalists let themselves be seduced from their pursuit of profits to the enchantments of art, they would be bankrupt before they knew where they were. You cannot combine the pursuit of money with the pursuit of art.

HENDERSON: Would it not be better for film magnates to engage first-rate authors to write directly for the films, paying them handsomely for their work, rather than pay enormous prices to an author of novel, story, or play, and then engage a hack at an absurdly low price to prepare a scenario?

SHAW: Certainly not first-rate authors: democracy always prefers second-bests. The magnates might pay for literate subtitles; but one of the joys of the cinema would be gone without such gems as "Christian: Allah didst make thee wondrous strong and fair." Seriously, though, the ignorance which leads to the employment of uneducated people to do professional work in modern industry is a scandal. It is just as bad in journalism. In my youth all writing was done by men who, if they had little Latin and less Greek, had at any rate been in schools where there was a pretence of teaching them; and they had all read the Bible, however reluctantly. Nowadays that has all gone: literary work is entrusted to men and women so illiterate that the mystery is how they ever learned their alphabet. They know next to nothing else, apparently. I agree with you as to the scenarios founded on existing plays and novels. Movie plays should be invented expressly for the screen by original imaginative visualizers. But you must remember that just as all our music consists of permutations and combinations of twelve notes, all our fiction consists of variations on a few plots; and it is in the words that the widest power of variation lies. Take that away and you will soon be so hard up for a new variation that you will snatch at anything—even at a Dickens plot—to enable you to carry on.

HENDERSON: . . . Have you in mind any definite suggestions for the further artistic development of films?

SHAW (*explosively*): Write better films, if you can: there is no other way. Development must come from the centre, not from the periphery. The limits of external encouragement have been reached long ago. Take a highbrow play to a Little Theatre and ask the management to spend two or three thousand dollars on the production, and they will tell you that they cannot afford it. Take an opium eater's dream to Los Angeles and they will realize it for you: the more it costs the more they will believe in it. You can have a real Polar expedition, a real volcano, a reconstruction of the Roman Forum on the spot: anything you please, provided it is enormously costly. Wasted money, mostly. If the United States Government put a limit of twenty-five thousand dollars to the expenditure on any single non-educational film, the result would probably be an enormous improvement in the interest of the film drama, because film magnates would be forced to rely on dramatic imagination instead of on mere spectacle. Oh, those scenes of oriental voluptuousness as imagined by a whaler's cabin boy! They would make a monk of Don Juan. Can you do nothing to stop them?

HENDERSON: The only way to stop them is with ridicule. That is why I am making you talk. . . . The triumph, almost the monopoly of the American film is uncontested. But are American films superior to all others?

SHAW (*decisively*): No. Many of them are full of the stupidest errors of judgment. Overdone and foolishly repeated strokes of expression, hideous make-ups, close-ups that an angel's face would not bear, hundreds of thousands of dollars spent on spoiling effects that I or any competent producer could secure quickly and certainly at a cost of ten cents, featureless over-exposed faces against under-exposed backgrounds, vulgar and silly subtitles, impertinent lists of everybody employed in the film from the star actress to the press agent's office boy: these are only a few of the *gaffes* American film factories are privileged to make. Conceit is rampant among your film makers; and good sense is about non-existent. That is where Mr. Chaplin scores; but Mr. Harold Lloyd seems so far to be the only rival intelligent enough to follow his example. We shall soon have to sit for ten minutes at the beginning of every reel to be told who developed it, who fixed it, who dried it, who provided the celluloid, who sold the chemicals, and who cut the author's hair. Your film people simply don't know how to behave themselves: they take liberties with the public at every step on the strength of their reckless enterprise and expenditure. Every American aspirant to film work should be sent to Denmark or Sweden for five years to civilize him before being allowed to enter a Los Angeles studio.

HENDERSON: Well! that's that! And how surprised and pained some American producers will be to read your cruel words! But . . . can plays of conversation—"dialectic dramas"—like yours be successfully filmed?

SHAW: Barrie says that the film play of the future will have no pictures and will consist exclusively of sub-titles.

HENDERSON: I wonder if conversation dramas are not on the wane—since the public in countless numbers patronizes, revels in the silent drama.

SHAW: If you come to that, the public in overwhelming numbers is perfectly satisfied with no drama at all. But the silent drama is producing such a glut of spectacle that people are actually listening to invisible plays by wireless. The silent drama is exhausting the resources of silence. Charlie Chaplin and his very clever colleague Edna Purviance, Bill Hart and Alla Nazimova, Douglas Fairbanks and Mary Pickford, Harold Lloyd and Buster Keaton, have done everything that can be done in dramatic dumb show and athletic stunting, and played all the possible variations on it. The man who will play them off the screen will not be their superior at their own game but an Oscar Wilde of the movies who will flash epigram after epigram at the spectators and thus realize Barrie's anticipation of more sub-titles than pictures.

HENDERSON: If that is true, then why—since wit and epigram are your familiar weapons—why have none of your plays been filmed?

SHAW (*deadly resolute*): Because I wouldn't let them. I repeat that a play with the words left out is a play spoiled; and all those filmings of plays written to be spoken as well as seen are boresome blunders except when the dialogue is so worthless that it is a hindrance instead of a help. Of course that is a very large exception in point of bulk; but the moment you come to classic drama, the omission of the words and the presentation of the mere scenario is very much as if you offered as a statue the wire skeleton which supports a sculptor's modelling clay. Besides, consider the reaction on the box office. People see a Macbeth film. They imagine they have seen Macbeth, and don't want to see it again; so when your Mr. Hackett or somebody comes round to act the play, he finds the house empty. That is what has happened to dozens of good plays whose authors have allowed them to be filmed. It shall not happen to mine if I can help it.[1]

1. The first Shaw plays to be filmed were: *How He Lied to Her Husband* (1930) directed by Cecil Lewis, *Arms and the Man* (1932) directed by Cecil Lewis, and *Pygmalion* (1938) directed by Anthony Asquith and starring Leslie Howard (Higgins) and Wendy Hiller (Eliza Doolittle). Shaw received an Academy Award (1938) for writing the year's best screenplay—*Pygmalion*.

Heinrich Mann

On *The Blue Angel:*
Heinrich Mann to Karl Lemke

March 15, 1930
at present: Nice, Hotel de Nice

Dear Mr. Karl Lemke;

I shall have to face anyway the question which you pose in your letter. The film will be shown to me in Paris in the near future. In Berlin I saw certain parts of it but never the whole thing, since my departure intervened. Having seen it in its entirety, I shall know more than I do now about the problems involved in the transfer from the literary to the cinematographic medium. But even judging by my present knowledge, I am convinced that the operation was successful in the case of *The Blue Angel.* Some sort of transition is imperative in every instance—that much I have learned while collaborating on the film. The adapters of the novel simply must build a bridge to the film, for a true novel cannot be filmed integrally. It has many sides, only one of which faces the film, which has to be shot in its own terms, as has here been the case in my opinion. This was done, by the way, with the help of seven persons

From Heinrich Mann's *Briefe an Karl Lemke, 1917–1949* (Berlin: Aufbau-Verlag, 1963), pp. 34–36. By permission of the publisher. Translated by Ulrich Weisstein.

Der Blaue Engel (The Blue Angel, 1930) directed by Josef von Sternberg, starred Emil Jannings and Marlene Dietrich. The film was based on Heinrich Mann's novel, *Professor Unrath oder Das Ende eines Tyrannen,* 1905.

altogether. You must not think that the director himself made all the decisions. I had a voice, and so did, in addition, two other authors [Carl Zuckmayer and Karl Gustav Vollmöller], a script writer [Robert Liebmann], a representative of the [film company] UFA [Erich Pommer] and, finally, [Emil] Jannings and [Josef von] Sternberg.

The decisive split between the film and the novel is due to an idea conceived by Emil Jannings who, from the very beginning, thought of his part in cinematographic terms. Sternberg wanted to enlarge on the scenes set in the harbor dive, a location dear to this director of films about the underworld.[1] The action now has a new twist, and the problems are slightly different; but this does not affect the characters, who remain basically the same. They now disport themselves in the film rather than in the novel, which changes their actions but not their nature. From another of his mental predispositions, Unrat [the professor, Emil Jannings' role] may well end as a clown (as he does in the movie) instead of as a croupier (as he does in the novel). The action unfolds along the same lines but is simplified in view of the fifty million viewers Sternberg envisages.

The more insight I gained, the more I abandoned the literary point of view, and the farther I was from exclaiming: "How much you have changed!" The plot of the film differs only in the second half from that of my novel. But even if it were totally different, I would still welcome it that these characters, bursting forth with life, have been transplanted just as they are. And even a few of my lines have been salvaged.

I probably will have to broach these views in public and I take the pleasure of communicating them to you as a kind of warming-up exercise. Please do not quote them literally but

1. Josef von Sternberg's films prior to *The Blue Angel* include *Underworld* (1927), a gangster melodrama, and *Docks of New York* (1928) which has a fog-drenched harbor setting.

merely use them, if you wish, in order to characterize my attitude
toward the film.

Looking forward to a continuation of our dialogue, I remain

Cordially yours,

Heinrich Mann.

HEINRICH MANN

The Blue Angel Is Shown to Me

The events which unfold there came first to my attention while
I was watching a play in Florence. During the intermission, a
newspaper was sold in the theater which reported from Berlin
the story of a professor whose relations with a cabaret singer
had caused him to commit a crime. I had barely finished reading
the few lines when the figure of Professor Unrat, that of his
seductress, and even the place of her activities, the Blue Angel,
arose in my mind's eye.

At that time, I was young enough for the experiences of my
boyhood still to be close and at instant recall. As a child, one
does not yet know a host of people; they do not crowd each
other out, and each one appears as soon as his tone is sounded.
Professor, for me, meant simply high school teacher. The
unusual linking of a professor with a *chanteuse* immediately

From Heinrich Mann, *Das öffentliche Leben* (Berlin: Zsolnay, 1932), pp.
325–329, by permission of the Aufbau-Verlag. Translated by Ulrich Weisstein.

suggested to me a stern but inexperienced man who, usually lording it over his students, now becomes less than a student, a mere toy in the hands of a girl. Once and for all, the girl looked as she would have had to look in order to make an aging man forget all his principles. As for the joint, it was always called the Blue Angel, was located in a side street near the harbor and suffused with the odor of tar, beer, and powder. The hearts of the boys who secretly sneaked there had beaten violently. Accordingly, the professor I envisaged during that intermission possessed a number of boyish traits.

From the very start, I knew him inside out. He and his fate had only to be elaborated and put down on paper. They had made their appearance without my having to invent them. A chance report had summoned them, and a vision had introduced them to me.

A few days later, by the way, the Italian newspapers rounded out the story. The *chanteuse*'s friend was actually a journalist covering the stock market and calling himself professor. He probably was the very opposite of my fictitious character who had gained so firm a foothold on my imagination.

The figure of Professor Unrat and the novel by that name are pretty old hat by now. The novel has been read by numerous generations of readers, and for many the figure has become one of those close acquaintances one frequently thinks of. For among the people we know intimately there are, upon careful reflection, more imaginary than real ones.

A novel is a world in itself, for it does not count in vain on man's greatest and most fatal gift, his imagination. We build a city, a house, a room and fill the latter with people. We place other people in other rooms, lead the ones to the others, and, while they move, their fate is decided. Our fellow beings are in a dither because an unusual event and an extraordinary character have come to the fore. We stage these events, although only verbally. Still, they are made visible to the imagination. Our work is that of an extremely independent and ingenious stage director, and viewed from this angle, writing a novel is equivalent to putting on a play.

Is that the reason why, from the start, I felt sympathetic toward the film *The Blue Angel*? A film is no novel; its action cannot unfold exactly as it does in literature, for the streets, as well as human lives, require different perspectives. Like the other collaborators on the film, I, too, endeavored to effect the transition from one medium to the other. The director (Sternberg) and the actor Jannings had to have clear sailing when their work began.

Finally, the strange moment arrived when, together with Jannings (who wore the mask of Professor Unrat), I found myself in the professor's messy bedroom. Jannings sat on the bed, with shelves full of dusty books above him. Dusty books everywhere, and a stove pipe ran right through the room. The technicians were working on their cameras, and we had to wait until they were ready. Then I recalled the first appearance of this "Unrat": Florence, the intermission—a long time ago. Here he was and he had not changed a bit.

He had gone through many experiences in the meantime and had passed through different times and heads. But he still loved the same kind of women, was as ponderous and innocent as before, and was headed for exactly the same fate. A great actor, Emil Jannings, had borrowed his shape and was now displaying it to me. He had enlarged on the figure, following its innermost nature, for in the novel Unrat does not die; but Jannings knew and realized the manner of his death.

The director, Sternberg, knew every step which this and the other figures were to take through the little town. He knew exactly what gestures, sounds, noises, songs and screams were in store for it. The corners and nooks of the plastically reconstructed city and street came to life for him even before the actors made them lively. I, for my part, remembered all these corners from the past. Not only Professor Unrat's messy bedroom but the entire Blue Angel from top to bottom had been revived in the studios of Neubabelsberg. I passed through the hall and climbed the winding stairs, as I might have done previously. Everything seemed to have returned uncannily out of the blue. In Neubabelsberg, there were two steps at the entrance to the Blue Angel, and I was immediately convinced that the same was true of its model. The rather shady lane passing by the cabaret was certain to lead into the once familiar city. At any rate, it led to the downfall of the figure that was still close to me.

Later on, I repeatedly watched the shooting and felt sympathetic toward the work of the actors, as I always do. I was unable to see the completed film in Berlin. The producer, Erich Pommer, had to go to Paris and was kind enough to bring the film to Nice, where I was then dwelling. Here he showed it to me.

This happened in a large and empty theater at the beach, in the morning and while the cleaning ladies were at work. The operator had some trouble with the reels since the sound track system was technically rather advanced. Even the French exclamations which resounded through the building made me feel how long a road the Blue Angel and its protagonist had travelled—from the port city in the North, where they acted out their story with me as their only witness, to the beach in the South where they were now shown to me.

There were only three spectators in the large French theater; and we saw the admirable Jannings smile—the gentle, childlike smile of a late and dangerous happiness breaking forth and shining through an unhappy face. Many people in several continents will soon have occasion to see it, too. While they look at these gaudy pictures and this gaudy world, they ought to sense the terror of a fate lived to its bitter end.

Thomas Mann

On the Film

I sometimes allow my thoughts to dwell on the film—one day I shall be uttering them at length. But just now all I can say is, that lately I have come to entertain feelings for this phenomenon of our time that amount to a lively interest, even almost to a passion. I go often to the cinema; for hours on end I do not tire of the joys of spectacle spiced with music; whether it be travel pictures, scenes from the wild, the weekly news of the world, a diverting piece of tomfoolery, a "thriller" or a "shocker," or a touching tale of love. The actors must be good to look at, with a gift of expression, vain if you like but never unnatural; the "story" itself may be vastly silly, provided—as is nearly always the case to-day—the silliness or sentimentality is set in a frame of scenic and mimic detail which is true to life and to reality, so that the human triumphs persistently over the crude falsity of the performance as a whole.

I used the word phenomenon above—and advisedly, since in my view the film has little to do with art, and I would not therefore approach it with criteria drawn from the artistic sphere, as do certain humanistic-minded and conservative souls, who then in sorrow and contempt turn away their eyes from the offending spectacle as from a base-born and inordinately democratic

From *Past Masters,* by Thomas Mann, translated by H. T. Lowe-Porter. Published 1933 by Alfred A. Knopf, Inc. Reprinted by permission. All rights reserved.

form of mass entertainment. For me, I despise it myself—but I love it too. It is not art, it is life, it is actuality. Compared with art's intellectual appeal its own is crudely sensational; it is the same as that of life itself upon a passive onlooker, who at the same time is aware that he himself is pretty comfortable and that what he sees is "nothing but a play." At the same time his sensations are heightened by the accompanying music. But now tell me: why is it people weep so, at the cinema? Or, rather, why do they fairly howl, like a maidservant on her afternoon out? We all went to the first performance of *The Big Parade*[1] and met Olaf Gulbransson at the exit. That jolly and muscular Eskimo was drowned in tears. "I haven't wiped my face yet," said he by way of excuse: we stood there together for a while, quite simply, unaffectedly, with streaming eyes. Is that the mood in which one turns away from a work of art, leaves a picture, puts down a finished book? It is true, elderly gentlemen do shed tears, at *Alt Heidelberg,* when they hear *"O alte Burschenherr-lichkeit";* but even elderly gentlemen do not weep over Shakespeare, or Kleist, or Gerhard Hauptmann. Say what you like, the atmosphere of art is cool; it is a sphere of spiritual valuations, of transmuted values; a world of style, a manuscript world, objectively, in the most personal sense, preoccupied with form; a sphere of the understanding—*"denn sie kommt aus dem Verstande,"* says Goethe. It is chaste and elegant, it is significant, it is serene; its agitations are kept sternly at second hand; you are at court, you control yourself. But take a pair of lovers on the screen, two young folk as pretty as pictures, bidding each other an eternal farewell in a real garden, with the grass waving in the wind—to the accompaniment of the meltingest of music; and who could resist them, who would not blissfully let flow the tear that wells to the eye? For it is all raw material, it has not been transmuted, it is life at first hand; it is warm and heartfelt, it

1. Directed by King Vidor (1925), starring John Gilbert. One of MGM's most successful movies at the box office.

affects one like onions or sneezewort. I feel a tear trickling down in the darkness, and in silence, with dignity, I rub it into my cheekbone with my finger-tip.

And the film has, quite specifically, nothing to do with the drama. It is narrative in pictures. That these faces are present to your sight does not prevent their greatest effectiveness from being in its nature epic; and in this sphere, if in any, the film approaches literary art. It is much too genuine to be theatre. The stage setting is based upon delusion, the scenery of the film is nature itself, just as the fancy stimulated by the story creates it for the reader. Nor have the protagonists in a film the bodily presence and actuality of the human figures in the drama. They are living shadows. They speak not, they are not, they merely *were*—and were precisely as you see them—and that is narrative. The film possesses a technique of recollection, of psychological suggestion, a mastery of detail in men and in things, from which the novelist, though scarcely the dramatist, might learn much. That the Russians, who have never been great dramatists, are supreme in this field, rests, without any doubt in my mind, upon their narrative skill.

As an author I have not as yet had much luck with the films. *Buddenbrooks*[2] has been filmed, but hardly to the satisfaction of the friends of that book. Instead of narrating, only narrating, and letting the characters speak for themselves, what has been made of it is a poorish play of merchant life, in which not much remains of the book save the names. A very good Berlin producer did think for a while of filming *The Magic Mountain;* which is not surprising, for a bold treatment of it might have produced a wonderful spectacle, a fantastic cyclopædia, with a hundred digressions into all points of the compass: visions of

2. *Buddenbrooks* has been filmed twice: (1923) directed by Gerhard Lamprecht and (1959) directed by Alfred Weidenmann. Other Mann works that have been filmed include: *Confessions of Felix Krull* (1958), *Tonio Kroger* (1968) and *Death in Venice* (1970).

all the worlds of nature, sport, research, medicine, politics, all grouped round an epic core. What might not have been made simply of the chapter "Snow," with its Mediterranean dream poem of humanity! But it is not to be. Such a production made too great material and intellectual demands. *Royal Highness* is under consideration. It is simple and should succeed; there are good rôles, including that always irresistible one of a good dog; and though the subject-matter might be reminiscent of *Alt Heidelberg,* with good settings and well-chosen actors it should be a pleasing piece and very likely a successful one.

Bertolt Brecht

Concerning Music for the Film

----

1. *Are Theatrical Experiences Applicable to the Film?*

The special nature of the experiments conducted by the German theater of the pre-Hitler years enables us to use some of its experiences for the film as well—provided this is done with extreme caution. The German theater (of the twenties) owed more than a little to the film. It made use of epic, gestic and montage elements germane to the latter, and even employed the film itself by using documentary material. On the part of some aestheticians, protests were raised against the theatrical use of cinematographic material—unjustly so in my opinion. For in order to preserve the theatrical nature of the theater, one does not have to banish the film but only needs to use it theatrically. The film, too, can learn from the theater and make use of theatrical devices. But that does not necessarily mean that one should offer a photographic record of a theatrical performance. Actually, the film constantly uses theatrical elements. The less aware of this fact it is, the less successfully it uses them. It is, in fact, quite depressing to see how much bad theater it produces. The turn toward more intimate aspects and toward the use of preconceived types, as well as the rejection of histrionics (antihamism), which occurred during the transition from the silent film to the sound film, has deprived the film of

From Brecht's *Schriften zum Theater* (Frankfurt: Suhrkamp, 1963), III, 288–289, 294–295, 298–301, by permission of the publisher. Translation copyright 1972 by Stefan Brecht. Translated by Ulrich Weisstein.

much expressiveness without freeing it from the clutches of the theater. One only needs, standing in the foyer, to listen to these antihams in order to realize immediately how operatically and unnaturally they speak.

. . . .

8. *The Sense of Logic*

As previously stated, cinematographic music is often used to "drown out" logical absurdities, leaps and inconsistencies of the action. It is easy for the composer to concoct a kind of artificial logic by evoking the sense of fatalism, inevitability, and so on. In such cases, the composers furnish the logic as certain cooks supply vitamin tablets with their dishes. Actually, the composer's knack for bringing out, with a few sleights of hand, the constructional logic inherent in his pieces and for thus causing us to enjoy the logic *qua* logic, could become significant for the film if it were properly harnessed. With the help of such music, apparently incoherent events can be linked and contradictory ones structurally integrated. To put it differently: if the music causes the audience to "take in details" and rationalize, the film writer can portray the course of an action much more dialectically, i. e., in all its paradoxicalness and incoherence. If, for example, a man is to be shown as being influenced by a) his father's death, b) an upward trend in the stock market, and c) the outbreak of a war, the montage can be richer, more complex or, simply, more extended if the music guarantees the integration of these factors. In the documentary film, [Hanns] Eisler and [Joris] Ivens have used music in this manner by juxtaposing two major processes—the conquest of arable land through the construction of the Zuiderzee dam and the destruction of Canadian wheat for the sake of price stabilization—in one film. . . .[1]

1. An allusion to the film *Zuiderzee* (Holland, 1931/33), directed by Joris Ivens; montage by Helen van Dongen. See further: Joris Ivens, *The Camera and I,* New York, 1969, and Hanns Eisler, *Composing for the Films,* London, 1961.

. . . .

14. *The Separation of the Elements*

Perhaps it would be advisable, at this point, to mention certain far-reaching experiments which, cinematographically, have, so far, been used only in the documentary film—that is to say, a very limited area—whereas in the theater they have already acquired considerable importance. I am referring to the separation of the elements constituting the theatrical work of art which was primarily effected in pre-Hitlerian Germany. That is to say, the music and the action were treated as totally independent ingredients. The musical pieces were visibly inserted into the action, and the style of acting changed as songs were introduced or a dialogue musically underlined. Generally, the orchestra remained fully visible and was integrated with the action by means of special lighting. The setting itself constituted a third, independent factor. Thus it became possible to introduce passages in which the music and the setting collaborated even in the absence of action, as in *Man is Man,* where a little serenade was played while slides were concurrently projected. In the opera *Rise and Fall of the [City of] Mahagonny,*[2] the same principle was used in a different way. Here the three elements —action, music, and setting—appeared jointly but separately in a scene which shows a man eating himself to death. The actor enacted the suicidal feast in front of a huge picture portraying an over-lifesize feaster, while a chorus narrated the event in chanting. The music, the setting and the actor thus independently portrayed the same event. These examples are somewhat extreme, and I don't believe that anything similar can be done in the present-day movies. I have mentioned them mainly in order to show what is meant by the separation of the elements. This principle, at any rate, made it possible to use music of intrinsic value to enhance the overall effect of a play. Three of

2. The two works mentioned are by Brecht.

the best German composers of our day—[Hanns] Eisler, [Paul] Hindemith and [Kurt] Weill—participated in the experiment.

. . . .

15. *The Separation of the Elements in the Art Film*

Used with discretion, the principle of the separation of the elements of "music" and "action" could also serve to produce some novel effects in the movies, provided that the composer is not consulted after the fact, as is now customary. He would have to participate from the start in planning the intended cinematographic effects. For, on principle, the music can assume certain functions, which ought to be reserved for it. If, for example, one is willing and able to use the music for expressing human emotions, all sorts of actions which, otherwise, would serve to express the mental phenomena in question, would become superfluous. The ripening of a man's decision to act, for example, could be portrayed pantomimically; that is to say: the man could be shown by himself, pacing up and down, while the music would assume the task of drawing his emotional curve. The fewer gestures the actor uses in the process, the stronger the effect is likely to be. In such a scene, the music acts quite independently and makes a genuine dramatic contribution. Let us consider another possibility: a young man rows his sweetheart out onto the lake, causes the boat to capsize and lets the girl drown.[3] Here the composer can do one of two things. By means of the accompanying music he can anticipate the audience reaction in building up tension, stressing the heinousness of the crime, and so forth. But he can also depict the serenity of the natural scene, the indifference of nature, or the ordinariness of the event, which, after all, is a mere excursion. If he chooses this latter alternative, he assigns to the music a considerably more independent role by causing the murder to appear much more frightening than unnatural.

3. The allusion is to a climactic episode of Dreiser's *An American Tragedy*. The filmic treatment of this episode is discussed at length by Eisenstein in his essay, "A Course in Treatment," in *Film Form* by S. M. Eisenstein.

Graham Greene

Three Reviews

A Midsummer Night's Dream

I sometimes wonder whether film reviewers are taken quite
seriously enough. Criticism, of course, may not be quite in our
line, but the production of *A Midsummer Night's Dream* has
demonstrated beyond doubt that no one can shake a better
tambourine or turn a better table. We are superb mediums, or is
it an intuitive sympathy with the poet which enables a Mr.
Luscombe Whyte (to be remembered for his appreciation of
Sam Goldwyn's "classic tragedy," *The Dark Angel,* and to be
distinguished from Mr. Pedro de Cordoba who was a Crusader)
to tell us that Shakespeare "had he lived now" would have
approved of Herr Reinhardt's film version of his play? "He had
a mind which must have chafed at the limitations of candle-lit,
small stages and curtains. He would have conjured up mad
woods with twisted trees, peopled with fantasies clothed in
visibility." A pregnant sentence, that, straight from the ouija
board.

Unfortunately the mediums differ. Mr. Sidney Carroll tells
us with an even greater air of authority that Shakespeare would

From *The Spectator* (London), October 18, 1935, p. 606. By permission of
Mr. Graham Greene, Laurence Pollinger Ltd., Martin Secker & Warburg Ltd.,
and Simon & Schuster Inc. *A Midsummer Night's Dream* (1935) was directed
by Max Reinhardt and William Dieterle; it starred James Cagney (as Bottom),
Joe E. Brown, Hugh Herbert, Dick Powell, Olivia De Havilland, Mickey
Rooney, Victor Jory, and Ian Hunter.

not have liked the film. It is his obligation, he says, "as a man of English descent on both sides for generations to try to protect our national poet dramatist from either idolatry or desecration." As I have said, apart from criticism, there is little we film critics cannot do.

Alas! I failed to get in touch with Shakespeare (my English descent is less pure than Mr. Carroll's), but I feel quite sure that Anne Hathaway, "had she lived now," would have thought this a very nice film (I am uncertain of the Dark Lady of the Sonnets). She would have liked the chorus of budding Shirley Temples drifting gauzily up the solid Teutonic moonbeams, and I am sure she would have liked the Bear. For Herr Reinhardt is nothing if not literal, and when Helena declares, "No, no, I am as ugly as a bear; For beasts that meet me run away for fear," we see a big black bear beating a hasty retreat into the blackberry bushes. All the same, I enjoyed this film, perhaps because I have little affection for the play, which seems to me to have been written with a grim determination on Shakespeare's part to earn for once a Universal certificate.

But Herr Reinhardt, lavish and fanciful rather than imaginative, is uncertain of his new medium. Although in his treatment of the Athenian woodland, the silver birches, thick moss, deep mists and pools, there are sequences of great beauty, there are others of almost incredible banality. After an impressive scene when Oberon's winged slaves herd Titania's fairies under his black billowing cloak, we watch a last fairy carried off over a slave's shoulder into the night sky. It is very effective as the slave sinks knee deep into the dark, but when the camera with real Teutonic thoroughness follows his gradual disappearance until only a pair of white hands are left twining in the middle of the Milky Way, the audience showed its good sense by laughing.

Much of the production is poised like this on the edge of absurdity because Herr Reinhardt cannot visualise how his ideas will work out on the screen. We are never allowed to forget the stage producer, a stage producer, though, of unlimited resources with an almost limitless stage. At every passage of dialogue we are back before footlights and the camera is focussed relentlessly on the character who speaks. The freer, more cinematic fairy sequences are set to Mendelssohn's music, and this is the way Shakespeare's poetry ought surely to be used if it is not to delay the action. It must be treated as music, not as stage dialogue tied to the image of the speaker like words issuing from the mouth of characters in a cartoon.

The acting is fresh and vivid for the very reason that it lacks what Mr. Carroll calls "proper Shakespearian diction and bearing." I do not want to be ungrateful, the film is never dull, and the last sequences, when the human characters stream up the stairs to bed, and the fairies flood in and fill the palace in their wake, was a lovely and effective visualisation of "the sweet peace," "the glimmering light," "the dead and drowsy fire."

Modern Times

I am too much an admirer of Mr. Chaplin to believe that the most important thing about his new film is that for a few minutes we are allowed to hear his agreeable and rather husky voice in a song. The little man has at last definitely entered the contemporary scene; there had always before been a hint of "period" about his courage and misfortunes; he carried about with him more than the mere custard pie of Karno's day, its manners, its curious clothes, its sense of pathos and its dated poverty. There were occasions, in his encounters with blind flower girls or his adventures in mean streets or in the odd little pitchpine mission halls where he carried round the bag or preached in pantomime on a subject so near to his own experi-

From *The Spectator* (London), February 14, 1936, p. 254. By permission of Graham Greene, Laurence Pollinger Ltd., Martin Secker & Warburg Ltd., and Simon & Schuster Inc.

Modern Times (1936) was directed and produced by Chaplin; it was his second film of the sound period.

ence as the tale of David and Goliath, when he seemed to go back almost as far as Dickens. The change is evident in his choice of heroine: fair and featureless with the smudged effect of an amateur water-colour which has run, they never appeared again in leading parts, for they were quite characterless. But Miss Paulette Goddard, dark, grimy, with her amusing urban and plebeian face, is a promise that the little man will no longer linger at the edge of mawkish situation, the unfair pathos of the blind girl and the orphan child. One feels about her as Hyacinth felt about Millicent in [Henry James's] *The Princess Casamassima*: "she laughed with the laugh of the people, and if you hit her hard enough would cry with their tears." For the first time the little man does not go off alone, flaunting his cane and battered bowler along the endless road out of the screen. He goes in company looking for what may turn up.

What *had* turned up was first a job in a huge factory twisting screws tighter as little pieces of nameless machinery passed him on a moving belt, under the televised eye of the manager, an eye that followed him even into the lavatory where he snatched an illicit smoke. The experiment of an automatic feeding machine, which will enable a man to be fed while he works, drives him crazy (the running amok of this machine, with its hygienic mouth-wiper, at the moment when it has reached the Indian corn course, is horrifyingly funny; it is the best scene, I think, that Mr. Chaplin has ever invented). When he leaves hospital he is arrested as a communist leader (he has picked up a red street flag which has fallen off a lorry) and released again after foiling a prison hold-up. Unemployment and prison punctuate his life, starvation and lucky breaks, and somewhere in its course he attaches to himself the other piece of human refuse.

The Marxists, I suppose, will claim this as *their* film, but it is a good deal less and a good deal more than socialist in intention. No real political passion has gone to it: the police batter the little man at one moment and feed him with buns the next: and there is no warm maternal optimism, in the Mitchison manner, about the character of the workers: when the police are brutes, the men are cowards; the little man is always left in the lurch. Nor do we find him wondering "what a socialist man should do," but dreaming of a steady job and the most bourgeois home. Mr. Chaplin, whatever his political convictions may be, is an artist and not a propagandist. He doesn't try to explain, but presents with vivid fantasy what seems to him a crazy comic tragic world without a plan, but his sketch of the inhuman factory does not lead us to suppose that his little man would be more at home at Dneiprostroi. He presents, he doesn't offer, political solutions.

The little man politely giving up his seat to the girl in the crowded Black Maria: the little man when the dinner-bell sounds tenderly sticking a spray of celery into the mouth of the old mechanic whose head has been caught between the cog-wheels: the little man littering the path of the pursuing detectives with overturned chairs to save his girl: Mr. Chaplin has, like Conrad, "a few simple ideas"; they could be expressed in much the same phrases: courage, loyalty, labour: against the same nihilistic background of purposeless suffering. "Mistah Kurtz— he dead."[1] These ideas are not enough for a reformer, but they have proved amply sufficient for an artist.

Romeo and Juliet

"Boy Meets Girl, 1436"—so the programme heads the story of *Romeo and Juliet,* which it tells with some inaccuracy; but this fourth attempt to screen Shakespeare is not as bad as that. Unimaginative, certainly, coarse-grained, a little banal, it is frequently saved—by Shakespeare—from being a bad film. The

From *The Spectator* (London), October 23, 1936, p. 679. By permission of Graham Greene, Laurence Pollinger Ltd., Martin Secker & Warburg Ltd., and Simon & Schuster Inc.

Romeo and Juliet (1936) was directed by George Cukor.

1. See Joseph Conrad's story, "Heart of Darkness."

late Irving Thalberg, the producer, has had a funeral success second only to Rudolph Valentino's, but there is nothing in this film to show that he was a producer of uncommon talent. He has made a big film, as Hollywood recognises that adjective: all is on the characteristic Metro-Goldwyn scale: a Friar Laurence's cell with the appearance, as another critic has put it, of a modern luxury flat, with a laboratory of retorts and test-tubes worthy of a Wells superman (no "osier cage" of a few flowers and weeds); a balcony so high that Juliet should really have conversed with Romeo in shouts like a sailor from the crow's nest sighting land; a spectacular beginning with the Montagues and Capulets parading through pasteboard streets to the same church, rather late, it appears from the vague popish singing off, for Benediction; Verona seen from the air, too palpably a childish model; an audible lark proclaiming in sparrow accents that it is not the nightingale; night skies sparkling with improbable tinsel stars; and lighting so oddly timed that when Juliet remarks that the mask of night is on her face, "else would a maiden blush bepaint my check," not Verona's high moon could have lit her more plainly.

But on the credit side are more of Shakespeare's words than we have grown to expect, a few more indeed than he ever wrote, if little of the subtlety of his dramatic sense which let the storm begin slowly with the muttering of a few servants, rather than with this full-dress riot. The picture has been given a Universal Certificate, and one was pleasantly surprised to find how safely our film censors had slumbered through many a doubtful passage: even "the bawdy hand of the dial" had not disturbed the merry gentlemen's rest. The nurse's part has suffered, but more from Miss Edna May Oliver's clowning than from a censor. This part and Mercutio's suffer most from overacting. Mr. John Barrymore's middle-aged Mercutio is haggard with the greasepaint of a thousand Broadway nights. Mr. Basil Rathbone is a fine vicious Tybalt, and Mr. Leslie Howard and Miss Norma

Shearer spoke verse as verse should be spoken and were very satisfying in the conventional and romantic and dreamy mode (one still waits to see lovers hot with lust and youth and Verona fevers, as reckless as their duelling families, "like fire and powder which as they kiss consume").

It is the duels and violence which come off well, Mercutio's death and Tybalt's, and, more convincing than on the stage, the final fight with Paris in the tomb, but I am less than ever convinced that there is an aesthetic justification for filming Shakespeare at all. The effect of even the best scenes is to distract, much in the same way as the old Beerbohm Tree productions distracted: we cannot look and listen simultaneously with equal vigilance. But that there may be a social justification I do not dispute: by all means let Shakespeare, even robbed of half his drama and three-quarters of his poetry, be mass produced. One found oneself surrounded in the theatre by prosperous middle-aged ladies anxiously learning the story in the programme for the first time; urgent whispers came from the knowing ones, as Romeo went down into the Capulet tomb, preparing their timorous companions for an unexpected and unhappy ending. It may very well be a social duty to teach the great middle-class a little about Shakespeare's plays. But the poetry—shall we ever get the poetry upon the screen except in fits and starts (the small scene between Romeo and the ruined apothecary he bribes to sell him poison was exquisitely played and finely directed), unless we abjure all the liberties the huge sets and the extras condemn us to? Something like Dreyer's *Passion of Jeanne d'Arc,* the whitewashed wall and the slow stream of faces, might preserve a little more of the poetry than this commercial splendour.

Louis Aragon

What Is Art, Jean-Luc Godard?

What is art? I have been asking myself this question ever since I saw Jean-Luc Godard's *Pierrot le fou* [1966], in which Belmondo-the-Sphinx asks an American producer the question, "What is the cinema?" There is one thing of which I am sure; and thus I can begin all this, in spite of my trepidations, by an assertion which, at least, stands like a solid beam driven into the middle of a swamp: art, today, is Jean-Luc Godard. It is perhaps for this reason that his films, and in particular this film, have provoked insult and scorn; people say things about Godard's films that they would never say about a current commercial production, they allow themselves to go to extremes having nothing to do with criticism: they attack the man.

The American, in *Pierrot le fou,* says about the cinema what one could say about the Vietnam war, or any war for that matter. And the statements have a strange ring to them when they are considered in the context of that extraordinary scene in which Belmondo and Karina, in order to earn some money, improvise a little play before an American couple and their sailors, somewhere on the Riviera. He plays Uncle Sam, she plays the niece of Uncle Ho. . . . "But it's damn good, damn good!" exclaims (in English) the delighted sailor with the red

From Les Lettres françaises, no. 1096 (9–15 September 1965), pp. 1, 8. Translated by Royal S. Brown. Reprinted by permission of Aragon and Les Lettres françaises.

beard . . . because the film is in color, of all things. But I'm not going to tell you what happens in the film, like everybody else. This is not a review. Furthermore, this film defies review. You might as well go count the small change in a million dollars!

What if Belmondo, or Godard, had asked me, "What is the cinema?" I would have answered in a different way, by talking about certain people. The cinema, for me, was at first Charlie Chaplin, then Renoir, Buñuel, and now Godard. That's all; it's quite simple. Somebody is going to say I'm forgetting Eisenstein and Antonioni. You're wrong, I'm not forgetting them. Or several others, for that matter. But I'm not talking about the cinema, I'm talking about art. Therefore, the question must be discussed in this context, in the context of another art, of one art with another one, a long history, in order to resume what art has become for us—I mean contemporary art, a modern art, painting for example. In order to characterize it through its personalities.

Painting, in the modern sense of the word, begins with Géricault, Delacroix, Courbet, Manet. And then the multitude follows. Finding its *raison d'être* because of these painters, or in using them as a starting point, or in opposing them, or in going beyond them. A flourishing such as has not been seen since the Italian Renaissance. In order to be entirely summed up in a man named Picasso. What interests me, for the moment, is this period of pioneers in which one can still compare the young cinema to painting. The game of saying who Renoir is, or who Buñuel is, doesn't amuse me. But Godard is Delacroix.

First of all because of the way his work has been received. At Venice, it would appear. I wasn't at Venice, and I didn't belong to the juries that handed out the prizes and the Oscars. I saw, I found myself seeing *Pierrot le fou,* that's all. I won't talk about the critics. They're good enough at dishonoring themselves! Nor am I going to contradict them. There were some, of course, who were taken by the film's grandeur—Yvonne Baby, Chazal,

Charpier, Cournot. . . . All the same, I can't pass up this chance
to mention Michel Cournot's extraordinary article—not so much
because of what he says, which manifests an almost exclusive
obsession with the reflections of personal life in the film (for
Cournot, like so many others, is intoxicated by cinema-truth,
whereas I much prefer cinema-lie).* But all right! at least we
have here a man who lets himself go when he likes something.
Furthermore, he knows how to write, if you'll pardon the expression—even if there is only one left, to me, that's important.
I love language, marvelous language, delirious language—nothing is rarer than the language of passion in this world, where we
live with the fear of being caught unawares, a fear that goes
back, you'd better believe it, to the flight from Eden, to that
moment when Adam and Eve notice they are naked, before the
invention of the fig leaf.

What was I talking about? Ah! yes[1]; I love language, and it's
for that reason that I love Godard. Who is completely language.

No, that's not what I was talking about; I was saying that
Godard's work has been received like Delacroix's. At the Salon
of 1827, which is just as good as Venice, Eugène had hung up
his *La Mort de Sardanapale,* which he called his *Massacre no. 2,*
because he too was a painter of massacres and not a painter of
battles. He had had, he says, a number of difficulties with "the
jackass members of the jury." When he saw his painting on the
wall ("My little daub is perfectly placed") next to the paintings
of the other artists, it gave him the impression, he said, "of a
première where everybody would boo." This, before the booing
ever started . . .

It happens that I went to look at *La Mort de Sardanapale* a
little while ago. What a painting this "massacre" is! Personally,
I greatly prefer it to *La liberté sur les barricades,* which I'm

* See *Le Nouvel observateur,* 1 Oct. and 3 Nov., 1965. [ed.]

1. For tic collectors: this is, in my writing, a tic. This note turns it into an
auto-collage.

sick and tired of hearing about. But that isn't really the question here. The problem is just how the *art* of Delacroix resembles, in this case, the *art* of Godard in *Pierrot le fou*. Doesn't the relationship strike you immediately? I'm speaking for those who have seen the film. Apparently the relationship has not struck *them* immediately.

While I was watching *Pierrot,* I had forgotten everything one is apparently supposed to say and think about Godard. That he has tics, that he quotes all over the place, that he is preaching to us, that he believes in this or in that . . . in short, that he is unbearable, talky and a moralist (or an immoralist); all I could see was one single thing, and that was that the film is beautiful. Superhumanly beautiful. All you see for two hours is that kind of beauty which the word "beauty" defines quite poorly—what has to be said about this procession of pictures is that it is, that they are quite simply sublime. Today's readers are not very fond of the superlative. Too bad. I find this film shot through with a sublime beauty. The word is ordinarily reserved for actresses and for the special vocabulary of theatre people. Too bad. Constantly, sublimely beautiful. You'll notice that I hate adjectives.

Pierrot is, therefore (like *Sardanapale*), a color film. Using a wide screen. Which stands apart from all other color films because the use of a *means* in Godard always has an *end,* and because this means almost constantly involves its own self-examination. It is not simply because the film is well photographed and because the colors are beautiful. . . . It *is* well photographed, and the colors *are* beautiful. But there is something else involved. The colors are those of the world such as it is . . . how is it said? You have to have remembered: "How horrible life is! but it is always beautiful."[2] If it is said in other words in the film, it amounts to the same thing. But Godard does not stop with the world such as it is—for instance, suddenly the

2. This is not a quotation; all the sentences I may quote are the dreams of a deaf man.

screen becomes monochrome, all red, or all blue, as during the sophisticated cocktail party at the beginning, a sequence that probably provoked the initial irritation of a certain number of critics (which reminds me of a certain evening at the Champs-Elysées, during the premiere of a ballet for which Elsa [Triolet] had done the scenario, Jean Rivier the music, Boris Kochno the choreography, and Brassaï the settings; the name of the work was *Le Réparateur de radios,* and the audience went wild booing and hissing, because the ballet showed people dancing in a night club, and, after all, what would you expect? all the members of Parisian high society found themselves to be the target!). During the party sequence, the abandonment of polychromaticism without returning to black and white *means* J.-L. Godard's reflection on both the world, into which he introduces Jean-Paul Belmondo, and on the technical means of expression at his disposal. This is further born out when this scene is almost immediately followed by a color effect which is in turn followed by a shot of fireworks and then, slightly later, by the bursts of light that follow one another without any possible justification in a nocturnal Paris in which the passion of the hero for Anna Karina suddenly becomes a reality; this latter effect takes the arbitrary form of discs, of colored moons sweeping across the wind-shield like rain, coloring their faces and their lives with an arbitrariness that seems to deny the world while marking the entrance of a deliberate arbitrariness into their lives. For J.-L. G., color does not exist simply to show us that a girl has blue eyes or that a certain gentleman is a member of the Legion of Honor. By necessity, a film by Godard that offers the possibility of color is going to show us something that could not be shown in black and white, a kind of *voice* that cannot resound when colors are *mute.*

In Delacroix' pallet, the reds—vermilion, Venice red, the red lacquer of Rome or madder, mingling with white, cobalt and cadmium (does this represent a particular kind of Daltonism on my part?)—eclipse for me all the other hues, as if the latter were only put there to serve as a background for the reds. One might quote the words of Philarète Chasles concerning Musset— "He is a poet who has no color . . . ," etc. "Personally, I prefer gaping wounds and the vivid color of blood. . . ." This sentence, which has always remained in my mind, came back to me quite naturally when I saw *Pierrot le fou*. Not only because of the blood. Red sings in the film like an obsession. As in Renoir, where a Provençal house with its terraces reminds one here of the *Terrasses à Cagnes*. Like a dominant color of the modern world. So insistently does Godard use the color that when I came out of the film, I saw nothing else in Paris but the reds— signs indicating one-way streets; the multiple eyes of the red stop-lights in cochineal-colored slacks; madder-colored shops, scarlet-colored cars, red-lead paint on the balconies of run-down buildings, the tender carthamus of lips; and from the words of the film, only the following sentence, which Godard has Pierrot say, remained in my mind: "I can't stand the sight of blood," which, according to Godard, comes from Federico Garcia Lorca. From which work? What does it matter. . . . from the *Lament on the Death of Ignacio Sanchez Mejias*[3], I can't stand the sight of blood, I can't see, I can't, I. . . . The entire film is nothing but this immense sob caused because the hero is unable to, because the hero cannot stand to see blood, or to shed it, to be obliged to shed it. A madder, a scarlet, a ver-milion, a carmine-colored blood, perhaps . . . the blood of the *Massacres de Scio,* the blood of *La Mort de Sardanapale,* the blood of July 1830, their children's blood that will be shed in the three *Médée furieuse* paintings (the one from 1838 and the ones from 1859 and 1862), all the blood that covers the lions

3. In the *Llanto por Ignacio Sanchez Mejias* (1935), the sentence is not formulated in the same manner. It is in the second part of this poem, entitled *La sangre derramada* (wasted blood), that you find the refrain "Que no quiero verla!" ("How I don't want to see it!"). Godard told me: "It's Lorca, but it could just as well not be Lorca!"

and tigers in their battles with horses. . . . Never has so much blood flowed on the screen, red blood, from the first cadaver in Anna-Marianne's apartment until her own blood; never has blood on the screen been so conspicuous as it is in the automobile accident, in the dwarf killed with a pair of scissors, and I don't know what else, "I can't stand the sight of blood; *Que ne quiero verla!*" And it isn't Lorca but the car radio which coldly announced the death of 115 Viet-Cong soldiers. . . . Here, it is Marianne who speaks up: "It's terrible, isn't it, how anonymous it is. . . . They say 115 Viet-Cong, and it doesn't really mean anything. And yet they were all men, and you don't know who they are, whether they loved a woman, whether they had children, whether they'd rather go to the movies or the theatre. You don't know anything about them. All they say is that a hundred and fifteen were killed. It's just like photography, which has always fascinated me . . ." Here, you don't see the blood, or its color. But everything seems to revolve around this color, in an extraordinary way.

For nobody knows better than Godard how to show the order of disorder. Always. In *Les Carabiniers* [1963], *Vivre sa vie* [1962], *Bande à part* [1964], this film. The disorder of this world is its basic matter, arising from the modern cities, shining with neon and formica; in the suburban areas or in interior courtyards, which nobody ever sees with an artist's eyes; the twisted girders, the rusty machines, the trash, the tin-cans—this whole shantytown of our lives; we couldn't live without it, but we conveniently put it out of our minds. And from this, as well as from automobile accidents and murders, Godard creates beauty. The order of what by definition cannot have any order. And when the two lovers, who have been thrown into a muddled and tragic adventure, cover up their tracks by blowing up their car next to a wrecked car, they cross France from the north to the south, and it seems that, in order to continue covering up their tracks, they once again, they still have to walk through water, in order to cross that river which could be the Loire . . . and later on in that lost area near the Mediterranean where, while Belmondo is beginning to write, Anna Karina walks (in the water) in a kind of hopeless rage from one end of the screen to the other while repeating the following sentences like a song for the dead: "What is there to do? Don't know what to do. . . . What is there to do? Don't know what to do. . . ." All this concerning the Loire. . . .

As I watched this river, with its islets and its sand, I thought that at least it is the one you see in the background in the *Nature morte aux homards* (which is in the Louvre), which Delacroix is supposed to have painted at Beffes, in the Cher River near the Charité-sur-Loire. This strange arrangement (or disorder) of a hare and a pheasant with two lobsters (cooked vermilion red) on the net of a hunting bag and a rifle, all in front of the vast landscape with the river and its islands may very well have been painted for a general living in the Berri province; it nonetheless remains an extraordinary slaughter, this *Massacre no. 2-bis,* which was done around the same time as *La Mort de Sardanapale* and which appeared next to the latter painting in the Salon of 1827[4]. It represents the trying out of a new technique in which the color was mixed with a copal varnish. All of the nature scenes in *Pierrot le fou* are similarly varnished with some kind of 1965 copal, which makes it seem as if we are seeing these sights for the first time. What is certain is that there was no predecessor for the *Nature morte aux homards,* that meeting on an umbrella and a sewing machine on a dissection table in a landscape, just as there is no other predecessor than Lautréamont to Godard. And I no longer know what disorder is, and what order is. Perhaps Pierrot's madness is that he is there to put into the disorder of our era the stupefying order of pas-

4. And why, in the foreground, is there a blue Wyvern, a heraldic animal found in various legends of the Beri region? And what about the hunter who had cooked his lobsters!

sion. Perhaps. The desperate order of passion (one sees despair in Pierrot from the very beginning, the despair of his own marriage, on the one hand, and the passion, the lyricism that represent his only hope of escaping from it).

The year that Eugène Delacroix, suddenly, left for Morocco, crossing France through "snow and bitter, freezing cold . . . a gust of wind and rain," 1832, there was no Salon at the Louvre because of an outbreak of cholera in Paris. But in May a charity exposition replaced the Salon, and here five small paintings lent by a friend represented the absent Delacroix. Three of them seem to have been done in rapid succession, probably during the period 1826–1827—the *Etude de femme couchée* (or *Femme aux bas flancs*), which is in the Louvre; the *Jeune femme caressant un perroquet,* which is in the Lyons museum; and *Le Duc de Bourgogne montrant le corps de sa Maîtresse au Duc d'Orléans* (I have no idea where this one is located)[5].

These paintings were done in the midst of Delacroix' relationship with Mme. Dalton, but it is impossible to know who the three nude women of these works actually were, or even whether it was the same woman. No doubt the *Jeune femme au pereoquet* has the same heavy eyelids one sees in the *Dormeuse,* which apparently is Mme. Dalton. But neither one resembles the portrait of this lady done by Bonington. In Delacroix' *Journal,* a number of young women who came to pose for him make a brief appearance, and the artist made notes about each one of them in a very particular kind of code. Whatever the case may be, *Le Duc de B. etc.* is held to be the sequel to the first two *Etudes,* and nobody doubts that there was a strip-tease coincidence

5. The person in question here is Louis I of Bourgogne, the lover of the Queen of France Isabeau de Bavière and of her uncle from Orleans, Philippe le Hardi. It is not hard to understand why these three paintings were not shown with the *Sardanapale* in 1827 and that the absence of Delacroix was necessary in order for the "friend" who owned them (probably Robert Soulier) to send them to the exposition of 1832. It is not hard to imagine the scandal they provoked in the midst of a cholera epidemic.

between this painting and life, Eugène no doubt being the Duc de Bourgogne and his friend Robert Soulier, le Duc d'Orléans. And everyone knows how Mme. Dalton went from one to the other. But the perversity of the painter is not really the point here—in *Pierrot le fou,* it is Belmondo who plays with a parrot. And I'm not saying all this to show how, if I wanted, I too could indulge in the delirium of interpretation. Furthermore, isn't this the answer to the question I started off with? Art is the delirium of the interpretation of life.

If I wanted to, furthermore, I would approach J.-L. G. from the painters' side to show the origin of one of the characteristics of his art for which he is the most often reproached. Quotations, as the critics call them; collages, as I propose they should be called (and it seems to me that Godard, in his interviews, has used the same term). Painters were the first to use collages, in the sense that Godard and I mean here, even before 1910 and their systematic utilization by Braque and Picasso; there is, for instance, Watteau, whose *L'Enseigne de Gersaint* represents an immense collage, in which all the paintings on the wall of the shop and the portrait that is being packed of Louis XIV by Hyacinthe Rigaut are *quoted,* as everybody likes to say. In Delacroix, all you need is a painting from 1823, *Milton et ses filles,* to find a "quotation" used as a means of expression. There was certainly some stimulus that made Delacroix use, as the subject of a painting, a man who cannot see, in order to show us his thought—the pale blind man is sitting in an easy-chair with his hand on an embroidered tapestry covering a table; his fingers seem to be feeling the colors of the tapestry, while there is a pot of flowers that escapes him. But below his two daughters seated on low chairs, one taking down the words of *Paradise Lost,* the other holding a musical instrument that has become silent, one sees an unframed painting on the wall showing Adam and Eve fleeing the Garden of Paradise and the Angel who is banishing them—defenseless, naked and ashamed. This is a collage intended to show us the invisible, i.e. the thought of the man with the empty eyes. This technique has not been lost since that time. There is the painting by Seurat, for instance, *Les Poseuses,* in which, in the painter's studio, three undressed women, the one at the right taking off some black stockings, are next to the huge painting of *La Grande Jatte,* which is quite appropriately "quoted" here so that the whole thing will be something else than what we call a strip-tease. And how about Courbet when he makes a collage of Baudelaire in a corner of his *Atelier?* In the same way, Godard, in *Pierrot,* stamps the letter with Raymond Devos before sending it, as he had done with the philosopher Brice Parain in *Vivre sa vie.* These are not characters from a novel; they are signs to show us how Adam and Eve were banished from Paradise.

Furthermore, if there is, in this area, a difference between *Pierrot* and Godard's other films, it lies in a certain overall impression that people will not fail to see as Godard simply trying to outdo himself. People have already been reproaching the director of *Le Mépris* [1963] and *Le Petit Soldat* [1960] for this technique for years now. They find it to be a mania they hope he will get rid of. The critics hope to discourage him, and they stand ready to applaud a Godard who would simply stop being Godard and make films the way everybody else does. They obviously have not succeeded, if this film is any indication. If anyone should be discouraged, it is the critics. The growth of this *system* of collages in *Pierrot le fou* is such that there are entire sections (*chapters,* Godard calls them) that are nothing *but* collages. The entire cocktail party at the bginning. Or even before that. The collages simply continue; everybody recognizes (because Belmondo holds the paper-back edition of Elie Faure's history of art in his hand) that the text on Velasquez that begins the whole story is by Elie Faure. On the other hand, they're not sure why, later on, Pierrot is reading the most recent printing of the *Pieds-Nickelés* comic strip. This in a story in which Belmondo waves a *Série Noire* novel about, as if to say "here is what a novel is really all about!" That gives me quite a laugh—when I was young, nobody said anything if I was found reading Pierre Louys or Charles-Henry Hirsch; but my mother forbad me to read the *Pieds-Nickelés*. I hate to think of what would have happened to me if she had ever caught me with a copy of *L'Epatant,* in which the comic-strip appeared. I don't know what the black-leather-jacket generation must think of the *Pieds-Nickelés;* but for people of my generation whose memories are not entirely grisly, the resemblance between the *Pieds-Nickelés* and the characters of the "organization" in the complicated game in which Pierrot has become involved is immediately evident—so much so, in fact, that this whole affair, when Belmondo reads *Les Pieds Nickelés,* takes on a slightly more complex meaning than it seems to have at first glance.

That is not the essential point—but when everything is said and done, you have to accept the idea that the collages are not illustrations of the film, but that they are the film itself. That they are the very matter of paintings, and that painting would not exist outside of them. Thus, all those who persist in taking the matter for a gimmick would be better off, in the future, changing records. You may hate Godard, but you cannot ask him to practice any other art than his own . . . the flute or water painting. You must see that Pierrot who is not named Pierrot and who screams at Marianne, "My name is Ferdinand!" finds himself next to a Picasso which shows the artist's son (Paulo, as a child) dressed up as a Pierrot-type clown. And certainly the large number of Picassos[6] on the wall does not manifest any

6. Picassos . . . the industrialization of the work of art has become a new sociological phenomenon. And you can have on your walls (in a smaller version than the original) the *Guernica,* for instance, as a permanent explanation of Algeria, of Vietnam, of Santo Domingo, of the Indo-Pakistani conflict (an "up to date" remark). . . . Snobbery is out of date. A Picasso means something and is taken by the everyday spectator for what it has to tell—once again, we are right in the middle of the era of the *Massacres de Scio,* of the *Sardanapale* era.

desire on Godard's part to show off his talents as a connoisseur, certainly not when Picassos can be bought at your local neighborhood department store. One of the first portraits of Jacqueline, in profile, shows up, somewhat later, with the head pointed downward because in the world and in Pierrot's brain, everything *is* upside down. Not to mention the resemblance between the hair painted on the canvas and the long, soft locks of Anna Karina. Or Godard's obsession for Renoir (Marianne is named Marianne Renoir). Or the collages involving advertising ("There was the Greek civilization, the Roman civilization, and now we have the ass-hole civilization. . . ."), beauty products, underwear.

What Godard is particularly reproached for are his spoken collages—too bad for those who did not react, in *Alphaville* (which is not my favorite Godard), to the humor of having Pascal quoted by Eddie Constantine as he is being questioned by the robot-computer. Godard is also reproached, along with everything else, for quoting Céline. In Pierrot, it happens to be *Guignol's Band*—but if I were to start talking about Céline, this could go on forever. I prefer Pascal, no doubt, and I certainly cannot forget what the author of *Voyage au bout de la nuit* became. But this does not prevent the fact that *Voyage,* when it appeared, was a damn beautiful book, and that subsequent generations, who lose themselves in the novel, find us unjust, stupid and partisan. And we are just that. These are misunderstandings between a father and a son. But you can't solve them by commandments: "My young Godard, thou shalt not quote Céline!" And so he quotes him, fancy that.

As for me, I am quite proud to have been quoted (or "collaged") by the creator of *Pierrot* with a regularity that is none the less remarkable than the determination Godard shows as he shoves Céline in your face. None the less remarkable, but much less remarked upon by the critics, either because they haven't read my works, or because I annoy them just as much as Céline, but offer them fewer reasons to attack than Céline, so that only their irritation remains and they use the weapon of silence, an irritation that becomes worse because it remains mute. In *Pierrot le fou,* a large extract of *La Mise à mort . . .*—a good two paragraphs; I don't know all my works by heart, but I can certainly recognize them when I hear them—spoken by Belmondo shows me once again the kind of secret understanding that exists between this young man and me on certain essential things—let him find his tailor-made expression either in my works, or elsewhere, where I have my dreams (the cover of *L'Ame* at the beginning of *La Femme mariée;* the French translation, *Admirables fables,* done by Elsa of Mayakovsky's work, on the lips of the partisan girl about to be shot in *Les Carabiniers* [1962–63]). When Baudelaire, in his poem "Les Phares," had used Delacroix ("Lac de sang, hanté des mauvais anges . . . ") in a "collage," the aged painter wrote to him, "A thousand thank-you's for your good opinion—I owe you a great many just for *Les Fleurs du mal;* I've already talked to you about your volume in passing, but it deserves a great deal more. . . ." And when, at the Salon of 1859, the critics assassinated Delacroix, it was Baudelaire who took his side and answered for him, and the painter wrote to the poet, "Since I've had the good fortune to please you, 1 can console myself over the reprimands I received. You treat me in a manner that is usually reserved for *great people who have died.* You make me blush while making me very happy at the same time. That is the way we're made."

I'm not quite sure why I'm quoting this, why I'm making a *collage* of this in my article—everything is backwards here, except that, actually, when in that intimate little theatre where only Elsa sat there with me, I heard these words that I knew but did not immediately recognize, I blushed in the darkness. But I'm not the person who resembles Delacroix. It's the other one. That child of genius.

Here I am back at the beginning. What is new, what is great, what is sublime always provokes insults, scorn and outrage. And this is always more unbearable for an older man. At the age of sixty-one, Delacroix met with the worst affront given by those who hand out glory. How old is Godard? And even if the game had been lost, the game is won, he can believe me on that. . . .

How many films has Godard already shot? Every one of us is a Pierrot le fou in one way or another, Pierrots who sit down on the railroad tracks, who wait for the train to come and run over them and who dash out of the way at the last minute, who continue to live. Whatever the ups and downs of our lives may be, and whether or not they resemble Pierrot's. Pierrot blows himself up, but at the last second he decided he didn't want to. Nothing is over, particularly since others will follow the same path, only the date will change. How alike it all is. . . .

I set off to talk about art. And I've only talked about life.

Part Three

Authors on Screenwriting

Henry Arthur Jones

The Dramatist and the Photoplay

The dramatist wins enduring renown by his dialogue, and by his dialogue alone. To write a successful play he must of course have other gifts and acquirements. He must call in the scene-painter, the upholsterer, the costumer, the electrician, and other adjutants to help him to express himself. But his dialogue alone has permanent value; all the rest of his trappings are perishable. The difference between *Macbeth* or *Hamlet* and a stock melodrama is that *Macbeth* and *Hamlet* can be read and studied as literature. That is the reason they have held their place in our theater for three hundred years. That is also the chief reason why they often fail on our modern stage. They are literature. They demand serious thought and feeling from an audience. They ask for examination, and offer emotional and intellectual enjoyment on these grounds.

It is clear that the film cannot afford the quality and kind of pleasure that spoken drama can give—the pleasure of literature.

Again, the voice has always been the chief gift of the actor, his chief means of swaying his audience and stirring their emotions. It is mainly by the voice that the actor gets his finest and worthiest effects. What the dramatist has written falls dead upon the stage unless it is vitalized by the actor.

It is clear that, as the film play forbids the dramatist to use his chief and highest means of expression, so also it forbids the actor to use his chief and highest means of expression.

Originally published in *The Mentor,* 9 (July 1921), p. 29.

What balancing advantages and compensations has the film to offer to the actor and the dramatist? To the film actor and actress it offers universal, though not immortal, fame, by displaying their pictures in every city of the civilized world, perhaps in five hundred theaters on the same night. It further offers to star performers an enormous salary.

What are the advantages offered the dramatist? In the volume, variety, and impetus of its action—that is, in the very essence of drama—in its swift, vivid, multiple transformations, its startling command of contrasts, its power of concentration on valuable minutiae, its capacity for insinuation and flashing suggestion—in all these truly dramatic qualities the film play offers to the dramatist an infinitude of opportunity compared with the spoken drama.

Aristotle compared the limitations of the drama with the expanses of the epic. But, compared with the film, even the epic, the novel, becomes a tedious chronicler of events.

The film is a bungler at comedy, except of the rude and boisterous kind which Thalia reproves. But the film invites and welcomes Romance and Imagination and opens a large field for their exploits. Now, imagination, from Shakespeare downwards, is largely shut out from our modern stage, with its pert vulgarity and dictionary of slang. Tongue-tied already, and almost banished from the spoken drama, imagination may perhaps find a home in the film theater. She will be deprived of speech, but how rarely she is allowed to open her lips upon the regular stage! May not Imagination find utterance in the vast pictorial resources and devices of the film theater, throw her magic beams amongst its fascinating lights and shadows, and employ the quick vibrations and successions of the screen to tell larger stories of human life than are being told today upon the stage of the spoken drama.

Tom Antongini

D'Annunzio and Film

D'Annunzio's first contact with the world of the cinema came in 1911, at the Hôtel Continental in Paris. Two Italian movie magnates (I am withholding their names because they wouldn't forgive me an anecdote concerning them which I don't feel like keeping from my readers) who had come from Paris, invited d'Annunzio and me to a private luncheon at the above mentioned hotel.

The Parisian custom is to resolve important business matters, even the establishment of large banks (I am not speaking of ministerial crises), at table. During the fish course (sole meunière, served with a superb Sauterne—if it's a small bank, the Sauterne may be replaced by a modest Graves) the nature of the business at hand is established. With the appearance of lamb chops "à la Villeroy," everything is in full swing; part of the capital is underwritten. By the time the peach melba is served the president is named, and over liqueurs—probably a fine old brandy—the bank itself is organized. The Italian movie producers simply followed the French tradition—a tradition which is very much justified, since during a good dinner the spirit inclines to propositions which would never be considered in an office.

From Tom Antongini, *Vita Segreta di Gabriele D'Annunzio,* Arnoldo Mondadori, 1938. Translated by Judith Turner. Published here, in translation, by permission of Arnoldo Mondadori Editore, Milano, Italy.

These producers had agreed between themselves on an offer, but they hadn't considered their guest. At that time d'Annunzio drank only water and was therefore always very clearheaded. Thus it came about that he extorted two thousand lire from his hosts for each plot adapted from his works. Two thousand lire! A munificent sum in 1911—a sum which brought a badly repressed, complacent smile to the face of that same d'Annunzio who, eighteen years later (that is, May 1929), wrote me apropos of an offer to adapt to film his poem "The Woman of Pisa": "The reasons which prevent me from accepting the offer made in response to my very modest demand have been explained. Five hundred thousand lire in advance, in addition to a percentage of the gross, is the minimum sum for such plots as I can create[1] . . . You should see how elaborate the contract is!"

But then, let's descend from this seventh heaven and return to the less extravagant era of a mere two thousand lire per plot. The 1911 contract, if not actually signed, was at least defined along general lines, and d'Annunzio was perhaps the most satisfied of all the parties. He still remembers that happy time, and he is especially fond of retelling a little story connected with that historic luncheon. The two producers, even though they knew their own business very well, felt uncomfortable on principle, not considering themselves the intellectual equals of their guest. However, partly because the poet was so very cordial, and partly because they made free with the red burgundy and white bordeaux, they became braver and began to chatter away freely. By the time the fruit was served, they were expounding on every subject—art, literature, politics, psychology and so on—absolutely shamelessly. And, d'Annunzio enjoyed himself immensely. Finally they caroled, "You know, it's incredible! Instead of feeling nervous and inferior, we felt com-

1. The poem "The Woman of Pisa or Perfumed Death" [1938] is to be published by Calmann Lévy.

fortable with you right away—we dare to talk to you as if you were an ordinary person!"

"But," said d'Annunzio, with a little smile, "what you don't know is that I am just like Orpheus."

"Yes indeed," laughed one of the producers, "like Orpheus." And turning to me he added, "What an extraordinary man! How cultured! He knows absolutely everything!" And in a low tone, "You put me on to this Orpheus afterwards, get it?"

However, I judged it preferable to leave him in blissful ignorance.

Having signed the famous contract, d'Annunzio gave no further thought to it. The art of the cinema was still at its dawning (I can't say "first cry," because, thank God, sound films hadn't yet been developed). The poet paid less attention to the adaptation of his works to the screen than a composer would pay to a provincial organ grinder's variation on one of his arias. He was never concerned with the way in which his stories were interpreted and realized. It wasn't until ten years later, in a theatre in Fiume, that Commander d'Annunzio, by mere chance, was present at the showing of one of the adaptations of his stories. It was the first film version of "Leda without the Swan." From beginning to end the poet split his sides laughing; he considered the film puerile and exaggerated. This was the first and only time that d'Annunzio ever saw a film of one of his works.

And, I can assure you that d'Annunzio never saw *Cabiria* [directed by Piero Fosco who was also called Giovanni Pastrone, 1914].* This denial, precise because categorical, will surely stupefy certain people. It will seem less astonishing when they are informed of the authentic history of that film, known in its

* The film starred Italia Almirante and Lidia Quaranta. Approximately 8,500 feet long, it told the story of Fulvio, a Roman, and Cabiria, a slave girl from Sicily, during the Second Punic War.

entirety to only four persons in the world. Of these four, three (that is, d'Annunzio and the two producers of the film) have no interest in revealing it. The fourth person is myself.

It all began in June, 1913. D'Annunzio was without a cent—a condition as normal for him as for another god-fearing man to have red hair or a nervous twitch. At the point he lived at 47 Avenue Kléber [in Paris], in a charming apartment which he embellished with the customary trappings of cushions and draperies. This was the apartment in which, much later, the outbreak of the European war took him by surprise. At one of the many confrontations with his balance sheets, to which he habitually invited me in order to hear my inspired plans for making money, the poet read me a letter he had received a few days before. This letter was rather strange, both in form and content, and since the original has remained in my possession I don't want to deprive my readers of it.

> Sir:
>
> At the risk of being unceremoniously consigned to the wastebasket, we are forced to confess that we are movie producers. We beg your forgiveness if, by presenting ourselves thus indirectly and covertly, we have incurred your displeasure. It is not cowardice that drives us to trickery, but the knowledge of the wrongs committed by the producers who snubbed you or made light of your great name.[2]
>
> In short, we have a project in mind which would mean profit and almost NO disturbance to you—and which would not reflect on your good name.
>
> Would you be willing to authorize us to come there at your convenience to submit it to you?
>
> With profound respects. . . .

Whoever sent this letter had unconsciously (I say "unconsciously" because he didn't actually know the poet and knew

2. The authors of the letter were alluding to some vicious criticism of preceding films based on d'Annunzio's works.

still less of his temperament) struck two notes which would bring him consideration: first, the fact that he recognized that the profession of producer wouldn't get him as far as, for example, being a lawyer or a shoe salesman; second, that he aroused d'Annunzio's curiosity by the hint, especially piquant at this critical moment, of possible easy gain with almost no (the word "no" was written in capital letters) disturbance. In fact, the letter had a magical effect.

D'Annunzio gave it to me and put me in charge of meeting with the author in my office in Paris to see how much truth and reliability there was in this mysterious proposal. My office was at 62 Rue la Boétie. At that time I managed a fashion magazine which brought me small profit and great annoyance. Signor [Giovanni] Pastrone (the letter writer's name) came as soon as he was invited, and revealed his very American proposal to me. I call it "American" because it was well worked out, bold, and very quickly understood.

"I have finished a magnificent film which may run as long as three hours," he said. "I have with me some still photographs made from at least two hundred frames of the picture and which give an accurate idea of the *mise en scène*. The captions are ready and so is the film title. But even if I swear with modesty that my film is as good as can technically be produced by the film industry, I can't say as much for the captions or the title. Besides, I need an author's name. It must be a big, world-famous, irreproachable name. And so I thought—at least my colleagues and I have dared to dream—of Gabriele d'Annunzio. For the rather pedestrian work of providing new captions, and especially for the acknowledgment of the film which would be ornamented by his great name, I am authorized to pay fifty thousand lire."

I no longer remember if the two words which indicated the numbers were pronounced unclearly, perhaps because Signore Pastrone had a slight cold, or if, because of the tension of the moment, I'd misunderstood him. The fact was that I was not perfectly sure if I'd exactly comprehended the words indicating the amount. It seemed enormous to me; and, for that time, it really was. The best going rate in Europe (America counted for less than nothing) was three or four thousand lire. Being offered fifty thousand lire at that time was like being offered a couple of million today. At any rate I didn't believe it advisable to indicate my agonized uncertainty as to the amount.

I told Signor Pastrone that I would refer the offer to d'Annunzio the next day; I filled him in about my boss's character, that I couldn't foresee what his answer would be, and so forth. I ended by giving Signor Pastrone an appointment for the following evening. That day I took care not to speak to the poet about the proposal. I knew his mentality then as well as I know it today. If a sum is proposed to d'Annunzio as the maximum figure that will be offered, two minutes later he begins with that sum fixed in his mind as the lowest possible sum he will accept. Thus, it often happens that the business at hand goes up in smoke, to the poet's great disadvantage.

I met Pastrone the next evening and told him that I'd not yet had the chance to speak to d'Annunzio about the offer. However, this time, as we discussed the business again, I broached the subject of the fee, cocking my ear so that not a syllable would escape me. The sum was stated for the second time and very clearly. Fifty thousand lire. There was no longer any doubt. I took my leave of Signor Pastrone and that same evening discussed the offer with d'Annunzio. Actually, as was my custom when dealing with him, I said at first that they had offered me twenty thousand lire, waited until he had raised the price to forty thousand lire, and left him to sleep on it. Then, the next day, I pretended to have wrenched not only the requested forty thousand lire out of Pastrone, but a round fifty thousand.

Having signed the contract, the producer began, as is usual, to complain. He kept demanding to be given the finished work; for

Pastrone every loss of time was equivalent to the loss of a good deal of money. I had at my disposal only one way to oblige the poet to work—that was to make him understand that, in spite of the greatest deference, admiration and sympathy (and the more you get, the more you want) the movie director had for the Great Italian Poet, he would not be given the famous cheque if the captions weren't written and the title not announced. D'Annunzio, who, when he couldn't do anything less, knew how to be understanding and very reasonable, accepted the conditions and, armed with the photos Pastrone had brought him and the existing captions, started work.

Deciding on the title was a ten minute affair. For d'Annunzio, thinking up a title isn't a difficulty, but a pleasure. In his life he'd probably thought up ten thousand names, nicknames, and titles! I believe the film, when it arrived in Paris, was called *Triumph of Love,* or something like that. D'Annunzio smiled at so much ingenuousness, and, fifteen minutes later, entitled it *Cabiria.* Those who know mythology understand that *Cabiria* means "born from fire." However, it's a sonorous, easy name which anyone could easily remember. The name *Cabiria* was joyously welcomed by the interested parties.

When he got to the characters' names and the captions, the going got harder. D'Annunzio had never been a man who did sloppy work. He had to meditate, to examine, to document. For example, he would never consider giving a Chaldean name to a Carthaginian, or one of Egyptian origin to a Hebrew. To d'Annunzio, such inaccuracy would be an enormity. Therefore, the work necessitated a certain amount of time. Pastrone was going crazy. He had figured that d'Annunzio would be able to get everything done in two or three days with the help of a typist, and so he gave himself no peace. He came to my house five or six times a day, telegraphed to Turin, and implored me to intercede with the poet on his behalf. Finally, after Pastrone had suffered for a good two weeks, d'Annunzio solemnly announced that he was almost finished. Pastrone, soured by recent disappointments, didn't put any faith in this talk. On the contrary he was so perturbed at the possibility that the d'Annunzian proclamation might hide a trap, that the poet, at the last minute, could take flight, renouncing the fifty thousand lire without so much as a fare-thee-well, that he established himself in the entrance hall of the poet's apartment on the Avenue Kléber and stayed put. Don't imagine that the phrase "established himself in the entrance hall" is simply figurative.

Pastrone passed the day there and slept there. I don't know if he got a mattress from d'Annunzio's man-servant, but I can swear that Pastrone was present in the entrance hall for one entire day and night and that he sent the porter to get him sandwiches at mealtimes. The poet at last understood that there was small chance of evading destiny, and that, willy-nilly, he was obliged to earn that fifty thousand lire. And so, in three days *Cabiria* was finished—without Pastrone's Piedmont obstinacy it would perhaps never have been completed, at least with Gabriele d'Annunzio as its author.[3]

And now that you know the true story of the great d'Annunzian film, I leave it to you to imagine with what moral satisfaction he heard Porel, the great vaudeville director, say (and he was certainly not the only one to say it), "Your genius is once again spectacularly confirmed. *Cabiria* is a true masterpiece." Of all d'Annunzio's work on *Cabiria* there remains only a brief, three page outline. It shouldn't surprise the reader that the captions were written in French, since, during his stay in France, the poet often wrote his personal notes in that language. From these three pages I may conclude that, at first, d'Annunzio had actually intended to write the whole story of *Cabiria* so as to

3. "A Greek-Roman-Punic drama, in the style of *Quo Vadis*?" That same d'Annunzio publicly described it thus. A description of this kind would have been enough—at least for those who knew the poet's character—to conclude that he was not really the only author of it.

conform to the greater part of the stills taken from the film; however, he wished to reserve the right to demand additions or modifications. Ultimately, faced with such pressure, he limited himself to "draping" Pastrone's puppets with his incomparable literary style. In his attitude toward the film, d'Annunzio was like those fathers who know that one of their children is not theirs, but the offspring of an attentive friend who often comes to dinner and sometimes takes the wife dancing, and who thus cannot manage, in spite of all efforts, to treat that child like the others although the poor little thing is in no way guilty. The poet never liked *Cabiria* and always avoided seeing it.

His small liking for this lovely natural child of his was again shown in correspondence concerning the staging of *Honeysuckle* at Porte-Saint-Martin theatre. At that time, *Cabiria* was beginning to make a hit in the Italian movie houses. In a letter answering Hertz and Coquelin, the directors of that theatre, he touched upon the earnings the film brought him, and let it be supposed that his great concern for the maintenance of his racing greyhounds led him to write the famous movie script. Pastrone noticed the letter which had been printed by several newspapers, was annoyed by that sort of self-depreciation—after all, d'Annunzio *had* written the script—and wrote to the poet. D'Annunzio, always ready to make up for the injuries he had inadvertently caused others, had me publish a sort of advertisement in the Parisian newspapers which I will reprint in its entirety. Although it appeared under my signature, it is d'Annunzio's work from start to finish. In this article he brought up the greyhounds again, but the tone is skillfully modified and for good reason:

> Various newspapers have printed inexact reports of the mediocre success of a film based on a story by Gabriele d'Annunzio, which a large company in Turin has produced with a magnificence heretofore unknown in cinematic circles. This report had its

origin in the Roman public's revolt against the un-
couth manager, who was so bold as to charge the
extraordinary prices which the public is resigned to
paying for the opening night of a tragedy by the
master, for the first showing of his film. But, for two
weeks, in Rome, Naples, Milan, Turin, and here, the
houses have always been packed and people have
been turned away. Besides, Signor d'Annunzio, who,
after all, is a wise man, would never have consented
to join the fortunes of his substantial kennels to such
a fragile and trembling thing as is called "film" unless
it were sure to succeed. On presenting the story he
received one hundred thousand francs ("cash on the
barrel-head," as Piron would say) which assured him
of red meat for his greyhounds, at least for six
months. And the proof of *Cabiria*'s success lies in the
fact that that same company has requested another
subject, for the same price, adding a percentage of the
cash gross. This will guarantee not only six more
months of the well-known red meat, but also a few
sweets, and, for hunting trips, egg yolks and one hun-
dred-year-old brandy.

The readers of the Parisian newspapers found the communiqué
well written. They also recognised the master's style—in fact
there were murmurings among the editorial staff that the poet's
secretary knew how to write as well as his boss.

From that time on, d'Annunzio's relationship with the film
world consisted of an unbroken sequence of offers, of counter-
proposals, of stories sketched and then abandoned, of payments
in advance never followed by the delivery of a manuscript, and
so it went. D'Annunzio had the habit of promising, hand on
heart, a comedy or tragedy written for every actress (I won't
say only the beautiful ones, but at least pretty ones) when he
was "on the threshhold of possession." After *Cabiria,* with the
same solemnity, he began to promise established actresses and
aspiring actresses of this still silent art form that, when they
crossed his threshhold, they would be heroines in his film

scenarios. Naturally, the stars and starlets were quick to communicate d'Annunzio's promises to film directors and to producers. I leave it to you to imagine the results of such "private communications" in the reserved and austere group which made up film society.

In reality, from 1913 on, d'Annunzio conceived and wrote only one work for camera—*The Innocents' Crusade*. In fact, the story, *The Man who Stole the Mona Lisa,* which the poet arranged for film, is merely a revision, or, better still, a transformation of a story which d'Annunzio wrote for the editor, Pietro Laffitte, who promised to print it in the supplement of the daily *Excelsior*. But *The Innocents' Crusade,* which was later published, could never be used. Technical reasons (for example, the employment of large numbers of children) made shooting the film almost impracticable. Besides, such a subject would not have interested the movie-going public. As I have said, the work has been published and anyone who reads it can see how inappropriate it is for the purpose intended by the author. However, it is inexplicable that *The Man who Stole the Mona Lisa* didn't come to the attention of those whose job it is to hunt for film stories. The plot goes beyond the usual tedious machinations to which America was accustomed from the start, and which then spoiled the more refined tastes of the Europeans. Barring necessary modifications, to which d'Annunzio certainly would have acquiesced, it had all the qualifications for interesting any public. And, if, after *Cabiria* (which was an indisputable and sensational triumph), d'Annunzio never wrote the script of another film, I must conclude that the only reason he didn't find buyers was the lack of sensitivity which the directors and producers of large film companies exhibited for about twenty years (except for rare and respectable exceptions).

The war [of 1914–18] not only stopped d'Annunzio's literary production, but, internationally at least, it thwarted his plans for film. Only at Fiume did his plans come close to realization.

The film to be produced had the unprecedented look of a "saga." Again I conducted the negotiations. Thus I can describe the strange stages of these particular dealings, which make the poet's psychology especially clear. Two Americans, impeccable from the standpoint of seriousness and financial potential (one of them brought the personal guarantee of Witney Warren, a famous American architect and a very good friend of d'Annunzio's), came to see me in Fiume at the Hotel Europa in the spring of 1920 to propose the following deal for d'Annunzio. The poet was to write a film about Fiume for them during the three months covered by the contract. For the story line, they wanted any subject which related to the city and the life of Fiume during its months of passionate struggle. They themselves would film the background without the Commander [d'Annunzio] even noticing it. This plan was, incidentally, quite feasible. Every day the Commander passed regiments and shock troops in review, received deputations, visited outlying posts, traveled through the city in a car and on foot, presided at military exercises, solemnly commemorated dates and events, and talked to the crowd from the balcony of the Governor's palace. Nothing, then, could be easier for the film-makers, who had only to follow the poet as he went about his manifold activities, for a few weeks' time. The poet's actual work would be reduced to the writing of a twenty or thirty page summary of any fictional subject he might choose. The work was infinitely less complex and fatiguing than, for example, writing a novel. In short, it was a task which d'Annunzio would have been able to complete splendidly in three or four days of mental preparation and as many days again to get it all down on paper. I have already said that, for d'Annunzio, the most important part of his work was the mental preparation, even if it is a question of a creation one hundred times more complicated—requiring his maximum literary effort—than a movie script.

When I told the Commander about the Americans' presence

at Fiume and their offer, he barked, "Get the contract! And accept a minimum of two hundred thousand lire, since, as you know, I need money very, very badly!" Not only was this an old subject for both of us, it was also, at that point, absolutely true. From that day on I walked, ate, smoked—in short, lived— with these two Americans; I worked so well that their confidence in the Commander reached a peak; thus I was able to convince them to prepare the draft of a contract which gave d'Annunzio eight hundred thousand lire at the time he gave them the finished manuscript. All this took place, of course, before I consulted d'Annunzio. At this time, such a sum of money was pure hyperbole. Finally I brought these two men into the presence of the Commander; their attitude toward him was something like that of a Catholic toward a relic of the true cross. They brought the agreement, already duly drawn up on legal paper. It had cost me ten days' work and, at that point, lacked only the Commander's signature. The Commander received the Americans at the palace, in the private study which adjoined his bedroom. In this room he used to discuss highly confidential matters with his followers and organize those magnificent political and military coups which allowed him and his legions to amuse themselves, all unknown to Europe, for about two years.

Battered into suitability, the contract was read and signed by both factions. Only a few times in my life have I seen d'Annunzio happier after reaching an agreement. The mirage of nearly a million lire earned in a few days (he had reduced the work that much) seemed to make him twenty years younger. We must not forget that the conquest of Fiume had represented a complete arrest of all his literary output and, consequently, a real financial disaster. In this he was more like a Garibaldi than a Cortez or a Pizarro since he had gained almost no material advantage from his exceptional position. Mr. Wilbur H. Williams (such was the name of the principal producer from overseas) left Fiume a few days later in precisely the same mental state as d'Annunzio; he was also convinced that he had concluded a good piece of business, an agreement which would bring huge financial gains. And I received from d'Annunzio an expensive cigarette case—a reward for the work I did on his behalf. On the case, which I still have, the following words are incised in the Commander's handwriting: "Fiume fire, thickening smoke." It will be seen, in a moment, how I was the only one who earned anything out of the deal, and how one of d'Annunzio's most beautiful contracts was dissolved in that "smoke."

The American left with the reciprocal understanding that he would return to Fiume a month later to shoot the scenes of real life which would serve as the cornerstone of the picture. D'Annunzio spent four days shut up in his apartment, receiving very few people. I attributed this to the mental gestation which precedes every one of the poet's literary works, but I was mistaken. After a few days, when it seemed like a good time to bring up the subject, I asked the Commander if he'd made any progress. I was informed that he had not as yet "put his mind to it." But, he added that he needed greater quiet and above all, absolute, undisturbed solitude, at least for a week, if he were going to succeed at his task. Since Fiume was quiet then I advised him to entrust the maintenance of his duties to General Ceccherini, in whom he had full confidence, and to impose absolute solitude on himself. He did just that. Another week passed, during which the Poet remained almost invisible. When he again contacted the external world he immediately called me to him. But, it wasn't hard to read in his face that expression which all people who know they are at fault have—especially children who haven't done their homework. D'Annunzio attributed the fact that he had nothing to show for that week of tranquility—that he was still at the beginning of his work—to everything except the real reason (and I didn't need him to inform me of it since I'd known him for a long time). The real reason was that d'Annunzio could not do anything that he didn't want to do—not even for a king. His famous will power had failed disgracefully to sustain him. The eight hundred thousand lire remained in the pockets of Mr. Wilbur H. Williams.

D'Annunzio's attitude toward recent cinematic creations and toward film personalities whose fame had spread all over the world was very strange. At best, he had vaguely heard of their names and their fame. A few years ago, in my covert dual capacity of friend of the poet and director of a movie company, I showed him about twenty of the most popular and respected films by American, French, German and Russian filmmakers. In the undisturbed quiet of Vittoriale, for more than twenty evenings, from nine till two in the morning I showed films starring Mary Pickford, Douglas Fairbanks, Harold Lloyd, Brigitte Helm, Dolores del Rio, Charlie Chaplin, Adolphe Menjou, Greta Garbo, and several Soviet films with Russian interpreters. The audience consisted of d'Annunzio, two of his guests, me, my daughter, and the men and women who made up his domestic staff (all of them, since d'Annunzio, with his inexhaustible kindness, always brought them together when he thought that they could in some way enjoy themselves or share in one of his pleasures).

I deemed his opinions of great interest, not only because they were the expression of his genius, but also because previously he had seen almost no film except for *The Ship* [1927], directed and adapted by his son Gabriellino, and produced by Ida Rubinstein. Of course, the films were shown without any musical accompaniment, and thus lacked all trappings. An absolute silence, broken only by an occasional word from the poet, was maintained. I have rarely seen d'Annunzio more interested in a show; no particular escaped him. He often wanted a film to be reshown, at least in part. Above all, the perfection that cinematic tricks had attained amazed and interested him. He didn't believe his eyes. The film directors' inventions, and the possibilities represented by each more daring film, made him extremely curious. Chuckling, he declared, "I wouldn't be capable of inventing things like that!"

Of all the famous actresses who peopled the screen, the one who least interested him was Mary Pickford.[4] But if my saying this should come to the ears of the famous *"Rosita,"* she shouldn't be disturbed for nothing. I know nothing of her private life, not having the honor of being acquainted with her, but certainly, on the screen, she is the least seductive of all the stars in the cinematic heavens; thus, she is the woman who least corresponds to the poet's feminine ideal. He likes all that is elaborate and exceptional in women and considers qualities like simplicity, sweetness, ingenuousness, archness—Mary Pickford's principle qualities—second rate. In him, besides the man there is the artist; from a strictly artistic point of view Mary Pickford's qualities would prevent her from playing any of the creatures born of d'Annunzio's fantasies—Ippolita Sanzio, Elena Muti, Isabella Inghirami, Silvia Settàla, la Pisanella, la Foscarina, Basiliola, Giuliana Hermil, to name only a few of the greatest. Naturally, for opposite reasons, as much human as artistic, he found Dolores del Rio and Brigitte Helm interesting and, as was predictable, he found Greta Garbo very interesting indeed. Besides the aesthetic delight Dolores del Rio gave him, he owed her some small recognition as he said, "I finally know the entire story of Tolstoy's *Resurrection,** which I've never had the patience to read to the end." He judged Charlie Chaplin, whom he knew mainly by reputation, to be an exceptional artist (d'Annunzio saw *The Gold Rush* and *The Circus*), only regretting that Chaplin had allowed himself to become typed. However, among all the films which were shown to him, Ufa's *Metropolis* [1926] and *Siegfried* [1925—both films directed by Fritz Lang]—and [Pudovkin's] Russian film taken from Gorky's

4. "She has an unexpressive mouth," he said, "and moves awkwardly."

* D'Annunzio saw *Resurrection* [1927] directed by Edwin Carewe, in which Dolores del Rio played Katusha.

novel, *Mother* [1928], interested him the most. *Metropolis* so enthralled him, especially technically, that he wanted the film shown twice. . . . He enjoyed Douglas Fairbanks' ingenuous performances and giggled like a girl at Harold Lloyd in the well-known film* *I Prefer the Elevator.*[5]

Not long after these showings, d'Annunzio expressed a desire to get seriously involved, if not in new creations, at least in adapting stories drawn from his works and in personally directing their execution according to the new concepts and possibilities inspired by the films which I had brought to Vittoriale. He wrote to a friend, at that time the head of a film company, who wanted to get the rights to the plot of *La Pisanella* to adapt it to film:

> My right eye, while it hasn't yet succumbed, has become a pretty poor viewer. During the long evenings of "movie month," a thousand images were superimposed on persistent fits of blindness. I have lived in a constant hallucination. Again tonight Zorro and Alberic possessed my bedroom, giving me no peace.[6] I have been able to ascertain the limits reached by moving art; and I know that the outer limits are still very far away. You won't deny that throughout my life Ulysses' bow has been offered to me to bend. Here again the bow confronts me. As with *Cabiria,* I have again taken up the position of surpassing the limits which have been reached. I begin to muse, to search, and to experiment. May the eleventh muse, Kinesis, help me! I have told Tom that I would be very happy if you would dare to animate my

---

* Possibly a reference to *Safety Last* (1923). There is no Harold Lloyd Film titled *I Prefer the Elevator.*

5. If the fact that up to that time I had not yet offered to show d'Annunzio some Italian films seems strange and disagreeable to some readers, I will limit myself to stating the sadly inarguable fact that till then there didn't exist a single film circulating in Italy which was worthy of being seen.

6. He is alluding to Douglas Fairbanks' film, *The Mark of Zorro* [1920] and to the character Alberic in the Ufa film *Siegfried,* [1923] directed by Fritz Lang.

> *Pisanella,* the most plastic and varied of my poems.
> If the great Bakst were alive, with what zeal he
> would help you!

This letter, dated December 7, 1928, would perhaps have resulted in something tangible, if the decline of the Italian film industry—the birth of which had given hope to so many who were interested in the resurgence of the Italian cinema—hadn't brought d'Annunzio's last project to nothing. And, at that time, this was a real loss for Italian art, since d'Annunzio's interest in movies was, from this time on, very strong—so strong that even during the war he wrote to me about the adaptation of the story *San Sebastiano,* saying: "I may need, after the war, to found a large movie company in order to produce four or five films in accordance with my theory. Movies are still in their infancy."

The present spiritual position which d'Annunzio takes with regard to the eleventh muse is the following: a strong desire to create for film something absolutely unpublished and new in substance and in form—something which would, above all, eclipse and banish *Cabiria,* that ebullient child which he was forced to adapt; an equally strong wish that his new movie would have nothing in common with everything he had already created. "Expect from me," he said to me recently, "something exceptional!"

Will d'Annunzio succeed in this new task, as he has always previously succeeded in everything? An answer can't be given, since the future, in all d'Annunzian matters, has never been guided by logic or analogy.

W. Somerset Maugham

On Writing for the Films

I know very well that it is unbecoming in me to express my
opinion on the subject of writing for the screen, since I have
busied myself with the matter only for a few weeks. But in these
weeks I have learned a good deal and I pretend only to jot down
my first impressions. Everyone now allows that the pictures have
reached a stage where they can no longer be treated with a
contemptuous shrug of the shoulders. If you are of a pedagogic
turn of mind—as apparently many authors are in these days—
and wish to improve your fellow men, there is no medium which
gives you a greater opportunity. You read your newspaper
cursorily and what goes in at one eye goes out of the other. But
what you see at the pictures impresses you with peculiar force.
It may be deplored that the novelist and the playwright should
think it their business to preach; but apparently they often do,
too often, perhaps; and they are fortunate enough to find many
people who are willing to take them with the utmost seriousness.
They can certainly expound their views of life more effectively
on the screen than between the covers of a book or even within
the three hours' traffic of the stage. The screen is an unrivalled
method of propaganda. This was widely realized during the war,
but the means employed were ingenuous and sometimes defeated
their own object. Little allowance was made for the frailty of

Originally published in *The North American Review,* 213 (May 1921), pp.
670–675.

human nature, and the pill of useful information was so little coated with sugar that the wretched public refused to swallow it. I shall not forget seeing a picture in a remote province of China which showed the President of the French Republic shaking hands with the Minister of Public Works. This was designed to impress the wily Oriental with the greatness of France, but I do not believe it achieved its object. If on the other hand a writer aspires to be no more, and no less, than an artist, the film is not unworthy of his consideration. There is no reason why the picture should not be a work of art.

But on this question the attitude of many of those who are concerned with the production of pictures is somewhat depressing. For if you wander about the studios you will find that some of the more intelligent men you meet are frankly pessimistic. They will tell you that the whole business is no more than a trick. They deny that there can be any art in a production that is dependent on a machine. It is true that for the most part the attempts that are made at an artistic result support this argument. There are directors who desire to be artistic. It is pathetic to compare the seriousness of their aim with the absurdity of their achievement. Unfortunately you cannot be artistic by wanting to be so; but the lamentable results of these endeavors, often so strenuous and so well-meaning, must be ascribed rather to incapacity in those who make them than to unsuitability in the material. You will not achieve art in a picture by composing pompous titles or by bolstering up a sordid story with the introduction of a Russian ballet or a fairy tale. The irrelevant is never artistic. The greatest pest of the moment is the symbol. I do not know how it was introduced into the pictures but I judge that it was introduced successfully; the result is that now symbolism is dragged in by the hair. Nothing, of course, can be more telling, nothing has greater possibilities; but it must be used with tact, appositeness, and moderation. To my mind there is something grotesque in the way in which an obvious symbol gambols, like a young elephant, through the middle of a perfectly commonplace story. No, the gentlemen who direct pictures will not make them works of art in this fashion. I think they would be well advised to set about the matter more modestly. There is a good deal of spade work to be done first. The sets might occupy their attention. They have yet to discover the aesthetic value of simplicity. They will learn in due course that the eye is wearied by a multiplicity of objects. They will not crowd their rooms with furniture and knick-knacks. They will realize the beauty of an empty wall.

Then I think they can profitably occupy themselves with the subject of line. It is distressing to see, judging by the results, how little thought is given to the beauty that may be obtained from graceful attitudes and harmonious grouping. The lover can clasp his beloved to his heart in such a manner as to make an exquisite pattern; but unless he is a very fortunate young man, whom the gods especially favor, he will not do this by the light of nature. I have been amazed to see how often the lovely heroine has been allowed to be photographed in a position that makes her look like a sack of potatoes. I venture to think also that those directors who pursue beauty (I have nothing to say about those who merely want to produce a picture that will bring in a million dollars: I have no doubt they know their business much better than I do) might explore more systematically the photographic possibilities of atmospheric effect. The camera is capable of a great deal in this direction, and the delight of every audience at the most modest attempts in this field, such as scenes by moonlight, show that the public would not be unresponsive. There is immense scope for the director who wishes to make beautiful pictures; but the Reinhardt of the screen has not yet arrived.

It will appear from these observations that I think the director should be definitely an interpreter of the author. Since I am a writer it is perhaps natural that I should have little patience with his claim to be a creative artist. I think he has assumed this impressive rôle because in the past he has too often been asked to deal with material which was totally unsuited to the screen. He could produce a tolerable picture only by taking the greatest liberties with the story he was given, and so he got into the habit of looking upon the story as a peg upon which to hang his own inventions. He had no exalted idea of the capacity of his audience (the commonest phrase upon his lips was: Remember that my public doesn't consist of educated people. It is not a two-dollar public it is a ten- and fifteen-cent public); and—if I may say so without offense—he was no genius. The stories he offered to an eager world were inane. For the most part the motive was absurd, the action improbable, the characterization idiotic; and yet so novel was the appeal, so eager the desire for this new amusement, that the public accepted all these defects with a tolerant shrug of the shoulders. The mistake the director made was in supposing the public did not see that they were defects. The most successful showmen have always credited the public with shrewdness. Now that the novelty of the pictures has worn off, the public is no longer willing to take these defects so humorously. They find them inconvenient. It seems to me that a few years ago I did not see bored people in a cinema: now I see them all around me. They raise their voices in derision. It is refreshing to hear the burst of laughter which greets a pretentious title.

The picture companies are discovering, what the theatrical managers might have told them long since, that no matter how eminent your stars and how magnificent your production, if your story is bad the public will not bother with you. The picture companies have put a bold face on the matter. They have swallowed their medicine with fortitude. They have gone to the highways and hedges and constrained the author to come in. They have brushed aside his pleas that he had no wedding garment: the feast was set.

The story is now all the thing.

It remains to be seen how the author will meet the situation. I do not think it will be surprising if he does not create very great works of art, for they come as the gods will, sparingly, and should be accepted with surprise and gratitude, but not demanded as a right. It is very good to receive a barrel of caviare now and then, but for the daily meal one should be satisfied with beef or mutton. At all events there will be no excuse for the author if his stories are not coherent and probable, if his psychology (to use the somewhat pompous term by which the play of motive is known in the world of pictures) is not reasonable, and his characters and the incidents he chooses to illustrate them not true to life.

In the past probably the worst pictures have been those which were made out of plays. Because there are certain similarities between moving pictures and plays it was thought that a successful play would make a good picture and, what is more eccentric, that an unsuccessful play might do the same. The fact that a play had been acted in London or New York was supposed to be a valuable asset, and for all I know this may be a fact. But it was constantly found either that the play offered insufficient material, or material of a character that was useless on the screen. We have all seen pictures purporting to be versions of well-known plays and found the most outrageous travesties. And what is more, they were dull. The fact suggests itself that the play as a play is seldom suited for the screen. When you write a play you take an idea from a certain angle. You quickly learn how much you have to eliminate, how ruthlessly you must compress, and how rigidly you must stick to your point. But when the result of these efforts comes to the screen only a bare skeleton remains. The director is not to be so bitterly blamed when he claims that he has had to invent a story to clothe these naked bones. The technique of the modern stage is very sharply defined, and to my mind the modern play as it stands has very little to give the pictures. The moving picture much more suggests the plays of the Elizabethans. But of course an idea can be looked at in all sorts of ways and there is no reason why a story which has proved effective on the stage should not prove equally effective on the screen. It must be written entirely anew from that standpoint. I think a writer might make a good picture from a theme upon which he has already written a good play, but he will probably need incidents other than those which he has used in the play, and, it may be, different characters. He is absurd if he expects real invention to be done by the scenario writer to whom the management who has bought his play will entrust the work of arranging it for the screen. That is work that he alone can do. No one can know his idea as well as he, and no one can be so intimately acquainted with his characters.

I think there is more to be said for the screen version of novels, since here the case is reversed and it is not a matter of expansion and elaboration but of selection. I do not see why very good pictures should not be made from novels. They will serve as illustrations for those who have read them, and may induce those who have not to do so. This may be a good enough thing. It depends on the novel. For myself I look forward to the time when, the present dislike of costume having been overcome, all the great novels of our literature are shown on the screen. I hope, however, that the scenarios which must be prepared for this purpose will be devised by a writer who is not only acquainted with the technique of the film but is also a man of letters and of taste.

But in my opinion all this in relation to the screen is by the way. I venture to insist that the technique of writing for the pictures is not that of writing for the stage nor that of writing a novel. It is something betwixt and between. It has not quite the freedom of the novel, but it certainly has not the fetters of the stage. It is a technique of its own, with its own conventions, its own limitations, and its own effects. For that reason I believe that in the long run it will be found futile to adapt stories for the screen from novels or from plays—we all know how difficult it is to make even a passable play out of a good novel—and that any advance in this form of entertainment which may eventually lead to something artistic, lies in the story written directly for projection on the white sheet.

Bertolt Brecht

Concerning the Film (1922)

In my opinion, the following obstacles stand in the way of a writer's collaborating in the making of film scripts:

1. The film script is a kind of improvised script. The writer, coming from the outside, is not familiar with the needs and means of the various studios. No engineer designs a complex water works at random in the hope that one day he will find a firm urgently needing precisely this kind of plant.

2. The boys at the source are highly suspicious of the boys trying to get to the source. This aversion is shared by the boys who sit at the boys [sic!], and so on.

3. The competition between individual films resembles a race between coach horses, the greatest attention being paid to the purple mountings and the color of the nags. No poet could keep up with this pace.

4. If the movie industry thinks that *Kitsch* (cheap entertainment) tastes better than solid work, theirs is a venial sin engendered by an audience's unlimited capacity to consume *Kitsch* —in this case the devil swallows flies—, as well as by those poets who equate quality with boredom, the "slighted" poets who perform in private. Yet the error of the poets who consider films to be *Kitsch* but write for the films is unpardonable. There

From Bertolt Brecht, *Schriften zum Theater* (Frankfurt: Suhrkamp, 1963), by permission of the publisher. Translation copyright 1972 by Stefan Brecht. Translated by Ulrich Weisstein.

are successful films which affect even the people who regard them as *Kitsch;* but there are no successful films written by people who regard them as *Kitsch.*

5. It would be a major step in the right direction if at least the distribution of artistically valuable film plots could be organized.

T. S. Eliot

Preface to the Film Version
of *Murder in the Cathedral*

Murder in the Cathedral is, I believe, the first contemporary verse play to be adapted to the screen. That is in itself a justification for publishing this film script, apart from the value and interest of the illustrative matter. It is certainly the only excuse for a preface by the author of the play.

I should like, first of all, to make clear the limits of my collaboration. At the beginning, Mr. Hoellering asked me to make a film recording of the entire play in my own voice. This recording (which was only completed after a number of sessions) was to serve as a guide, for himself and for the actors, to the rhythms and emphases of the verse as I heard it myself. He tells me that he found this recording very useful: I only know that it suggested to him the possibility of using my voice for the words of the Fourth Tempter—after he had had the happy idea of presenting the Fourth Temptation merely as a voice proceeding from an invisible actor. (He did wisely in demanding of me another recording of this voice, made later after the filming of the scene: for no one—certainly not the author—can

From T. S. Eliot and George Hoellering, *The Film of Murder in the Cathedral,* Faber and Faber, London, 1952. Reprinted by permission of Faber and Faber Ltd.

Murder in the Cathedral (1951) directed by George Hoellering; Father John Groser played the role of Becket.

throw himself completely into any one part, when he is reading all the parts in succession).

After making this first recording, I wrote the preliminary scenes which he told me would be needed to turn the play into an intelligible film. He gave me the subject-matter of these scenes: I had only to provide the words. Of the necessity of these additional scenes I shall have something to say presently. As to the quality of the verse, I should like to say this: that if it seems inferior to that of the original play, I must ask the critic to observe that I had to imitate a style which I had abandoned as unsuitable for other purposes than that of this one play; and that to compose a pastiche of one's own work some years later is almost as difficult as to imitate the work of another writer. If the new lines are judged to be as good as the old ones, that may call into question the value of the play itself as a contribution to poetry; but I shall nevertheless conclude that the additions constitute a successful *tour de force*.

Beyond the execution of these two definite tasks, my collaboration in the making of the film seems to have been limited to frequent discussions with the producer, in which I accepted nearly all of his suggestions, to frequent visits to the workshop and the studio, and one or two lengthy arguments where differences of opinion arose. Such occasions were rare. I learned something about film technique. And, just as, in learning a foreign language, we learn more about the resources and limitations of our own, so I think that I learned something more about the theatre, in discovering the different resources and limitations of the screen.

The first and most obvious difference, I found, was that the cinema (even where fantasy is introduced) is much more realistic than the stage. Especially in an historical picture, the setting, the costume, and the way of life represented have to be accurate. Even a minor anachronism is intolerable. On the stage much can be overlooked or forgiven; and indeed, an excessive care for accuracy of historical detail can become burdensome and distracting. In watching a stage performance, the member of the audience is in direct contact with the actor, is always conscious that he is looking at a stage and listening to an actor playing a part. In looking at a film, we are much more passive; as audience, we contribute less. We are seized with the illusion that we are observing the actual event, or at least a series of photographs of the actual event; and nothing must be allowed to break this illusion. Hence the precise attention to detail given by Mr. Hoellering, an attention which at first seemed to me excessive. In the theater, the first problem to present itself is likely to be that of casting. For the Film of *Murder in the Cathedral,* Mr. Hoellering's first care was that the materials for the costumes should be woven in exactly the same way, from exactly the same materials, as they would have been in the twelfth century. I came to appreciate the importance of texture of material, and the kinds of folds into which the material falls, when fashioned into garments and worn by the actors, after I had seen the first photographing.

The difference between stage and screen in respect of realism is so great, I think, as to be a difference of kind rather than degree. It does not indicate any superiority of either medium over the other: it is merely a difference. It has further consequences. The film, standing in a different relation to reality from that of the stage, demands rather different treatment of *plot.* An intricate plot, intelligible on the stage, might be completely mystifying on the screen. The audience has no time to think back, to establish relations between early hints and subsequent discoveries. The picture passes before the eyes too quickly; and there are no intervals in which to take stock of what has happened, and make conjectures of what is going to happen. The observer is, as I have said, in a more passive state. The film seems to me to be nearer to narrative and to depend much more upon the episodic. And, as the observer is in a more passive state of mind than if he were watching a stage play, so he has to have more explained to him. When Mr. Hoellering pointed out to me that the situation at the beginning of the play of *Murder in the Cathedral* needed some preliminary matter to make it intelligible, I at first supposed that what he had in mind was that a film was aimed at a much larger, and therefore less well informed audience, ignorant of English history, than that which goes to see a stage play. I very soon became aware that it was not a difference between one type of audience and another, but between two different dramatic forms. The additional scenes, to explain the background of events, are essential for *any* audience, including even those persons already familiar with the play. On the other hand, I hope that no amateur stage producer will ever be so ill-advised as to add these scenes to his production. They are right for the film; they would ruin the shape of the play. In the play, there is not room, beside Thomas Becket, for another dominating character such as Henry II; but in the film, he is not only admissible, but necessary.

I then discovered another interesting and important difference. The speeches of my Four Knights, which in the play are addressed directly to the audience, had to be completely revised. (Mr. Hoellering himself is responsible for the ingenious rearrangement and abbreviation; and I am responsible only for the words of the new ending of the scene.) This also is a consequence of the *realism* of film: the *Stilbruch*—as such an abrupt change is aptly called in German—would be intolerable. (It took me some time, and much persuasion, to understand the difference, and accept it.) For one thing, the camera *must never stand still*. An audience can give their attention to four men actually speaking to them; but to look at the picture of the same four men for that length of time would be an intolerable strain. Furthermore, having once got away from the scene of the murder, it would be impossible to get back to it. Therefore the speeches have to be adapted so as to be spoken to the crowd assembled at the cathedral; and when the third knight turns at last to address the audience, he must make his point very quickly and clearly, so that his hearers may return at once to the illusion of being eye-witnesses of an event which took place nearly eight hundred years ago.

In looking at a film we are always under *direction of the eye*. It is part of the problem of the producer, to decide to what point on the screen, at every moment, the eyes of the audience are to be directed. You are, in fact, looking at the picture, though you do not realise it, through the eyes of the producer. What you see is what he makes the camera see. The fact that the audience's vision is directed by the producer of the film has special consequences for a verse play. It is important, first, that what you see should never distract your attention from what you hear. I believe this presented Mr. Hoellering with some of his most difficult problems. No one perhaps but I, who followed the creation of the film from beginning to end, can appreciate these difficulties, and Mr. Hoellering's success in solving them. Several visual effects, magnificent in themselves, were sacrificed because he was convinced that the audience in watching them would cease to attend to the words. Second, the fact that the illustration of the words by the scene is, so much more positively than on the stage, an interpretation of the meaning of the words, points to the conclusion that only a producer who understands poetry, and has taken a good deal of trouble to grasp the value of every line, is competent to deal with such a play at all. If the production of this film of *Murder in the Cathedral* leads—as I hope it may—to further experiment in the cinema with verse by living poets (and with plays written by poets *for* the cinema, not merely adaptations from the stage) the results can only be successful where there has been close co-operation and understanding between author and producer.

The play was originally written to be performed under the special conditions of the Chapter House at Canterbury, accepting the limitations and exploiting the special advantages of such a setting. Allowing for the great differences of aim and technique between stage and screen, I think that in some respects—notably in the treatment of the choral passages—this film version makes the meaning clearer, and in that way is nearer to what the play would have been, had it been written for the London theatre and by a dramatist of greater experience. I leave Mr. Hoellering to draw attention to some of the changes and developments from the producer's point of view.

Truman Capote

The Writer and Motion Pictures

INTERVIEWER: You've written for the films, haven't you? What was that like?

CAPOTE: A lark. At least the one picture I wrote, *Beat the Devil*,[1] was tremendous fun. I worked on it with John Huston while the picture was actually being made on location in Italy. Sometimes scenes that were just about to be shot were written right on the set. The cast were completely bewildered—sometimes even Huston didn't seem to know what was going on. Naturally the scenes had to be written out of a sequence, and there were peculiar moments when I was carrying around in my head the only real outline of the so-called plot. You never saw it? Oh, you should. It's a marvelous joke. Though I'm afraid the producer didn't laugh. The hell with them. Whenever there's a revival I go to see it and have a fine time.

Seriously, though, I don't think a writer stands much chance of imposing himself on a film unless he works in the warmest rapport with the director or is himself the director. It's so much a director's medium that the movies have developed only one writer who, working exclusively as a scenarist, could be called a

From *Writers at Work: The Paris Review Interviews,* edited by Malcolm Cowley. Copyright © 1957, 1958 by *The Paris Review,* Inc. Reprinted by permission of The Viking Press, Inc. Title supplied.

1. *Beat the Devil* (1954) directed by John Huston, starred Robert Morley. Humphrey Bogart and Peter Lorre.

film genius. I mean that shy, delightful little peasant, Zavattini. What a visual sense! Eighty per cent of the good Italian movies were made from Zavattini scripts[2]—all of the De Sica pictures, for instance. De Sica is a charming man, a gifted and deeply sophisticated person; nevertheless he's mostly a megaphone for Zavattini, his pictures are absolutely Zavattini's creations: every nuance, mood, every bit of business is clearly indicated in Zavattini's scripts.

2. Zavattini's scripts include: *Shoeshine* (1946), *Bicycle Thief* (1948), *Miracle in Milan* (1951) and *Umberto D* (1952).

William Faulkner

The Writer and Motion Pictures

INTERVIEWER: Can working for the movies hurt your own writing?

FAULKNER: Nothing can injure a man's writing if he's a first-rate writer. If a man is not a first-rate writer, there's not anything can help it much. The problem does not apply if he is not first rate, because he has already sold his soul for a swimming pool.

INTERVIEWER: Does a writer compromise in writing for the movies?

FAULKNER: Always, because a moving picture is by its nature a collaboration, and any collaboration is compromise because that is what the word means—to give and to take.

INTERVIEWER: Which actors do you like to work with most?

FAULKNER: Humphrey Bogart is the one I've worked with best. He and I worked together in *To Have and Have Not* and *The Big Sleep*.[1]

INTERVIEWER: Would you like to make another movie?

FAULKNER: Yes, I would like to make one of George Orwell's *1984*.[2] I have an idea for an ending which would prove the thesis

From *Writers at Work: The Paris Review Interviews,* edited by Malcolm Cowley. Copyright © 1957, 1958 by *The Paris Review,* Inc. Reprinted by permission of The Viking Press, Inc. Title supplied.

1. Hemingway's *To Have and Have Not* (1944) directed by Howard Hawks; other film versions were made: in 1951 (*The Breaking Point*), and in 1958 (*The Gun Runners*); *The Big Sleep* (1946) was directed by Howard Hawks.

2. *1984* (1956) was directed by Michael Anderson; the screenplay by William P. Templeton and Ralph Bettinson.

I'm always hammering at: that man is indestructible because of his simple will to freedom.

INTERVIEWER: How do you get the best results in working for the movies?

FAULKNER: The moving-picture work of my own which seemed best to me was done by the actors and the writer throwing the script away and inventing the scene in actual rehearsal just before the camera turned. If I didn't take, or feel I was capable of taking, motion-picture work seriously, out of simple honesty to motion pictures and myself too, I would not have tried. But I know now that I will never be a good motion-picture writer; so that work will never have the urgency for me which my own medium has.

Part Four

The Hollywood Experience

William Faulkner

My Hollywood Experience

INTERVIEWER: Would you comment on that legendary Hollywood experience you were involved in?

FAULKNER: I had just completed a contract at MGM and was about to return home. The director I had worked with said, "If you would like another job here, just let me know and I will speak to the studio about a new contract." I thanked him and came home. About six months later I wired my director friend that I would like another job. Shortly after that I received a letter from my Hollywood agent enclosing my first week's paycheck. I was surprised because I had expected first to get an official notice or recall and a contract from the studio. I thought to myself the contract is delayed and will arrive in the next mail. Instead, a week later I got another letter from the agent, enclosing my second week's paycheck. That began in November 1932 and continued until May 1933. Then I received a telegram from the studio. It said: *William Faulkner, Oxford, Miss. Where are you? MGM Studio.*

I wrote out a telegram: *MGM Studio, Culver City, California. William Faulkner.*

The young lady operator said, "Where is the message, Mr. Faulkner?" I said, "That's it." She said, "The rule book says that

From *Writers At Work: The Paris Review Interviews,* edited by Malcolm Cowley. Copyright © 1957, 1958 by *The Paris Review* Inc. Reprinted by permission of The Viking Press, Inc. Title supplied.

I can't send it without a message, you have to say something." So we went through her samples and selected I forget which one—one of the canned anniversary greeting messages. I sent that. Next was a long-distance telephone call from the studio directing me to get on the first airplane, go to New Orleans, and report to Director [Tod] Browning. I could have got on a train in Oxford and been in New Orleans eight hours later. But I obeyed the studio and went to Memphis, where an airplane did occasionally go to New Orleans. Three days later one did.

I arrived at Mr. Browning's hotel about six p.m. and reported to him. A party was going on. He told me to get a good night's sleep and be ready for an early start in the morning. I asked him about the story. He said, "Oh, yes. Go to room so and so. That's the continuity writer. He'll tell you what the story is."

I went to the room as directed. The continuity writer was sitting in there alone. I told him who I was and asked him about the story. He said "When you have written the dialogue I'll let you see the story." I went back to Browning's room and told him what had happened. "Go back," he said "and tell that so and so—never mind, you get a good night's sleep so we can get an early start in the morning."

So the next morning in a very smart rented launch all of us except the continuity writer sailed down to Grand Isle, about a hundred miles away, where the picture was to be shot, reaching there just in time to eat lunch and have time to run the hundred miles back to New Orleans before dark.

That went on for three weeks. Now and then I would worry a little about the story, but Browning always said, "Stop worrying. Get a good night's sleep so we can get an early start tomorrow morning."

One evening on our return I had barely entered my room when the telephone rang. It was Browning. He told me to come to his room at once. I did so. He had a telegram. It said: *Faulkner is fired. MGM Studio.* "Don't worry," Browning said. "I'll call that so-and-so up this minute and not only make him put you back on the payroll but send you a written apology." There was a knock on the door. It was a page with another telegram. This one said: *Browning is fired. MGM Studio.* So I came back home. I presume Browning went somewhere too. I imagine that continuity writer is still sitting in a room somewhere with his weekly salary check clutched tightly in his hand. They never did finish the film. But they did build a shrimp village—a long platform on piles in the water with sheds built on it something like a wharf. The studio could have bought dozens of them for forty or fifty dollars apiece. Instead, they built one of their own, a false one. That is, a platform with a single wall on it, so that when you opened the door and stepped through it, you stepped right on off to the ocean itself. As they built it, on the first day, the Cajun fisherman paddled up in his narrow tricky pirogue made out of a hollow log. He would sit in it all day long in the broiling sun watching the strange white folks building this strange imitation platform. The next day he was back in the pirogue with his whole family, his wife nursing the baby, the other children, and the mother-in-law, all to sit all that day in the broiling sun to watch this foolish and incomprehensible activity. I was in New Orleans two or three years later and heard that the Cajun people were still coming in for miles to look at that imitation shrimp platform which a lot of white people had rushed in and built and then abandoned.

Theodore Dreiser

The Real Sins of Hollywood

----

*An Arraignment of America's Powerful
Motion-Picture Industry*

I believe that motion pictures offer great possibilities as a
medium of art. The pictorial effects on the screen are real, while
those on the stage, especially outdoor scenery, are artificial. The
camera can interpret as well as create by moving rapidly to any
idea or any place in the world. In that respect a movie is more
like a novel than is the limited legitimate drama.

Yet does Hollywood make anything at all of art in motion
pictures? Is Hollywood's attitude sympathetic and creative or
base and destructive? Nearly a year ago, when I was in California, I talked with the executives of Paramount, Universal,
Warner Brothers, and Metro-Goldwyn-Mayer. I found them all
to be business men; none was in any sense imaginative, creative,
or colorful. Mr. Zukor, Mr. Lasky, Mr. Thalberg, and others
are not artists but business executives. Of course, there would be
less cause for complaint on this score if these business men
allowed the writers, directors, and players whom they employ
and control to exercise freely their artistic perceptions and
capabilities. But that is something they certainly do not allow. I
talked seriously on this problem with these gentlemen and many
others, and here is the gist of our conversations.

From *Liberty,* June 11, 1932, pp. 6–11. Copyright 1932 Liberty Publishing
Corp. Reprinted by permission of Liberty Library Corporation.

These movie representatives admitted that they would prefer, for example, to buy the title only of, let us say, Eugene O'Neill's *Strange Interlude,* their reason being that the play itself was far above the head of the average individual with whom the moving-picture theaters have to deal. But with the title in their possession as property, their writers could make a movie script of parts which at least would bear some resemblance to Mr. O'Neill's story. They then said this was necessary because really all that the great American public knew about this drama was that Eugene O'Neill had had a big success in New York City called *Strange Interlude.* Sock one for America!

Movie officials went on to point out the truth that this work was a deep psychological study, and that the greater part of the movie audiences would not understand it even though it were portrayed on the screen with all possible fidelity to the original. They brought out the point that whenever artistic films were released to theaters in small towns in Kansas, North Dakota, etc., the managers of these wired back that their audiences didn't want these films, and they would have to close their theaters unless they received more popular films.

I, too, can understand that motion pictures are a business and their existence depends on their financial return. It is, however, a deeper problem.

But in this matter of bringing the motion-picture standards down to the intelligence, moral views, etc., of the masses, I was surprised to find that this was held to be a necessity not only by motion-picture magnates but by the law. For when I tried, in the Supreme Court in New York, last July, to restrain Paramount from showing the movie of my book, *An American Tragedy,*[1] on the ground that by not creating the inevitability of circumstance influencing Clyde, a not evil-hearted boy, they had reduced the psychology of my book so as to make it a cheap

1. Directed by Josef von Sternberg, starring Phillips Holmes and Sylvia Sidney.

murder story, I lost the case. But when I read the court's decision, a light broke upon me. For, said the learned court:

"The producer *must* [italics are mine] give consideration to the fact that the great majority of the people composing the audience before which the picture will be presented, will be more interested that justice prevail over wrongdoing than that the inevitability of Clyde's end clearly appear."

Such being the case, that spells the end of art, does it not?

Despite this sweeping judicial opinion as to the intellectual level of the movies, the basis of my attack is that the picture corporations, with their monopoly, owe a certain percentage of their enormous profits to the artistic development of the film. For, assuming the correctness of their interpretation of the mass mind, should not a genuine effort be made now and then to portray a masterpiece of literature, or present a gifted actor or actress in some such fashion as to widen the appeal of masterpiece or artist, or both? I think yes. By so doing the general standard might be raised rather than left where it is, or lowered. But this, as I insist, the movies do not do—and it is their great sin.

It might be well to comment here on the strange and even unprecedented fate that has befallen this art form. Always heretofore art has meant individuality; the artist was of necessity an individual. But today it has become an industry, along with coal, iron, and steel, and in Wall Street journals and elsewhere it is called that. More, according to figures of not so long ago, the motion-picture industry rated among the largest in America. So for the first time, as you see, an art, so called, is discussed as representing an investment. This investment totals about $2,-500,000,000. The figures go on to show that about 10,000,000 tickets are sold daily to Americans desirous of imbibing this "art form." The average weekly attendance is, or was until recently, over 100,000,000.

More, the frenzy over this "art form," considering that there are only 125,000,000 persons in the United States, is terrific. Of course the American people are given ample opportunity to patronize this art medium; there are some 15,000 to 20,000 movie theaters throughout the country. In fact, the movie industry, with its enormous salaries to this and that star, its publicity, investment, etc., is holding its own as against even the steel industry, which pays its famous or infamous bonuses of millions to its executives. Can many Wall Street magnates in these days boast a salary greater than Constance Bennett's? All in all, movie salaries amount (or did until recently) to possibly $500,000,000 every year.

And in this connection it is also necessary to explain that one of the real artistic ills of the American movie companies, and hence their product, is that they are completely united. That is, they not only can but, as is common in all such situations, do exercise a despotic power as to how anything is to be done, also why, where, by whom. In other words, there has been established by a more or less purely commercial and so business-minded group a material tyranny over a new and even beautiful art form.

For example, since 1922 the Motion Picture Producers and Distributors of America has existed. Its membership now includes Paramount Publix (formerly Famous Players-Lasky), First National, Fox, Metro-Goldwyn-Mayer Distributing Corporation, Warner Brothers, Educational Film Exchanges, and eighteen other leading companies. These include all of the great producing firms, all important national distributors of films, and all of the largest movie theaters throughout the country, owned or leased for a long period by these companies. Thus they can exercise great power over any independent producer, distributor, or theater owner, as well as any artist, writer, dramatist, actor, or what have you, who must do business with them.

More, this unification of power or control has been extended all over the world by our American producing companies, who now own most of the important movie houses in foreign countries and so distribute their films there. And with this go their practical as well as artistic or inartistic standards, whatever the same may be. Yet whether these be good, bad, or indifferent, they now dominate moving pictures the world over. Thus, only two or three years ago, Latin America became the largest importer of American film. Yet the American pictures shown in Europe make more money for the American companies.

Of course, the American moving-picture market is now the largest in the world, being relatively equal to the European. The American movie giant bestrides the world; it not only possesses the vast American market but also about 60 per cent of the entire foreign market!

More, our American companies sell most to England, Australia, Canada, and France, then Argentina, Brazil, and, farther down the list, Germany. Only a few years ago the great difficulty over languages arose because of the talkies, but that is being surmounted. Already in France, for instance, Paramount has leased a large studio near Paris. This studio, completed in April, 1931, made, during eight months, over 160 pictures in fourteen languages. I feel compelled to add that this studio of Paramount's is there and again referred to as a "plant." That isn't like the younger generation calling a spade a spade, but rather like a shining, tinny ghost over beauty.

But, this industry or octopus being what it is, what does it do with its far-reaching equipment, its possibilities? For, of course, these powerful extensions, all functioning from a common center, hold within their grip the culture and education of the world.

What are the marks of beauty attained by it?

How far do moving pictures go in any effort toward art or its perfection?

To begin with, it is important to note that the motion-picture companies have the world's treasures of literature at their disposal, also many of the most talented actors and actresses from the legitimate stage; also finances with which to accomplish their purposes. But what do they do?

I have read recently forty-five reviews or criticisms of forty-five motion pictures produced since 1925, all based upon famous novels, plays, etc., and all reviewed by men or women supposed to be alert and searching students of this industry or art. According to those reviews, twenty movies were unlike the original masterpiece or did not convey the idea of it, while seventeen movies were judged as adequately representing the novels or plays upon which they were based.

It is not so much a belittling as a debauching process, which works harm to the mind of the entire world. For the debauching of any good piece of literature is—well, what? Criminal? Ignorant? Or both? I leave it to the reader.

Of the above twenty movies tampered with, three definitely changed the story in important phases. For instance, in the 1931 Universal production of *Frankenstein,* based on Mary Shelley's book, since the movies cannot see a nice hero harmed, the monster which Frankenstein, the scientist, creates merely batted him around, whereas in the novel the monster finally kills the scientist. And in *Notre Dame,* the priest, the archvillain in the story, became, of course, the priest's brother.[2]

There are innumerable instances of popular novels and plays purchased by the movie companies and then so altered as to be decidedly unrepresentative of the original. In the play *Coquette,* the "ruined" heroine killed herself, hoping to save her father. In the movie version, the girl is not "ruined"; her father only thought she was, and, realizing his mistake, kills himself. *The Easiest Way* was screened with a different ending from the play,

2. *Frankenstein* (1931) directed by James Whale; starring Colin Clive as Frankenstein and Boris Karloff as the Monster. *The Hunchback of Notre Dame* (1923) directed by Wallace Worsley; starring Lon Chaney, Patsy Ruth Miller, and Ernest Torrence.

and *Cardboard Lover* was changed completely in content. *Ramona* lost the greater part of its dramatic value on the screen, since they eliminated about one-third of the story. *The Bridge of San Luis Rey* as transferred to the screen became, according to the critics, "a muddled and unconvincing story"; and *Redemption,* the 1930 rendition of Tolstoy's *The Living Corpse,* was "dull, halting, and artificial."

In two of these twenty films I have referred to above, the main variance was improper characterization. In the movie version of *Du Barry,* for instance, done in 1930 by Norma Talmadge, the lines were criticized by even the movie critics as being so "verbose and poorly written" that they did not in the least approximate the true characterization. And in Ernst Lubitsch's version of Oscar Wilde's *Lady Windermere's Fan,* done in 1925, the characters, according to the New York Times review, "didn't in any way resemble Wilde's."[3] Yet it would seem as though anyone observing and feeling the life about him would understand that a drama with certain happenings and moods is dependent not only upon the particular personality of each character, and the particular manner in which those personalities affect each other, but the most careful recreation of the various situations in which they find themselves.

Yet in six of the twenty movies above referred to as not truly portraying their originals, the main fault was failure to catch

3. *Coquette* (1929) was directed by Sam Taylor and starred Mary Pickford. *The Easiest Way* (1931), based on a play by Eugene Walter, was directed by Jack Conway and starred Adolphe Menjou and Constance Bennett. *Cardboard Lover* (1928), directed by Robert Z. Leonard, starred Jetta Goudal and Nils Asther. *The Bridge of San Luis Rey* (1929) was directed by Charles Brabin and starred Lily Damita and Ernest Torrence; Thornton Wilder's novel was adapted for the screen a second time, in 1944, when the picture was directed by Rowland V. Lee. *Redemption* (1930) was directed by Fred Niblo and starred John Gilbert, Renee Adoree, and Conrad Nagel. *Du Barry* (1930) was directed by Sam Taylor. *Lady Windermere's Fan* (1925) starred Ronald Colman, Irene Rich, and May MacAvoy. There were several film versions of *Ramona.* Dreiser is probably referring to the 1928 version which starred Dolores Del Rio.

the spirit of the author, his real meaning or mood! So it was with *Quo Vadis, The Taming of the Shrew, Mother's Cry,* and *Quality Street.*[4] The cinema *Taming of the Shrew,* according to its cinema critics, was betrayed by typical Hollywood slapstick. In it, for example, Douglas Fairbanks was Douglas Fairbanks and none other most of the time; he forgot that Shakespeare wrote this play around a character, Petruchio, and not around himself as an athletic and grimacing motion-picture star.

Again, in the *Camille* of Norma Talmadge, done in 1927, the classic of the younger Dumas was deliberately changed in tone. In fact, Mordaunt Hall of the *New York Times* observed that this *Camille* was "but a faint reflection of the classic, and those who expect something of the real character of Marguerite Gautier as she was impersonated by Sarah Bernhardt, Duse, Réjane, and others, will be keenly disappointed." He added that "this is not due to Miss Talmadge's acting, for she is lovely and sincere in her performance, but rather to Fred Niblo's direction and the others who revamped the scenario."[5]

Not only are masterpieces of literature thus ruined by poor movie adaptations of the stories, but motion-picture actresses, many of them quite talented, are forced to repeat themselves in a series of rapid-fire, mediocre movie stories, all commonplace or bad, until finally the public, sick of the stories, though not necessarily of the star, becomes sick of the star, whereupon Hollywood throws her out and substitutes a new face which it values commercially, no matter how blank that new face may be.

Thus, after Evelyn Brent, under contract to Paramount, did a splendid piece of work as Natacha in *The Last Command,*

4. *Quo Vadis* (1925), directed by Arturo Ambrosio, starred Emil Jannings. *The Taming of the Shrew* (1929), directed by Sam Taylor, starred Douglas Fairbanks and Mary Pickford. *Mother's Cry* (1930), from the novel by Helen Grace Carlisle, was directed by Hobart Henley and starred Dorothy Peterson and David Manners. *Quality Street* (1927), based on Barrie's play, was directed by Sidney Franklin and starred Marion Davies and Conrad Nagel.

5. *Camille* (1927), directed by Fred Niblo, starred Norma Talmadge, Gilbert Roland, and Maurice Costello.

with Jannings, and in *Beau Sabreur*,[6] she was afterward cast in a veritable cyclone of bunk, in order, I presume, to make money. And indeed, the names of her pictures are a revelation of what is here asserted: such elevating productions, for instance, as *His Tiger Lady, The Mating Call, Darkened Rooms, Fast Company*.

So, too, with Esther Ralston, whose career with Paramount began with *Peter Pan, Beggar on Horseback*, and *The Goose Hangs High*.[7] Then, after her reputation had been established, she was run through such cheap, albeit money-making, trash as *The Trouble with Wives, Fashions for Women, Love and Learn*, etc. Personally, I cannot understand the petty, degrading forces that would move people to create such complete travesties upon art. More, I still believe that the movies can be artistic and at the same time successful.

Pola Negri is an outstanding example of the sacrifice of a star to commercialism. Lilian Gish is another. But to further emphasize this sacrifice of really valuable artists, one may take Rudolph Valentino, the one movie actor who waged a real fight against the great companies' conduct in this respect. He maintained publicly and at law that he was being deliberately debased in order to make money for Paramount. Valentino, catapulted to fame and appreciation in *The Four Horsemen*, one of the few very good photoplays, was immediately thereafter, and because of the nature of his contract with Famous Players-Lasky, cast in *The Sheik* and *The Young Rajah*.[8]

6. *The Last Command* (1928), directed by Josef von Sternberg, starred Emil Jannings, Evelyn Brent, and William Powell. *Beau Sabreur* (1928), directed by John Waters, starred Evelyn Brent, Noah Beery, Gary Cooper, and William Powell.

7. *Peter Pan* (1924) was directed by Herbert Brenon. *Beggar on Horseback* (1925) was directed by James Cruze. *The Goose Hangs High* (1925) was also directed by Cruze.

8. *Four Horsemen of the Apocalypse* (1921) was directed by Rex Ingram. *The Sheik* (1921) was directed by George Melford. *The Young Rajah* (1922) was directed by Philip Rosen.

Enraged at such casting, in September, 1922, he served notice on Famous Players-Lasky that he was dissatisfied with the management and direction of his films and asked to be released from his contract. In his own words, he "hated" *The Sheik,* and added that his interest in pictures was artistic, not commercial, and that his pictures to date had not lived up to his artistic ambitions. Famous Players-Lasky immediately thereafter obtained a temporary court order, and later a permanent one, prohibiting Valentino from contracting with any other movie producer during the term of his contract with them, and when this was appealed to a higher court, he lost.

Later, in July, 1923, Valentino contracted to make pictures for another movie corporation entitled Ritz-Carlton, this contract to go into effect after his Famous Players contract had expired. According to his agreement with that concern, he was to have full artistic freedom. Thereafter, for reasons unknown to me, but within six months, Valentino was back with Famous Players. Probably he realized that the smaller company, with nowhere near the resources of Famous Players-Lasky—no control, say, of thousands of moving-picture houses—would be throttled and defeated by the all-powerful Famous Players group. And although upon his return he was granted some slight artistic privileges (not many, as we all know), his success thereafter was small, and his death in 1926 makes useless speculation as to what his ultimate fate would have been.

Nonetheless, my contention is that actors and actresses like Valentino, Garbo, and Dietrich, or any others sufficiently gifted to present the higher art forms, should be reserved by the moving-picture industry—some central board of art criticism, let us say—for at least one superior production a year. Such players as these might do wonders toward elevating motion pictures above their present level. Thus, and obviously, Marlene Dietrich could play Thaïs. Who can doubt that Greta Garbo would shine in Emily Brontë's *Wuthering Heights*?

At any rate, it is obvious to me that for the sake of the possibilities of the movies as an art, the best talent in it should on occasion be called upon not only to exercise its supreme capabilities, but aided in every way so to do. Yet is that ever thought of, let alone done? During the past ten or fifteen years, what arresting exemplifications, if any?

In the past, upon the legitimate stage at least, a great actor or actress was looked upon as a god or goddess of art. Now our wholesale movie and radio corporations have, by their own indifference or insensitivity or greed, or all three, ended that lovely illusion which clothed such stage geniuses as Sir Henry Irving, Ellen Terry, Edwin Booth, Joseph Jefferson, Constant Coquelin, Mary Anderson, Sarah Bernhardt. For by them was certainly evoked an artistic reality which in their followers flowered into something akin to worship. Who of the elders of this day does not recall Mary Anderson, Clara Morris, Maude Adams, Richard Mansfield? But show me the equivalent of any of them anywhere today! Yet perhaps an incident will convey more clearly what I mean.

In 1905, when Maude Adams opened at the Empire Theater in New York in Barrie's *Peter Pan,* the critics made fun of the play. Of what followed Mr. Alexander Woollcott has written, in the *New York Sun:*

> But Maude Adams had faith, and so did Charles Frohman. Through the first scanty weeks they held the Empire stage, and then gradually, as the Peter Pantheists found out how good and dear a play was waiting for them, the tide turned, and in the crowds that waited in the falling snow at the stage door after each performance, just for a glimpse of Miss Adams as she went to her carriage, you heard the overtones of a folkway and saw the beginnings of an immortality

And again, with the rank, greedy, insensitive, nonperceptive commercialism of this our movie world, contrast the temperaments as well as the financial and personal generosity of many of the above artists. In the 1860s, when Booth was at the zenith of his career, he invited the great German tragedian, Bogumil Davison, to play Othello while he himself took the lesser part of Iago. And even later, Booth played Iago when Salvini had the title rôle of Othello. He also played with such brilliant actresses as Charlotte Cushman and Helena Modjeska. And the late Sir Henry Irving and Booth alternated in playing Othello and Iago. More, Irving advertised actresses like Mrs. Sterling and Ellen Terry equally prominently with himself.

In consequence, and justly, these gifted players were looked upon with reverence. Young artists could but be inspired by such masters.

But compare these and their worship with the careers and personal evocations of our present-day motion-picture players. I know of no finer actress who has been cast in worse stories than Greta Garbo. It isn't that the original stories selected have not been good, but that uniformly they have been so wretchedly adapted or rewritten as to make them trash. Only recall *Inspiration*, one of Miss Garbo's plays, which Mordaunt Hall, the *New York Times* motion-picture critic, speaks of as "a sadly unconvincing talking pictorial conception of Alphonse Daudet's Sappho," itself a beautiful story.[9]

And as for *Susan Lenox,* by David Graham Phillips, itself by no means as imposing a piece of realism as it might have been, but good and capable of improvement in the movies if placed in a master's hands, that was made not merely into another very bad movie story, but so twisted and trashy a thing as to be sufficient to wreck even Garbo's appeal.[10] And yet, as Mr. Hall has said, since Garbo has never given anything but an excellent account of herself, it is a pity that she should not have had better stories.

9. *Inspiration* (1931) directed by Clarence Brown.
10. *Susan Lenox: Her Fall and Rise* (1931) directed by Robert Z. Leonard.

But does that mean anything to the master minds of the world's largest "art" industry? We know it does not. And for the reasons above pointed out: that it is the lowest, or at least the most popular, and so paying, level that is sought, and never with so much as a compromise, let alone a sacrifice, in favor of something really beautiful and worth while. Were I so minded, I could continue through a long list of instances of exploitation of excellent talent in poor stories, and for commercial reasons, with the consequent debasing of the players themselves. So much so that the moving-picture houses the world over are today only half or three-quarters filled.

The trouble is that the fate of these actors and actresses is, of course, largely, and I suppose I should say completely, determined by the companies which control them with contracts. For whereas ten years ago these contracts were usually for one picture or for a very short time, now contracts are made over a long period of years. Also, whereas in the beginning actors and actresses worked for eight, ten, or a dozen companies within a short period, now their destinies are all with one concern or with allied or similar companies, and their artistic freedom is exactly nothing.

Actually, the big companies control players' contracts in so drastic and shabby a way as to make their artistic future a nightmare, and the thought of every little upstart occupying an office chair is to prove himself greater and much more important than the genius who is still called upon to enthrall the public. They are told what and how and are charged to obey on pain of ostracism the world over. And yet Hollywood ventures to speak of the artists and the art of their purely commercial picture world!

This particular situation had its rise largely in the formation in 1916 of the Famous Players-Lasky Corporation from many producing companies. This company was even by then so powerful that it soon absorbed Paramount, its distributing company. This group, already controlling production and distribution, set upon a scheme to control exhibition of these films, and the plan turned out to be sure-fire. For immediately thereafter they bought or built 400 theaters, most of which they designated as first-run houses. These they made more luxurious and glittering than palaces or cathedrals. The vast clamor created over openings in these cathedrals brought a prestige and the enhanced value of advertising against which no one could compete. At that time this company, already controlling 75 per cent of the stars, was in a position so to exploit them as to dim the possibilities of any less-advertised star.

To show what power this particular company then wielded in the career of any of its stars—how and when, for instance, he or she was to be presented to the public—let me cite a Supreme Court case showing this company guilty under the Sherman Anti-Trust law. The court said that the practice of compulsory arbitration over disputes arising in connection with exhibitors' contracts was unlawful restraint of trade. Also, in connection with a First National case, the government attacked credit committees which restrained the freedom of sales of motion pictures. The *New York Times,* late in 1930, reported that the Supreme Court had held ten of the largest motion-picture producers and thirty-two distributing boards, controlling 98 per cent of the motion pictures, guilty under the Sherman Anti-Trust Act.

Well, as against such a united and plainly illegal trust front, what opportunity has the writer, player, director, actor—granting him art or genius—to do anything really worth while? What? And after the player has been so dogmatically and crassly exploited, what chance has he or she of retaining popularity? For, because of the dull pictures in which he or she is forced to appear, audiences, as I have said, grow tired not only of his or her face but of his or her work—which is all it is; whereupon the player is first dropped from the major contract list, and then later is let to the independents.

After that, however, the public hears almost nothing about these small-concern "stardoms." Or supposing the players remain under contract to the big companies, nevertheless their pictures become of such minor importance that they are finally dropped. Many such players so misused finally free-lance in the supporting cast of this or that trivial thing. Thus, Claire Windsor, after a five-year contract with Goldwyn, went to Tiffany-Stahl, and Jacqueline Logan starred in such little companies that her work was practically lost. So, like the fairly constant rainfall per year, it goes. A list in *Variety* of those who lost popularity in 1931 includes Vilma Banky, Monte Blue, Evelyn Brent, Dolores Costello, Marie Prevost, Norma Talmadge. All of these latterly have been in stupid pictures.

Of course, this exploitation of the star is done for money-making reasons. Sensational movies attract more people than others. And since neither the will nor the power to think and feel keenly the higher things of life has ever been encouraged by these movie masters, the movies themselves have become an enormous example of mental and so social frustration. Every crazy thing has been and still is forced upon the not very experienced and quite gullible public. For, as we all know, when notices of coming pictures are flashed on the screen, a note describing the picture's greatness appears, usually signed "Your Manager." And these "personal notes" appear all over the country before millions of people, vast numbers of whom do or did believe in the "greatness," "depth," "power," and what not of the coming Hollywood creation, although subsequently and because of this mechanical production contract system, against which the local theater manager has no redress, they are coming to learn what the word "hooey" means. Also, since there are no independent artistic production companies or theaters anywhere, these wares are what they must see or else stay at home.

Yet, as we all know, everything today is called "great." And in connection with that, I often wish that advertising ethics were a matter of law. For then when a really great play or novel was screened, the public, with some informative and helpful data on the subject thrown in for its enlightenment as well as enjoyment, might be aided mentally to sort the best from the worst. And how much better that would be! And, incidentally, how refreshing to see a plain old melodrama of the sob school labeled as such and not as the world's greatest screen production to date!

Hollywood, however, turning out 800 features a year, wants to get the people to the movies several times a week. It also knows that the bulk of the people can be attracted by the bizarre, the scandalous, the what not. Hence the preponderance of melodrama now flooding the country and, more completely than at any time in the past, even lumping all of the old-time stock companies together.

What is more, the movie companies have found a way to force these ignorant, albeit money-making, movies upon the public. This is none other than the block-booking system, adopted about 1915, by which a theater owner, in order to get a much desired picture of superior quality, has to take a whole block (fifteen or twenty) of mediocre pictures. This system, long since taken up by the combined producing and distributing companies, is still in force. And now that the theaters themselves, as well as the producing companies, are controlled by the same interests, pictures may be shown in these theaters because they own the theaters rather than because of the artistic merit of the film.

Finally, as I have said and illustrated, the real masterpieces of literature which Hollywood films, are notoriously botched or at best altered and changed to suit some sales agent's view of what is right and proper. And this countinghouse school of production becomes worse, not better. I even believe that Hollywood is becoming more erratic and superficial hourly. If you doubt this, read reviews of the old movies, or recall, if you will, that years ago *Les Misérables* was filmed most accurately according to Hugo's chapters.[11] Also the works of Balzac, Tolstoy, France, d'Annunzio, and others. In fact, even Hawthorne's book plan was used for the early filming of his *Scarlet Letter*.[12] And how he would have appreciated that today!

But let me finally point out here that in this matter of artistic standards, American movies compare most unfavorably with foreign productions. Of the reviews of forty-five movies of foreign as well as American origin examined by me, of nine foreign pictures, eight followed the original story; but of thirty-six American pictures, only nine followed the original story. So judge for yourself.

And of those pictures which according to American—not foreign—picture critics included both good acting and adequate representation of the original, seven were American and six foreign.

And yet the eminent Mr. Samuel Goldwyn said only the other day: "The Russian films are overestimated. There's too much education in the foreign celluloids. Americans don't go to the theater to be educated. When they want to be educated they go to schools."

Well, as we used to say when we were suddenly confronted with inexplicable signs and wonders—and say with reason: *"What do you know about that?"*

---

11. i.e. William Fox's production of 1917, starring William Farnum.

12. Presumably a reference to Victor Seastrom's version of 1926, starring Lillian Gish and Lars Hanson. The *New York Times* reviewer described it thus: "as faithful a transcription of the narrative as one could imagine."

F. Scott Fitzgerald

Letter to His Daughter

[*En route to Hollywood*]
[*July, 1937*]

Dearest Pie:

This may be the last letter for a time, though I won't forget the check when I get at my check book.

I feel a certain excitement. The third Hollywood venture. Two failures behind me though one no fault of mine. The first one was just ten years ago. At that time I had been generally acknowledged for several years as the top American writer both seriously and, as far as prices went, popularly. I had been loafing for six months for the first time in my life and was confident to the point of conceit. Hollywood made a big fuss over us and the ladies all looked very beautiful to a man of thirty. I honestly believed that with *no effort on my part* I was a sort of magician with words—an odd delusion on my part when I had worked so desperately hard to develop a hard, colorful prose style.

Total result—a great time and no work. I was to be paid only a small amount unless they made my picture—they didn't.

The second time I went was five years ago. Life had gotten in some hard socks and while all was serene on top, with your mother apparently recovered in Montgomery, I was jittery

Reprinted by permission of Charles Scribner's Sons from *The Letters of F. Scott Fitzgerald*, pages 16–17, edited by Andrew Turnbull. Copyright © 1963 Francis Scott Fitzgerald Lanahan. Title supplied.

underneath and beginning to drink more than I ought to. Far from approaching it too confidently I was far too humble. I ran afoul of a bastard named de Sano, since a suicide, and let myself be gypped out of command. I wrote the picture and he changed as I wrote. I tried to get at Thalberg[1] but was erroneously warned against it as "bad taste." Result—a bad script. I left with the money, for this was a contract for weekly payments, but disillusioned and disgusted, vowing never to go back, tho they said it wasn't my fault and asked me to stay. I wanted to get East when the contract expired to see how your mother was. This was later interpreted as "running out on them" and held against me.

(The train has left El Paso since I began this letter—hence the writing—Rocky Mountain writing.)

I want to profit by these two experiences—I must be very tactful but keep my hand on the wheel from the start—find out the key man among the bosses and the most malleable among the collaborators—then fight the rest tooth and nail until, in fact or in effect, I'm alone on the picture. That's the only way I can do my best work. Given a break I can make them double this contract in less [than] two years. You can help us all best by keeping out of trouble—it will make a great difference to your important years. Take care of yourself mentally (study when you're fresh), physically (don't pluck your eyebrows), morally (don't get where you have to lie) and I'll give you more scope than Peaches.

Daddy[2]

1. MGM's "wonder-boy" producer, Irving Thalberg; the model for the hero of Fitzgerald's unfinished, *The Last Tycoon.*

2. On Fitzgerald in Hollywood, see further: Aaron Latham, *Crazy Sundays,* 1971.

James T. Farrell

The Language of Hollywood

In America, a tremendous commercial culture has developed
as a kind of substitute for a genuinely popular, a genuinely
democratic culture, which would re-create and thus communicate how the mass of the people live, how they feel about working, loving, enjoying, suffering, and dying. This culture has
become a big business. It is capitalized at hundreds of millions
of dollars; it returns many millions in annual profits, rent, and
interest; and it employs thousands of men and women to whom
it pays additional millions as wages and salaries. At times,
the apologists and propagandists for these cultural industries
proudly boast of the "cultural" achievements of these industries:
on other occasions, however, they assert that these industries
produce entertainment, not culture. Let us not quibble over
words. The products of these industries (motion pictures, songs,
radio plays and soap operas, cartoons, and so on) re-create
images of life: they communicate feelings, no matter how banal
these may be; they externalize reveries; they fix ideals; they
embody and illustrate moral attitudes; they stimulate tastes
which in turn create attitudes—in brief, directly and by example,
suggestion, innuendo, fable, story, they tell huge masses of
people how and what to believe. If the performance of such

Reprinted by permission of the publisher, The Vanguard Press, from *The
League of Frightened Philistines* by James T. Farrell. Copyright, 1945, by
The Vanguard Press.

functions be described as something other than cultural, then the plain meaning of words is being inexcusably debased.

Usually, the debates concerning these industries—and especially the motion picture industry—are concerned with the problem of commercial versus artistic values. Critics of the motion picture industry generally claim that pictures are not artistic enough; their adversaries then reply that pictures are as artistic as they can be made, considering the fact that they must be produced for a profit. The claim that the function of pictures is to produce entertainment serves as a justification of the simple and admitted fact that the fundamental purpose of the motion picture studios is to make money. Not only in motion picture studios, but also in the offices of publishers and theatrical producers, a very common reason for the rejection of many books and scripts is that these do not promise to return a profit. The role of cash value in contemporary American culture is continuously acknowledged on many sides.

All this is common knowledge. It is clear that business considerations play a decisive role in all these fields. And art that we call good, art that we call bad, art that we call counterfeit—all are sold on the commodity market. But today, owing to basic economic causes, something of the most profound significance has happened in American culture: it has been invaded by finance capital. American commercial culture is owned and operated by finance capital.

The motion picture industry clearly illustrates what has happened. Back in 1931 the late Mr. Benjamin Boles Hampton's book, *A History of The Movies* was published; it revealed, as of that date, the change in the economic character of the motion picture industry. As is well known, and as Mr. Hampton clearly described, motion pictures were fathered in peep shows and nickelodeons by a motley crowd of carnival workers, hustling immigrants, and others. This novelty quickly interested the public—and it attracted a lot of nickels. In particular, men with a gambling temperament rushed into this new field in order to exploit it before the novelty wore off. However, it quickly became clear that motion pictures were more than a mere and transient carnivalistic attraction. A golden flood of silver began pouring in. And it was this, and not the cultural possibilities of the medium, that made it so attractive. The stage of novelty did not last long. A period of intense competition followed, punctuated by litigation over patents. The stage of competition led to the formation of a Trust, which would standardize trade, control production, eliminate independent producers, and (as Mr. Hampton indicated) mulct the exhibitors.

A bitter struggle ensued between the Trust and independents like Zukor and Laemmle. As is usual in the development of a new form of business under capitalism, this struggle was not carried on merely according to laws of competition and in accordance with the due processes of law provided by the courts. There were instances of violence: sluggers were hired, and they smashed cameras, studio, and other tangible assets of more than one independent. In general, the history of the rise of the motion picture industry parallels that of the rise of many other American industries.

The Trust was eventually defeated. It was more or less left to die its own death, a process that was related to its conservatism. One of the independents, Mr. Zukor, then rose until he became, perhaps, the most powerful figure in the new industry. This industry expanded rapidly. Movies became increasingly popular. Expenses, salaries, income, all sky-rocketed. This process continued toward the period of the talkies. The money spent, when one reads of it, seems like an orgy. It was paralleled with the boom time and the expenditures of the parvenu stars of that period. Stories and anecdotes of this are common gossip and parlor talk. One director is supposed to have had two stunning and sensational automobiles of a very expensive make and to have gone about Hollywood riding in one and being serenaded from the other by a hired jazz band.

But this period reveals something very important. The so-called normal and natural processes of capitalist competition become one of the fetters on production and expansion if we look at these from the point of view of society. Much waste, duplication and unnecessary costs of production, which are merely a result of the needs of competition, become inevitable. The uneven and continuing process of growth—that is, expansion—leads to more intense and persistent efforts to eliminate the smaller and more economically weak groups or individual entrepreneurs. In this period Mr. Zukor became so powerful in the industry that the federal government even investigated his power. At the same time, each new person, each new group that expanded, that attained power and an important place in the industry, quickly became conservative. Mr. Hampton pointed out that, generally, new capital, and, with it, new figures were needed for each innovation, such as three-reel films, five-reelers and so on. This is a very important fact in the history of the motion picture industry. It suggests how uneven its expansion has been—uneven in the tempo of the development of pictures as an industry, on the one hand, and as an art form, a mass cultural medium, on the other. From the very beginning, its attraction was that of the money it promised for those investing in it. At first this money was what many Hollywood persons would now refer to as peanuts, as coffee and doughnuts money. Then it was marked by gambling, speculation, the taking of risks. At this time there was manipulation, competition, maneuvering, struggles for control, This led, further, to the rise of new personalities, the entry of new capital, and to an intensification and extension of the struggle for control, which, in turn, was a struggle for a larger share of profits. This struggle, and the kind of economic expansion it predicated, continuously hampered the technical and artistic development of the motion picture. The feverish irregularity that characterized capitalism as a whole was revealed in the expansion of the motion picture industry. And there is nothing peculiar in the fact that at each innovation those who were powerful would resist change, arguing that innovations would not be good box office. In other words, the public was getting what it wanted, liked what it was getting, and introducing innovations was too risky. But changes were inevitable. The powerfulness of the medium, its potentialities which today are still far from being realized, made innovations inevitable on the technical side; the need for capital to expand made them inevitable on the economic side. By and large, the majority of those who rose in the evolution of the motion picture industry, some of them rising only to fall, were not personages who were seriously interested in culture, experienced in it, anxious to develop a new and great artistic medium. They were speculators, businessmen, gamblers, risk-takers. And the risk-taker of one year soon became the conservative of the next year. In this way, feverishly, irregularly, unevenly, competitively, the motion picture industry expanded until it became a miracle of this century. It grew so big that it could no longer be financed from within. One by one the movie kings went to the bankers. The industry, rising to the billion-dollar stage and becoming one of the 'most heavily capitalized of American industries, was soon based on huge *blocs* and coagulations of capital: it reached the stage where it was to become dominated by finance capital, where it was to be a virtual monopoly. Economic control passed from the hands of individuals; it resided in the hands of a very few individuals in association with the banks. Entrepreneurs of yesterday were forced out, or else they became managers instead of owners, that is, in the sense in which once they had been owners. This occurred not as a result of dastardly conspiracies but rather as a kind of logical result of the possibilities of this industry and the nature of capitalistic enterprise. The volume of business increased enormously, as we know. The investment in capital kept pace with this increase. The task of financing the industry became such that it was no longer possible for individuals to undertake it. There was nothing to do but call in the banks.

A number of years ago, the French writer, Léon Moussinac, began his book, *Panoramique du Cinema* [Paris, 1929], by juxtaposing quotations: one from the merchant stating that the film is not merchandise; another from the writer declaring that the film is not art. To the film-maker, it is better to believe, or pretend to believe, that the film be seen as art, to hope that it is art, to gain all the good will he can from prestige that thereby is cast upon films—the glow, the dignity, the respect that is granted to art and culture. To the writer, the character of the work he does, the way he is employed, the continuous manner in which he is blocked from creating as an artist make it indubitably clear to him that the film is merchandise. But the fact is that the film is both merchandise and art. It is merchandise—a commodity—and it is also an artistic production. It may be good, or bad, or it may be a fake and a counterfeit, but it is, nevertheless, an artistic, a cultural production. The contradictions between the film as merchandise and the film as art are central in the American motion picture. These contradictions are not general, formal, abstract. They appear as contradictions concretely, individually, in the making of films; in the give-and-take; in the conflicts among producers, directors, and writers that often occur when a film is being made:[1] in general, the results constitute some form of compromise generally weighted on the side of merchandise. Often this contradiction is concealed by

1. At the present time I am reading a recent book, *Hollywood Hallucination,* by Parker Tyler (published by The Creative Age Press, New York, 1944). It is too late for me to discuss Mr. Tyler's volume in this book, but he has some illuminating observations to offer on competitiveness as it revealed in the context of films. He points out that, because of a lack of unity of artistic conceptions, films reveal an inner competitiveness between those involved in the making of the movies—actors, camera men, costumers, and so on. His observation is just. And he provides many other stimulating insights

various apologetic arguments. For instance, Leo C. Rosten, in his book, *Hollywood: The Movie Colony and the Movie Makers* [New York, 1941], argues that motion pictures are a young industry, an artistic infant, and that, in consequence, one needs to judge them artistically with a certain, and at least relative, leniency. Further, he defends motion pictures by a formal comparison of the film with the printed word and points out how much rubbish, how much bad art, how much utter verbal junk is written, printed, and sold. He argues that if you make such a comparison, the motion picture industry is not alone to be criticized for its "bad" films, and especially not when it is further understood that it is an infant art, a child of this century. Such arguments, such apologetics teach us nothing; accept them and not only do we understand nothing, but, worse, we misunderstand everything. The reason so much junk is produced on a mass scale is because this is *so profitable*. The contradiction between the film as art and the film as merchandise has existed, and has been revealed at every stage of the development of the motion picture industry. Today, because of the size of the industry, and because of the fact that it is now socially organized under a monopolistic aegis, this contradiction can be more clearly, more sharply revealed. With this, the predominating, the almighty, role of the market is nakedly exposed. It is generally admitted that pictures have to make money. They have to make a lot of money. They have to keep making millions of dollars.

At the same time, the motion picture industry has become involved in the whole life of America in innumerable and complicated ways. It touches indirectly on the business life of the nation in a manner that needs to be understood, because this is

---

on the role of the camera, the character of love in films, and other aspects of the motion picture in America. I should urge everyone interested in the problems of the motion picture in this country to read Mr. Tyler's book, for I am confident that it will—despite difficulties in its style—reward him with fresh and suggestive perceptions.

one of the important specific factors that further focuses and widens this same contradiction. The element of competition in American economy has been heightened, generalized. It is now competition between huge combinations of capital that manufacture and sell different types of commodities. Each of these combinations must jealously guard its product, its good will, prestige, reputation. Indirectly, the motion picture plays an enormous role in causing the sale of various kinds of commodities. It influences styles in dress, in furniture, in the trade and art of the beautician; styles relating to many aspects of the leisure life of, and consumption of goods by, millions of Americans. Trade-marks, business reputations—all these are involved. If a film directly or indirectly endangers a trade-mark, a business reputation, etc., a studio can easily become involved in difficulties—even in expensive litigation—with the producers of the commodity so affected. Not only is the industry owned by the same class that owns all the major means of production of America, but, in addition, it occupies a special place whereby it indirectly affects the increase or decrease of sales of any number of commodities. More broadly, its films touch on the whole religious, political, and social life of America. And as a result of this fact, it is always in danger of becoming involved in difficulties and conflicts. The results of this situation, insofar as they relate to the contradiction between the film as merchandise and the film as art, are incalculable.

The motion picture industry is dominated by a few huge studios; the same is the case in radio. The success of *Reader's Digest* and of the Luce publications reveals the same tendency triumphing in journalism. Some of the consequences of this fact must be noted. It is seemingly paradoxical, but true, that the bigger a corporation producing for the consumer market, the more must it depend on good will. The profits of huge concerns are vitally affected by this fact. Good will, considered as an asset, is highly important. The motion picture industry, which has already revealed in practice how it must expand, demands the widest possible audience. It has something of a mass-production character and a mass audience. And thanks to the stakes involved in the industry, the need for profits and expansion(Hollywood is now on the eve of gaining tremendous control over the world film market), this leads to greater caution. On the whole, there is less willingness to take risks. Capitalism involves risks. But in the stage of finance capital, there is a reduction, a relative standardization, of risk. The greater disinclination to take risks is reflected in the economy of the industry. Its cost of circulation is increased, and because of this the calculations concerning cost of production and concerning profits are affected. Preparations for any "new" venture in films are made long in advance, with an expensive barrage of publicity and fanfare. This fact, in itself, offers eloquent testimony concerning the growing disinclination to take risks.

The star system is also a related and a rather peculiar feature of the social organization of Hollywood. The stars are now virtually walking possibilities of profit. Each major star represents a great asset. As such, he or she must be protected. The protection of stars further demands the reduction of risk. It is financially dangerous to put a star in a role in which he or she may seem unpopular to a considerable section of the audience. This fact has no necessary relationship to the abilities of the stars to play such roles: it is a matter of cold calculation. The element of prestige comes in. In every film in which a star appears, the film must be made according to that star's importance. A star must have expensive directors, expensive writers, and a story that usually is expensive. A star must appear in a film that costs a lot of money. The other actors must not take a film away from the star. This is of vital interest to the star in person; often it is important to the studio. Nowadays, stars, to a certain extent, are "made" by studios. They are trained, coached, treated by beauticians and cosmeticians, nursed and babied along, all at great cost and with the idea in mind that here is an investment that will realize much more than what it costs.

Factors such as these all play their respective roles (a) in the making of profits, (b) in the accumulation of capital and expansion of the market, and, as a consequence of this, (c) in creating the need for so much good will, spread over such a wide human area. Here we see a major reason why the Hollywood studio cannot permit as much freedom in the treatment of a subject as the Broadway producer can, who, in turn, can allow less freedom than the book publisher can. The bigger our cultural industries become, the greater are the restrictions they must impose on the choice and the handling of subject matter. These factors should explain why economic necessities dominate all other considerations. The aims and tastes of the men controlling the industries must be compatible with the economics. One producer may be more sincere, more artistic than another. But all must adjust themselves; all must work within this system.

There can be no doubt that individual taste plays its role in the making of films. What is notable concerning taste is that it is secondary, not decisive. The economic factors more or less map out the boundaries within which individual taste must function, and therefore the role of taste is often reduced to mere detail. Daring, experimentation, have a correspondingly similar role. One act of daring experiment and bold honesty may cost a million dollars. Similar risks taken by book publishers can be sustained more easily because the risks are not so great.[2] In addition, those who control the big studios are large-scale capitalists themselves, or they are managers for huge capitalist enterprises. And we have already mentioned, in a direct or indirect way, films touch on all the major economic, political,

2. It must be noted that the book industry is becoming big business and that a stage of combinations has now been reached.

social, and religious aspects of American life and that the industry needs good will. By representing life on the screen the movies affect every vital material and spiritual interest in American life. There are both objective and subjective interests for doing this. The men in control of the industry have the same class interests as do American capitalists as a whole. They tend to think and act according to their class interests. This is not a matter of dire conspiratorial ideas; it is an inevitable social phenomenon. It is folly to expect them wilfully to produce, and even to lose money on, art that will endanger their basic class interests. Honest art often threatens these interests. This means there is a double restriction imposed on the character of what is produced in motion pictures. Besides promising a profit, a picture must not seriously threaten the class interests of the owners.

Genuine works of art have something new and individual to convey. They reveal new aspects of life, of human feeling. They make us conscious of what hitherto has been hidden, concealed, not clearly grasped in our own consciousness. To assimilate true works of art is often painful, disturbing, difficult; we must make an effort; we must expand our boundaries of feeling and thinking. Growth and assimilation are almost always painful, disturbing, demanding. For we are then forced to change—to alter the force of habit. It is a truism that in a shoddy culture shoddy art generally gains quicker acceptance than does genuine art. The time required for the assimilation of new, more honest, more revealing pictures would be too long, and large losses would have to be sustained during that period. Again we see the role of the element of risk.

Now and then it may happen that a good picture is produced. This is exceptional, often accidental. Usually, bad pictures are produced, and the explanation is as follows: The aim of the studios is to gain a return on investment, to gain profits, rent, and interest. If returns on investment permit the studios to produce great art, then, and *then only,* will they do so; otherwise the artistic values—the truth values embodied in pictures—are, and will remain, merely secondary. In order to be a businessman in this system you must do what business requires; in order to be an artist you must meet the demands and responsibilities required by art. An artist must be sincere, honest, clear, and he must draw on his own inner life and inner tensions for his work. A businessman must stay in business. Q.E.D.!

My analysis can be extended to encompass the economic relationships that play an important role in other fields of culture as well as in the motion picture industry. I use the latter merely as an illustration. Hollywood is not a cause; it is an effect. But the relative purity with which it reveals tendencies now at work in American culture makes it a most illuminating illustration of what I want to convey. The rise of Hollywood to the realm of culture is a phenomenon somewhat analogous to that of the triumph of machine production during the industrial revolution. In the studios many separate crafts and arts are all linked together, mainly under one roof in one serial process. And this requires a large capital investment. This means that we have social methods of artistic creation and of film production carried on for private profits. But those who contribute artistically to this production—with rare exceptions—do not control it. They lose their independence as artists and craftsmen and become employees. Their economic relationship is thereby changed. Most writers, for instance, become wage-working writers. It is true that their wages are generally fantastically higher than those of factory workers, but that is not the decisive factor here. In the economic sense, most writers have a relationship to their employers similar to that of the factory worker to his boss. Just as the worker sells his labor power, so does the writer sell his skill and talent. What he then receives is a wage. All control over the means of his production resides in the employer. Thus, the writer suffers from the same kind of alienation as does the factory worker. He is alienated from control over his means of production, and over what he produces.

And there is a singular character to the alienation of the writer. His real means of production consists of his skill, his feelings, the needs that feed his work, his way of seeing life; in other words, his real means of production is his soul. This is what he sells. As a result of his economic relationships the writer may write what he feels and wants to write only if his employer allows him to do so. But the artist does not determine whether he will or will not do this.

Culture, art, is the most powerful means invented by mankind for preserving the consciousness of civilized man. It externalizes and communicates that which is most important in human life—man's inner life. But in Hollywood the writer who plays the role of the artist, who is ostensibly the creator, sells as a commodity his very ability to create. There is a clearcut difference between freely creating out of inner need and then selling the creation, and selling the very faculty of creating instead of the results of that creation. The writer may thus write out of his inner self only when his own needs, feelings, and attitudes coincide with the demands of his employer. The nature of these demands has already been uncovered in this analysis. Under such conditions free creation is not a conscious act of will; it is merely accidental, coincidental. Such being the case, it is not accidental, however, that so many Hollywood writers, once they become inured to their work, reveal a retrogression in consciousness. When they write they cannot draw fully on their needs and emotions. Much of their writing is reduced to the level of literary carpentering. They are fettered. And the fettered consciousness must retrogress. This is the real situation. Here we see the mechanism that takes those who should be artists and turn them into mere purveyors of entertainment. Let each make what he can of this situation in accordance with his values, his moral outlook, and with what he wants in life for himself and for his fellow man.

It has already been noted, in passing, that there is a huge capital investment in the distribution end of motion pictures. America—the world, in fact—is almost glutted with motion picture theaters, each of which also must return its profit, its rent, its interest. In many instances these are also organized into chains. Taken together, they constitute a huge and voracious mouth forever crying for commodities to be consumed. And they must be fed. They must stay open; they must have customers continually streaming to the box office. The studios must supply them. Halt this flow of commodities, and bankruptcies will follow. This need, more than any other, conditions the production schedules of the studios. Gigantic blocs of capital are involved in the total structure of the industry. Consequently it must find the widest possible market. This means that the largest possible audience is a necessity. Such an audience can be only a most heterogeneous one, encompassing all age, emotional, and mental levels, and it is only such an audience that will permit this industry to continue. There is no time for costly experiments for educating the tastes of this audience. Staple commodities, based on the lowest common denominator of the mentality and the emotional life of the audience, must be produced. Staple commodities in art, produced in this way, and in order to meet such requirements must mean, in the main, counterfeit art. This is a decisive prerequisite why the masses of the American people really "need" so much Hollywood "entertainment."

Actually, the motion picture industry needs the money of the American masses as much as they need the industry's entertainment. Thus we get an endless barrage of Hollywood publicity and of Hollywood advertising that almost batters the intelligence of the nation into insensibility. Hollywood must do this in order to give the public what Hollywood wants it to want. The audience cannot choose directly. It is not given proper alternatives. Usually it may choose one of various absurd pictures, or none of them at all. When choice is so restricted, it is meaningless to argue that the public really gets what it wants. Also, the contradictions we have observed in the motion picture industry are apparent in American society as a whole. The conditions of American life create alienated and truncated personalities, a fact that has already engaged the attention of more than one generation of sociologists, political scientists, psychologists, judges, social workers, and others. The conditions of earning one's bread in this society create the lonely modern man.

Such conditions help explain the need, sometimes feverish, for an entertainment that so repetitively presents the same reveries, the same daydreams, the same childish fables of success and happiness. So much of the inner life of men is dried up that they tend to become filled with yearnings and to need the consolation of these reveries about people who are happy, healthy, and always successful. Tastes are thus conditioned. Increasingly deprived of proper alternatives from which to choose, the American masses have also become habituated to this taste for the movies. The movies have thereby become a social habit. The kind of culture for profit which we now have would in any case have produced conditions which would aid in the creation of the necessary audience. The two have developed more or less harmoniously. Hence, parallel to the retrogression of consciousness in, say, the Hollywood writer, there is a more widespread and also more pernicious retrogression of consciousness in the motion-picture audience. Social and economic conditions have established the basis for this; the motion picture further enforces it. But such a process cannot continue indefinitely. Eventually a limit must and will be reached. Eventually, there will be a profound revulsion of popular taste.

But this will depend not only on the audience being saturated with what it is given; but, more than this, it will depend on fundamental changes that are economic, political, and social in character.

Most motion pictures enervate rather than energize. They distract the masses of the people from becoming more clearly aware of their real needs, their moral, esthetic, and spiritual needs; in other words, the motion pictures of today distract people from the real and most important problems of life. As such, they offer what William James aptly characterized as "a moral holiday." Moral holidays can be refreshing, but when a nation spends so much time on moral holidays, it presents a social problem that must be defined. The gap between the realities of life in our time and the way these are represented on the screen is a wide one. However, the masses of the people do not lose their real needs merely because these are not fulfilled in motion pictures.

It should now be clear that this commercial culture is a safety valve. Here, I offer—in opposition to the conceptions, the apologetics, the theorizations, of such a culture—a different idea of what a culture should do. It should help to create those states of consciousness, of awareness of oneself, of others, and of the world, which aid in making people better, and in preparing them to make the world better. Hollywood films usually have precisely the opposite effect; most of them make people less aware, or else falsely aware. This, to me, is the sense in which Hollywood films fail to fulfill the real cultural needs of the masses of the people. For really to try to satisfy that need, they must not merely envision the masses of the people as they were in the past and as they are now; one must also envision them as they might be; one must establish as a premise their great potentiality. In other words, one must think in terms of the future as well as of the past and of the present. Such a premise is essential if one ideal is a culture that is truly human, a culture that is truly free. Here, in essence, is the great ideal of a free, a human, a socialist, culture which was expressed by Friedrich Engels when he spoke of the possibility of mankind's escaping from the kingdom of necessity and entering the kingdom of freedom.

The content of motion pictures is so familiar to us that it need not be analyzed here in great detail. The values generally emphasized are those of rugged individualism. The lessons inculcated are those implying that the world in which we live, and have lived, is the best of all possible worlds. The dominant characteristics embodied in most motion picture heroes are those of the pioneer, plus those characteristics of the present either consistent with the practices, standards, and the mores of bourgeois America, or else in no vital contradiction to them. The past is re-created in accents of weak nostalgia; the present glorified. The future is promised as no different. All history is, in fact, gradually being revised on the screen until it begins to seem like some glamorous fable. Furthermore, pictures often embody within their very context a kind of visual and illustrative argument indicating that the function of the motion picture is entertainment; thus, the reliance placed on entertainment within the picture, which is itself an entertainment. And although heroes and heroines, on occasion, are given roles, for example, of social workers, which tend to suggest an improvement in the content of motion pictures, the change is merely superficial, and the heroes and heroines remain as absurd as before. Besides, the introduction of social workers as heroes is one indication of how Hollywood really meets social problems. It creates the impression that these problems are soluble by the exercise of individual good will, by babying and nursing the poor, and by eliminating struggle and effort on the part of the poor themselves. Social change is thus treated as purely individualistic. Often, and especially in films dealing with juvenile delinquency, the entire social problem treated is depicted as one caused by pure accident. The absurdity of the heroes and heroines in such films is therefore not the major point on which they should be criticized: the major criticism is that they give totally false impressions of the nature of social problems.

What characterizes almost all Hollywood pictures is their inner emptiness. This is compensated for by an outer impressiveness. Such impressiveness usually takes the form of a truly grandiose Belasco realism. Nothing is spared to make the setting, the costumes, and all of the surface details correct. These efforts help to mask the essential emptiness of the characterizations and the absurdities and trivialities of the plots. The houses look like houses; the streets look like streets; the people look and talk as people do; but they are empty of humanity, credibility, and motivation. Needless to say, the disgraceful censorship code is an important factor in predetermining the content of these pictures. But the code does not disturb the profits, nor does it disturb the entertainment value of the films; it merely helps to prevent them from being credible. The code isn't too heavy a burden for the industry to bear. In addition to the impressiveness of the settings, there is a use of the camera which at times seems magical. But of what human import is all this skill, all this effort, all this energy in the production of effects, when the story, the representation of life, is hollow, stupid, banal, childish? Because masses of people see these films, they are called democratic. In addition, there is often a formal democratic character embodied in the pictures. Common speech is often introduced; an ambassador acts like a regular guy named Joe; poor working girls are heroines, and, now and then, they continue to marry rich men; speeches are introduced propagandistically, in which the common man is praised, democracy is cheered, and the masses are flattered with verbiage. The introduction of such democratic emphases is an additional way of masking the real content of the picture; these emphases are pressed into the service merely to glorify the status quo.

Let us grant that, now and then, an unusual picture is produced—one different from those which I have characterized.
Let us not forget that *The Informer** was produced.[3] But can
one, or could even ten such films, justify a preponderance of
the vastly inferior pictures? One might ask a theologian: if a
man steals money, and uses some of it to have masses said for
the suffering souls in Purgatory, will he thereby redeem his
guilt for theft? To argue that because once in a while we get a
picture like *The Informer,* Hollywood is justified, is just about
the same as to argue that you should be forgiven for theft
because you have used some stolen money for the remission of
punishment, due to sin, of souls in Purgatory. I leave those
who argue in this manner to the theologians, who can explain
what is wrong with this kind of argument. And, similarly, the
argument that bad pictures are necessary to make money which
will permit the use of profits for good pictures is a fallacious
one. The reason this happens, when it does, is because of the
social organization of the industry, and I have already indicated
the structure of that.

Hollywood has not created all this counterfeit culture. It
borrowed most of what it has given us from tendencies that
antedate the appearance of the motion picture on the cultural
scene. In fact, other than in the technical realm, Hollywood has
invented very little. It has used the powerful inventions of the
cinema to repeat most of the cheap stories, the cheap plots, the
counterfeits, which have long been printed as stories in commercial magazines. Many of its jokes were familiar even to our
fathers, and perhaps our grandparents. Therefore Hollywood is
significant mainly because it is a clear-cut example of the de-

---

* [*The Informer* (1935) directed by John Ford, starring Victor McLaglen;
based on the novel by Liam O'Flaherty.]

3. I cite *The Informer* rather than a later film for a reason that should be
obvious: my overwhelming admiration for this film. It also is an instance, in
my opinion, of something more than rare; here, for once, the film was far
superior to the novel on which it was based.

velopment of commercial culture in the period of finance capital. Owing to its size, its wealth, its ability to reach such a mass audience, Hollywood has a penetrating influence in the whole field of culture, one which far exceeds that exerted in the commercial culture it inherited.

Its penetrating influence has long been observed in the drama and in the novel. Hollywood simplifications are introduced more and more into the characterizations of current novels, and this is but one example of the penetrating influences of the motion picture. At present, novels are sold for pictures even before they are written. One can guess what most such books will be like; or, if one wishes to know without trusting to a guess, one can read Louis Bromfield. Another penetrating influence of Hollywood on the novel is the stimulation it has given to a kind of hard-boiled realism that imitates all the manners of serious realistic writing but contains none of the inner meaning, the inner protest against evils, the revelation of the social mechanisms and social structures found in serious realism. This tendency is illustrated by such books as [James M. Cain's novel] *The Postman Always Rings Twice.*[4] The influence of the film industry is to be observed, also, in an incalculable way. For instance, there is the diversion of talent, the fettering of talent, in brief, the retrogression in consciousness about which I have already commented. A large proportion of the literary talent of America is now diverted to Hollywood and to radio writing. In many instances there is a certain inevitability in this. For, with the rise of these industries, the writers' situation is such that, on the whole, the book market (except in periods of war prosperity) can support relatively fewer of them. By and large,

4. An instance that can be cited here is the filming of James M. Cain's book, *Double Indemnity,* where the realism is utterly pointless and unilluminating. To have a suggestion of extra-marital sexual relationships, to have a husband murdered, to have the hero die at the end, and to present this story with touches of vernacular dialogue does not produce *meaningful realism.*

talent flows toward the highest bidder. A writer represents more than an individual talent; he represents so much social labor that had to be performed in order that he may have developed his talent. This social labor has been expended for the development of literary talent in America. Such talent, instead of returning honest work for the social labor that made its development possible, is used up, burned out, in scenario writing. This is a positive and incalculable social loss. And there can be little doubt of the fact that a correlation exists between the success of this commercial culture and the loss of esthetic and moral vigor in so much contemporary writing. This must be the result when talent is fettered and sold as a commodity, when audiences are doped, and when tastes are confused, and even depraved.

The culture of a society ought not to be viewed as a mere ornament, a pastime, a form of entertainment. It is the life, the consciousness, the conscience of that society. When it fails to serve as such, then it moves farther and farther away from the real roots of life. Such is precisely and unmistakably the situation in America, where we have this tremendous commercial culture spreading itself like an octopus. And consider how many lives, how much labor power, how much talent, how much of social goods is poured not only into Hollywood but into American commercial culture as a whole. The social cost is fabulous. We are familiar with the news telling us of the financial costs of pictures. A million dollars. More than that. And then we go once again and see what has been produced at such cost. Once again we see a picture so silly that it insults our intelligence. Once again the same old stupid and inept story of boy meets girl, framed, mounted, and glorified until it becomes a monumental absurdity. And so inured are most people to this that they do not even see anything wrong in it.

This entire structure can be metaphorically described as a

grandiose Luna Park of capitalism. And if the serious artist enters it, he well may quote these words from Dante: "All hope abandon, ye who enter here."

This is a culture that does not serve men; on the contrary, it makes men its servants. Its highest measure of worth is revealed in little numerals, written in black and red ink on sheets of paper that record profits and losses. Let those who favor this masquerade try to justify it. Far better is it to see it for what it is, and to renounce all the ideals and aims embodied by it. But the writer who does this places himself in that category described by one motion picture executive as "the irresponsible literati." Correct! Irresponsible to this system; responsible to an ideal of trying to show men what life is like now, of seeking to do what one can in the necessary effort of creating in men a consciousness of their problems, their needs, and their future that will help to produce a better society.

Part Five

Of Mice and Movie Stars

E. M. Forster

Mickey and Minnie

I am a film-fanned rather than a film-fan, and oh the things I
have had to see and hear because other people wanted to! About
once a fortnight a puff of wind raises me from the seat where I
am meditating upon life or art, and wafts me in amiability's
name towards a very different receptacle. It is a fauteuil. Here art
is not, life not. Not happy, not unhappy, I sit in an up-to-date
stupor, while the international effort unrolls. American women
shoot the hippopotamus with eyebrows made of platinum.
British ladies and gentlemen turn the movies into the stickies for
old Elstree's sake. Overrated children salute me from Germany
and France, steam tractors drone across the lengths and breadths
of Russia, with the monotony of wedding chimes. All around
me, I have reason to believe, sit many fellow film-fanneds, chaff
from the winnowing like myself, but we do not communicate
with one another, and are indistinguishable from ecstasy in
the gloom. Stunned by the howls of the Wurlitzer organ, choked
by the fumes of the cigars—and here I break off again, in a
style not unsuited to the subject. Why do cigars and cigarettes
in a cinema always function like syringes? Why do they squirt
smoke with unerring aim down my distant throat and into my
averted eyes? Where are they coming from? Where are we going
to? Before I can decide, the greatest super-novelty of all time

Originally published in *The Spectator*, London, January 19, 1934, pp. 81–82.
Reprinted by permission of *The Spectator*.

has commenced, Ping Pong, and the toy counter at Gamage's is exhibited as a prehistoric island. Or mayn't I have a good laugh? Why certainly, why sure, that's what we take your money for, a good laugh, so here's a guy who can't swim and finds he can racing a guy who can swim and pretends he can't, and the guy who can't get a laugh out of that had better—.

But now the attendant beckons, a wraith in beach pyjamas, waving her electric wand. She wants someone, and can it be me? No—she wants no one, it is just a habit she has got into, poor girlie, she cannot stop herself, wave she must, it is a cinema. And when she is off duty she still cannot stop herself, but fanned by she knows not what sits skirted and bloused in the audience she lately patrolled. I do think though—for it is time for optimism to enter—I do think that she will choose a performance which bills a Mickey Mouse. And I do hope that Mickey, on his side, will observe her fidelity and will introduce her into his next Silly Symphony, half glow-worm and half newt, waving, waving. . . .

What fun it would be, a performance in which Mickey produced the audience as well as the film! Perhaps Mr. Walt Disney will suggest it to him, and I will provide the title gratis: "Plastic Pools." We should see some gay sights in his semi-darkness, and more would get squirted about than smoke. Siphons that pour zig-zag, chocolates exploding into fleas—there are rich possibilities in the refreshments alone, and when it comes to Miss Cow's hatpins and fauteuils for the dachshund sisters, why should there be any limits? Yet I don't know. Perhaps not. "Plastic Pools" is withdrawn. For much as I admire Mickey as a producer, I like him as a lover most, and rather regret these later and more elaborate efforts, for the reason that they keep him too much from Minnie. Minnie is his all, his meinie, his moon. Perhaps even the introduction of Pluto was a mistake. Have you forgotten that day when he and she strolled with their kodaks through an oriental bazaar, snapping this and that, while their camel drank beer and galloped off on both its humps across the desert? Have you forgotten Wild Waves? Mickey's great moments are moments of heroism, and when he carries Minnie out of the harem as a pot-plant or rescues her as she falls in foam, herself its fairest flower, he reaches heights impossible for the *entrepreneur*. I would not even have the couple sing. The duets in which they increasingly indulge are distracting. Let them confine themselves to raptures appropriate for mice, and let them play their piano less.

But is Mickey a mouse? Well I am hard put to it at moments certainly, and have had to do some thinking back. Certainly one would not recognize him in a trap. It is his character rather than his species that signifies, which one could surely recognize anywhere. He is energetic without being elevating, and although he is assuredly one of the world's great lovers he must be placed at some distance from Charlie Chaplin or Sir Philip Sidney. No one has ever been softened after seeing Mickey or has wanted to give away an extra glass of water to the poor. He is never sentimental, indeed there is a scandalous element in him which I find most restful. Why does he not pick up one of the coins thrown to him in that Texas bar? Why does one of the pillows in *Mickey's Nightmare* knock him down? Why does Pluto—Or there is that moment in *Wild Waves* when Minnie through some miscalculation on her part is drowning, and he rushes for a boat. As he heaves it out of the sand two little blobs are revealed beneath it, creatures too tiny to be anything but love-items, and they scuttle away into a world which will scarcely be as severe on them as ours. There are said to be "privately shown" Mickeys, and though I do not want to see one, imagination being its own kingdom, I can well believe that anyone who goes so far goes further.

About Minnie too little has been said, and her name at the top of this article is an act of homage which ought to have been paid long ago. Never before has she headed an article in *The*

Spectator. Nor do we know anything about her family. When discovered alone, she appears to be of independent means, and to own a small house in the midst of unattractive scenery, where, with no servant and little furniture, she busies herself about trifles until Mickey comes. For he is her Rajah, her Sun. Without him, her character shines not. As he enters she expands, she becomes simple, tender, brave and strong, and her coquetry is of the delightful type which never conceals its object. Ah, that squeak of greeting! As you will have guessed from it, her only fault is hysteria. Minnie does not always judge justly, and she was ill advised, in *Puppy Love,* to make all that fuss over a bone. She ought to have known it belonged to the dogs. It is possible that, like most of us, she is deteriorating. To be approached so often by Mickey, and always for the first time, must make any mouse mechanical. Perhaps sometimes she worries whether she has ever been married or not, and her doubts are not easy to allay, and the wedding chimes in *Mickey's Nightmare* are no guide or a sinister one. Still, it seems likely that they have married one another, since it is unlikely that they have married any one else, since there is nobody else for them to marry.

What of their future? At present Mickey is everybody's god, so that even members of the Film Society cease despising their fellow members when he appears. But gods are not immortal. There was an Egyptian called Bes, who was once quite as gay, and Brer Rabbit and Felix the Cat have been forgotten too, and Ganesh is being forgotten. Perhaps he and Minnie will follow them into oblivion. I do not care two hoots. I am all for the human race. But how fortunate that it should have been accompanied, down the ages, by so many cheerful animals, and how lucky that the cinema has managed to catch the last of them in its questionable reels!

Jean Cocteau

Encounter With Chaplin

CHARLIE CHAPLIN, 11TH MAY—FATED ENCOUNTER
—A NEW LANGUAGE—ARTISTE IN THE STREET—AN
ART BARS ITSELF IN—PASSEPARTOUT'S LUCK—THE
END OF CHARLIE—WORK

Two poets follow the straight line of their destiny. It suddenly happens that these two lines intersect, forming a cross, or if you prefer, a star. My meeting with Charlie Chaplin remains the delightful miracle of this voyage. So many people have planned this meeting for us, tried to be its organisers. But on each occasion some obstacle arose and now chance—which poets know by another name—throws us together on an ancient Japanese cargo-boat, transporting merchandise on the China seas between Hongkong and Shanghai.

Charlie Chaplin is on board. It is a staggering piece of news. Later on, Chaplin was to say, "The real function of a person's work is to make it possible for friends like ourselves to cut out preliminaries. We have always known each other." But up to that moment I had no idea that the wish was mutual. Furthermore this voyage had taught me how capricious fame was. I had had, it is true, the pleasure of finding myself translated into all languages, but in some places where I expected friendship I

Excerpted from Jean Cocteau, *My Journey Round the World* translated by W. J. Strachan, Peter Owen, London, 1958. Published by permission of Peter Owen Ltd. Title supplied.

had met with a blank; elsewhere I expected a blank and had been overwhelmed with friendship.

I decided to write Chaplin a short note. I mentioned my presence on board and my affection for him. He came down to his dinner-table with Paulette Goddard.[1] His manner conveyed to me that he desired to preserve his incognito.

The truth of the matter was that my letter had not been handed to him. He did not know that I was on board the *Karoa* and did not connect me with the table-companion whom he could only half see. After dinner I returned to my cabin. I was undressing when I heard a knock at my door. I opened it. It was Charlie and Paulette. My note had just been delivered. Chaplin was afraid it might be a joke or a trap. He had hurried off to ask for a passenger-list from the purser, and then sure of his facts, decided to run down and reply in person.

No response could have been simpler nor more youthful. I was touched. I begged them to go and wait for me in their cabin and just give me time to slip on a dressing-gown and pass the news on to Passepartout, who was writing in the reading-room.

You can imagine the innocence, the violent and fresh impact of this extraordinary meeting for which our horoscopes alone had been responsible. I was meeting a myth in flesh and blood. Passepartout's eyes devoured his childhood's hero. Charlie Chaplin shook his white curls, removed his glasses, put them back, gripped my shoulders, burst out laughing, turned to his companion and kept repeating. "Isn't it marvellous? Isn't it marvellous?" I do not speak English; Chaplin does not speak French. Yet we talked without the slightest difficulty. What is happening? What is this language? It is *living* language, the most living of all and springs from the will to communicate at all costs in the language of mime, the language of poets, the lan-

1. Paulette Goddard, female lead in Chaplin's *Modern Times* (1936) and *The Great Dictator* (1940) married Chaplin in 1936; divorced him in 1942.

guage of the heart. Chaplin detaches every word, stands it on the table, as it were on a plinth, walks back a step, turns it where it will catch the best light. The words he uses for my benefit are easily transported from one language to the other. Sometimes the gesture precedes the words and escorts them. He announces each word first before pronouncing it and comments on it afterwards. No slowness, or only the apparent slowness of balls when a juggler is juggling with them. He never confuses them, you can follow their flight in the air.

The ingenuous Las Casas writing in his *Memoirs* about the Emperor Napoleon's bad English comments, "From this combination of circumstances was born a veritably new language."

It was certainly a new language that we were talking, that we brought to perfection and to which we stuck, to everybody's surprise.

This language was comprehended only by the four of us, and when they reproached Paulette who speaks French well, for not coming to our rescue, she replied, "If I help them, they will lose themselves in details. Left to their own devices, they only say the essentials." A remark which speaks volumes for her intelligence.

A necessary reserve stops me from telling you Chaplin's projects in detail. Precisely because he opened his heart to me I find it impossible to hand this wealth over to the public. What I am at liberty to say is that it is his dream to film the Crucifixion in the middle of a dance-hall where no one notices it. His Napoleon was to be a fantasy of the Elba period (a comic-opera Napoleon). From now on Chaplin is going to renounce "Charlie." "I am the most exposed of men," he said. "I work in the street. My aesthetics are those of a kick in the pants, and I am beginning to get it back." A remarkable statement and one which sheds light on one whole aspect of his character. In the modern jargon, he is suffering from a vast inferiority complex. It is equalled only by his rightful pride and a system of reflexes suitable for defending his solitude (which he finds painful) and allowing no one to encroach on his prerogatives.

Even friendship is suspect; the duties and inconveniences it entails. His instant taking to me was, it seems, unique, and it produced a kind of panic in him. I felt him withdraw into himself again, and close up after his expansiveness.

He is making his next film, in which he himself is not appearing, for Paulette. He is to shoot three episodes of it at Bali. He is busy with the script and never stops writing. He recites the dialogues to me. This film seems to be a kind of halt before a new cycle. But can he ever take leave of his "poor Pagliacci" theme, removed from the commonplace though it is by his genius? His next rôle is to be that of a clown, torn between the contrasts of real life and the "boards." How carefully he restricts himself to this facile, sentimental ballad theme which he redeems from banality by his attention to detail, so that the most easily satisfied as well as the most stolid audience could follow his progress on the tight rope.

I ought to have guessed that *Modern Times* [1936] was a terminal work by this sign; for the first time at the end of the film Charlie *does not walk off alone* down the road.

In any case Charlie was gradually shedding the type as he became the individual. The moustaches got smaller, the boots shorter, etc. If he is to take character parts, let us hope that one day he will give us Dostoievsky's *The Idiot*. Is not Prince Myshkin a hero after his own heart?

I spoke to him about *The Gold Rush* [1925] being one of those gifts in an artist's life. A work that seemed to have a blessed life from start to finish, to walk on a ridge of snow poised halfway between earth and heaven. I saw that my description was an accurate one and that he does indeed reserve a special place in his work for *The Gold Rush*. "The dance of the bread-rolls! That's what they all congratulate me on. It is a mere cog in the machine. A detail. If that was what they specially noticed they must have been blind to the rest!"

I remember that charming incident, that farce invented to dazzle the guests, that faculty for flying in one's dreams and imagining that one will be able to teach others how to do it and that one will still be able to fly when one wakes.

He is right; those who praised and mentioned only this particular item failed to understand this love-epic, this *chanson de gestes*. It is a film, finely balanced between life and death, waking and sleeping; it is the candle-light of sad Christmases. In it Chaplin lowers as it were the brothers Williamson's diving-bell to the depths of his nature. He turns over the pages in his flora and fauna of the great depths. In the cabin episode he combines the popular legends of the North with the chicken episode which is pure Greek comedy and tragedy.

"One hasn't always the luck to produce a work that grows like a tree every time. *The Gold Rush, A Dog's Life* [1918], *The Kid* [1921] are exceptional. I worked too long on *Modern Times*. When I had worked a scene up to perfection, it seemed to fall from the tree. I shook the branches and sacrificed the best episodes. They existed in their own right. I could show them separately, one by one, like my early one-reelers."

He mimed the cut scenes. He set his décor in the narrow cabin, directed his supers, played his own part. We shall never forget the scene in which he incites a town to revolt and holds up all the traffic on account of a piece of wood that he is trying to thrust into the gutter with his little cane.

Paulette went off for a few minutes. Charlie bent over and whispered in a mysterious voice, "And then I feel such pity." What? Pity for this thousand-spiked cactus, this little lioness with her mane and superb claws, this great sports Rolls with its shining leatherwork and metal? The whole of Chaplin is in that remark; that is what his heart is like.

Pity for himself, the tramp, pity for us, pity for her—the

poor waif whom he drags after him to make her eat because she is hungry, put her to bed because she is sleepy, snatch her away from the snares of city life because she is pure, and suddenly I no longer see a Hollywood star in her silver satin page-boy outfit nor the rich impresario with his white curls and salt and pepper tweeds—but a pale little man, curly-haired, with his comic cane, dragging away a victim of the ogre of capital cities and police-traps, as he stumbles along through the world on one leg.[2]

Chaplin is your good child who puts out his tongue as he works.

It was a child who came down to my cabin, a child who invited us to California, and it is a couple of children who after the filming of *Modern Times* decided on a five minute impulse to set off for Honolulu, travel round the world hand in hand.

I find it extremely difficult to fit the two pictures together. The florid complexioned man who is talking to me and the pale little ghost who is his multiple angel whom he can divide up like quicksilver. I gradually succeed in superimposing the two Chaplins. A grimace, a wrinkle, a gesture, a wink and the two silhouettes coincide, that of the fool of the Bible, the little saint in a bowler hat who tugs at his cuffs and straightens his shoulders as he enters paradise and that of the impresario pulling his own strings.

One evening he asked me to lend him Passepartout. He wanted to turn him into the star of the Bali film. He had been looking for the right man and had found him. Passepartout would be the ideal partner for Paulette, etc., etc. You can imagine Passepartout's excitement. Alas, it was our fault that the scheme could not be realised, for the sole condition was that

2. He owes his good fortune to the fact that his sympathy is his natural road whereas it usually diverts us from ours, and that the practice of his pity carries it on to its goal instead of spoiling and weakening it. (Author's note).

Passepartout should learn English in England in the next three months, a tour de force which he had made up his mind to accomplish but which circumstances and my work rendered impossible.

The fact remained, however, that Passepartout had encountered his "fateful moment on the high seas" as the fortune-teller had once predicted, which proves that young men should travel out and meet their fate half-way.

The miracle, as Passepartout said, without a hint of bitterness was that Chaplin should offer him the part. The luxury of his position was that he could not accept it. It changed his life into a fairy tale.

The project strengthened our bonds and brought us closer together. We joined forces, shared our meals and the journey alike; to such an extent did we form the habit of living together that we found it painful to part company at San Francisco.

Our encounter was not just a meeting of two artists full of curiosity about each other. We were sworn brothers, finding and understanding each other.

When Chaplin is working on a film, whether he locks himself up in his cabin or paces up and down his studio, he is completely absorbed in the job in hand. He takes his fear of being distracted from it to the point of rejecting life and confining himself within some simple problems and exhausting their possibilities. An old man's smile, a Chinese mother suckling her new-born baby, some detail observed in the poor quarter are all grist to his mill. He does not look any further and shuts himself up in his beloved work.

"I don't like work," said Paulette.

Chaplin loves it; and as he loves Paulette he makes work of that. The rest of life bores him. As soon as you distract him from his work, he becomes weary, yawns, stoops, his eyes lose their sparkle. He plunges into somnolence.

Chaplin should be pronounced in the French way, like the painter's family.

Two things about his ancestry are a source of pride to him; his French descent and his gypsy grandmother.

In physical and moral make-up, the little man of the films comes from the Jewish quarter. His bowler hat, overcoat, shoes, curly hair, his pity, his proud yet humble soul are the flower of the ghetto. Is it not a significant and admirable thing that Chaplin's favourite painting is Van Gogh's *The Old Shoe?*

12th May
Charlie is working.

Shut up in his cabin for the last two days, unshaven, in a suit which is too tight, his hair untidy, he stands fidgeting his glasses in those very small hands of his, setting in order sheets of paper covered with writing.

"I might get drowned bathing tomorrow" he confided to me at Shanghai. *"I* do not count. I don't exist. Only this paper exists and counts."

Rendez-vous at Hotel Cathay at five p.m. Dinner that reunites business men who have come from Hollywood.

All the time at table Charlie yawns. In this dance hall which is Chinese but is doing its best not to look so, only one plank of the floor speaks of China and on it we are to see an artiste who sums up this squalid town—in which Shanghai Lili Marlene would not find room to move and could only be *European*—sitting at the *Venus* under a bluish trellis among the "taxi-girls" (the name for girls of every race with whom you dance in exchange for a ticket—five for a dollar).

"The White Flower of Chinatown" was how Marlene Dietrich described herself, speaking into a boa of cockerel feathers. It is difficult to imagine this flower, in this cracked vase in which the flowers cannot be less than two nights old, on a dance floor.

Look at this pitiable dance which Charlie watches open-mouthed with his double chin resting on his tie and his brow furrowed with crows-feet. A poor red-head with her hair done like a female clown surmounted with a chimney sweep's hat, with one leg bare, the other in a pierrot's trousers, a draught-board between her thighs, gloves with red spangles, embarks on the first notes of Debussy's *Cakewalk*.

Picture to yourself this dimly lit stage surrounded by gowned Chinese who provide us with an exhibition of theological students dancing the tango, Chinese girls and half-castes hoping to be taken for patronesses, and under this spot-light, accompanied by an orchestra with gilt music-desks and green lanterns this woman saying to herself, "I am going to invent a modern number, an acrobatic dance, which will be a hotch-potch of our time, plus Pierrot's melancholy, clown's antics, grimaces of the devil, the agility of a ship's boy and the provocativeness of a vamp." And off she goes, leaping, falling with her toes turned in, putting out her tongue, sinking her head into her shoulders, making eyes, clawing the air, wagging an admonitory finger, pouting, pirouetting, hopping on one foot, rolling her hips, surveying the horizon under her raised hand and pulling on imaginary ropes—in short, all the usual routine.

This wretched woman sums up a Shanghai of which you get a front view when you try to interrupt the wild course of one-eyed coolies who only last four years, and gallop full pelt straight ahead without knowing where they are going.

The guests at the dance café rise to their feet and revolve on the floor. Chaplin remains at the table. He is ruminating. The people who look at him, trying to place him, are causing him visible embarrassment.

I have left him to himself. Some of my compatriots wanted me to join them at their table. He is sulking. He stretches over from his table to tell me about a cock fight in Spain. The impresario of the fight, a colossus with the hands of a marchioness, little dumpy white hands, the palms of which he rubs gently, voluptuously, in the blood. No other movement except a flutter of these fine hands and a slight quiver of his nostrils.

Suddenly Paulette gets up. She would like to "see Shanghai." But there is nothing to see. But it has to be "done." My French friends give me to understand that there is a secret Shanghai. They are racking their brains. Chaplin is returning to the hotel to sleep. He is going back to stow his fountainpen and camera safely away, precious machines from which the ink and images might escape and it is important for them to be wrapped up in cotton wool for the night. . . .

Carl Sandburg

Says Chaplin Could Play Serious Drama

Some day Charlie Chaplin is going to show the world a drama of serious acting.[1] The conventional joke to follow this suggestion is the query, "Is he going to play Hamlet?"[2] The answer is, "Nix, brother, he is not—not so anybody notices it—but howsumever, when he does get around to a production of anything approximating the sadness of the Hamlet play and a grave digger digging a grave and telling the spectators it is a grave matter—holding up the skull of a man and commenting on the jests that once fell from the lips—when Charlie Chaplin gets around to anything like that in seriousness—it will be a drama with clutches and high speed."

For Charlie, I found on visiting him in his unprofessional and confidential moods, is an artist of beautiful and gentle seriousness. Away back under all the horseplay—the east-and-west feet, the cane, the derby and the dinky mustache—is a large heart and a contemplative mind. He knows what he is doing nearly every minute.

Sometimes he refers to the time when he will put before the

Originally published in *The Daily News* (Chicago), April 16, 1921, p. 13. Reprinted by permission of *The Chicago Daily News*.

1. Sandburg's comments anticipate *A Woman of Paris* (1923) which Chaplin wrote and directed, but in which he did not act.

2. See Shaw's Preface to *Ellen Terry and Bernard Shaw: A Correspondence* (1931) in which GBS says that Charlie Chaplin is the only performer who reminds him of the great Shakespearean actor, Sir Henry Irving.

world a Chaplin film play without the east-and-west feet, the cane, the derby, the dinky mustache. Those who have seen him in his quiet, serious moods understand well that it will be a drama with punch, drive and terrible brooding pauses of high moments.

I have seen four or five renowned actors (most of them admit they are renowned) play Hamlet, but I have not seen any player better cast for the high and low spots of the life of the Prince of Denmark than this lithe mocker of a little mummer out at Hollywood, making farces for the world to laugh at.

Not often is the child joy and play heart of the world to be found in a man shrewd and aware of the hungers and dusts of its big streets and back alleys. Yet Chaplin in his gay moods— and his commonest mood is gaiety—is the universal child. I have heard children 4 or 5 years old bubble and ripple with laughter in the course of a Chaplin film. They answer to the child in him. *The Kid* is a masterpiece of expression of love for the child heart—love and understanding.

There is pathos about the rain-beaten, dusty walls of the city street where the scenes of *The Kid* were filmed. The walls are still standing about the center of the studio lot. And the thought comes to a looker-on, "These are unique walls, different from stage play scenery or exposition art works or any similarly transient creation. These walls and paving stones have already been seen by millions of people and will in future years be known to millions more who shall see *The Kid*."

The home of Chaplin is on a mountain side overlooking Hollywood and Los Angeles. In a night of blue air the city of Los Angeles is indicated by lights that resemble a valley of fireflies. Charades is a favorite game when there is company at the house. After the Japanese cook and waiters have served "everything there is," the guests go in for pantomimes, sketches, travesties, what they will.

Charlie was paired with a young woman who has done remarkable work in art photography "stills." All lights went out both in the drawing room where the spectators sat and in the dining room which was the improvised stage.

A door opened. Here was Charlie in a gray shirt, candle in his right hand, lighting his face and throwing shadows about the room. He stepped to a table with a white sheet over it. He drew back the sheet. A woman's head of hair, then a woman's face, appeared. He slipped his hand down under the sheet and drew out his fingers full of the pearls of a necklace. He dropped the necklace into his pocket, covered the face and head, picked up the candle and started for the door.

Then came a knocking, louder, lower, a knocking in about the timebeat of the human heartbeat. The man in the gray shirt set down the candle, leaped toward the white sheet, threw back the white sheet, put his fingers at the throat and executed three slow, fierce motions of strangling. Then he started for the door. Again the knocking. Again back, and a repetition of the strangling.

The third time there was no more knocking heard, no more timebeats in the time of the human heartbeat. He paused at the door, listening. He stepped out. The door closed. All was dark.

The guests were glad the lights were thrown on, glad to give their applause to the mocking, smiling, friendly host.

At the dinner Charlie mentioned how he once was riding with Douglas Fairbanks in a cab past some crowded street corner. And one of them said in a voice the passing crowds could not hear: "Ah, you do not know who is passing: it is the marvelous urchin, the little genius of the screen."

The ineffable mockery that Charlie Chaplin can throw into this little sentence is worth hearing. He holds clues to the wisdom and humility of his ways.

Every once in a while, at some proper moment, he would

ejaculate, "the marvelous urchin, the little genius of the screen," with an up-and-down slide of the voice on the words, "little genius" and "marvelous urchin."

Fame and pride play tricks with men. Charlie Chaplin is one not caught in the webs and the miasma.

Margaret Reid

Has the Flapper Changed?

F. Scott Fitzgerald Discusses the Cinema Descendants
of the Type He Has Made So Well Known

The term "flapper" has become a generalization, meaning almost
any *femme* between fifteen and twenty-five. Some five years ago
it was a thing of distinction—indicating a neat bit of feminity,
collegiate age, who rolled her stockings, chain-smoked, had a
heavy "line," mixed and drank a mean highball and radiated
"It."

The manner in which the title has come into such general
usage is a little involved, but quite simple. A young man wrote a
book. His heroine was one of the n. bits of f. referred to above.
"Flapper" was her official classification. The young man's book
took the country by, as they say, storm. Girls—all the girls—
read it. They read about the flapper's deportment, methods and
career. And with a nice simultaneousness they became, as nearly
as their varied capabilities permitted, flappers. Thus the fre-
quency of the term today. I hope you get my point.

The young man responsible for it all, after making clear—in
his book—the folly of flappers' ways, married the young person who had been the prototype for the character and started in
to enjoy the royalties. The young man was F. Scott Fitzgerald,
the book was *This Side of Paradise,* and the flapper's name was

From *Motion Picture Magazine* 33 no. 6 (July 1927), pp. 28–29, 104.

Zelda. So about six years later they came to Hollywood and Mr. Fitzgerald wrote a screen story for Constance Talmadge. Only people don't call him Mr. Fitzgerald. They call him "Scotty."

But we don't seem to be getting anywhere. The purpose of this discussion was to hear Mr. F. Scott (or Scotch) Fitzgerald's opinion of the cinema descendants of his original brain-daughter, the Flapper.

It was with an admirable attempt to realize the seriousness of my mission that I went to his bungalow at the Ambassador. Consider, tho! By all literary standards he should have been a middle-aged gentleman with too much waistline, too little hair and steel-rimmed spectacles.

And I knew, from pictures in *Vanity Fair* and hysterical first-hand reports, that instead he was probably the best-looking thing ever turned out of Princeton. Or even (in crescendo) Harvard —or Yale. Only it was Princeton. Add "It," and the charming, vibrant, brilliant mind his work projects. My interest was perhaps a bit more than professional.

There was a large tray on the floor at the door of his suite when I reached it. On the tray were bottles of Canada Dry, some oranges, a bowl of cracked ice and—three very, very empty Bourbon bottles. There was also a card. I paused before ringing the bell and bent down to read the inscription—"With Mr. Van Vechten's kindest regards to Scott and Zelda Fitzgerald." I looked for any further message on the other side, but there was none, so I rang the bell.

It was answered by a young man of medium height. With Prince-of-Wales hair and eyes that are, I am sure, green. His features are chiseled finely. His mouth draws your attention. It is sensitive, taut and faintly contemptuous, and even in the flashing smile does not lose the indication of intense pride.

Behind him was Mrs. Fitzgerald, the Rosaline of *This Side of Paradise*. Slim, pretty like a rather young boy; with one of those schoolgirl complexions and clear gray eyes; her hair as short as possible, slicked back. And dressed as only New Yorkers intangibly radiate smartness.

The two of them might have stepped, sophisticated and charming, from the pages of any of the Fitzgerald books.

They greeted me and discovered the tray hilariously.

"Carl Van Vechten's going-away gift," the First Flapper of the Land explained in her indolent, Alabama drawl. "He left this morning after a week's stay. Said he came here for a little peace and rest, and he disrupted the entire colony."

In the big, dimly lit room, Mrs. Fitzgerald sank sighing into a chair. She had just come from a Black Bottom lesson. F. Scott moved restlessly from chair to chair. He had just come from a studio conference and I think he'd rather have been at the Horse Show. He was also a trifle disconcerted by the impending interview. In one he had given to an avid press-lady the day before, he had said all his bright remarks. And he couldn't think up any more in such a short time.

"What, tho, were his opinions of screen flappers? As flappers? As compared to his Original Flappers?"

"Well, I can only," he began, lighting a cigaret, putting it out and crossing to another chair, "speak about the immediate present. I know nothing of their evolution. You see, we've been living on the Riviera for three years. In that time the only movies we've seen have been a few of the very old pictures, or the Westerns they show over there. I might," his face brightening, "tell you what I think of Tom Mix."

"Scotty!" his wife cautioned quickly.

"Oh, well. . . ."

Having exhausted all the available chairs in the room, he returned to the first one and began all over again.

"Have flappers changed since you first gave them the light of publicity? For better? For worse?"

"Only in the superficial matter of clothes, hair-cut, and wisecracks. Fundamentally they are the same. The girls I wrote about were not a type—they were a generation. Free spirits—evolved thru the war chaos and a final inevitable escape from restraint and inhibitions. If there is a difference, it is that the flappers today are perhaps less defiant, since their freedom is taken for granted and they are sure of it. In my day"—stroking his hoary beard—"they had just made their escape from dull and blind conventionality. Subconsciously there was a hint of belligerence in their attitude, because of the opposition they met—but overcame.

"On the screen, of course, is represented every phase of flapper life. But just as the screen exaggerates action, so it exaggerates type. The girl who, in real life, uses a smart, wise-cracking line is portrayed on the screen as a hard-boiled baby. The type, one of the most dangerous, whose forte is naiveté, approximates a dumb-dora when she reaches the screen. The exotic girl becomes bizarre. But the actresses who do flappers really well understand them thoroughly enough to accentuate their characteristics without distorting them."

"How about Clara Bow?"[1] I suggested, starting in practically alphabetical order.

"Clara Bow is the quintessence of what the term 'flapper' signifies as a definite description. Pretty, impudent, superbly assured, as worldly wise, briefly clad and 'hard-berled' as possible. There were hundreds of them—her prototypes. Now, completing the circle, there are thousands more—patterning themselves after her."

"Colleen Moore[2] represents the young collegiate—the care-free, lovable child who rules bewildered but adoring parents with an iron hand. Who beats her brothers and beaus on the tennis-

---

1. Clara Bow (1905–1965), the "IT" girl of the twenties. Her films included *Dancing Mothers* (1926) and *It* (1927).
2. Colleen Moore (1900–   ), star of such movies as *Flaming Youth* (1923), *Synthetic Sin* (1928) and *Lilac Time* (1928).

courts, dances like a professional and has infallible methods for getting her own way. All deliciously celluloid—but why not? The public notoriously prefer glamor to realism. Pictures like Miss Moore's flapper epics present a glamorous dream of youth and gaiety and swift, tapping feet. Youth—actual youth—is essentially crude. But the movies idealize it, even as Gershwin idealizes jazz in the *Rhapsody in Blue*.

"Constance Talmadge[3] is the epitome of young sophistication. She is the deft princess of lingerie—and love—plus humor. She is Fifth Avenue and diamonds and Catalya orchids and Europe every year. She is sparkling, and witty and as gracefully familiar with the new books as with the new dances. I have an idea that Connie appeals every bit as strongly to the girls in the audience as to the men. Her dash—her *zest* for things—is compelling. She is the flapper *de luxe*.

"I happened to see a preview the other night, at a neighborhood movie house near here. It was Milton Sills' latest, I am told. There was a little girl in it—playing a baby-vamp. I found that her name was Alice White.[4] She was a fine example of the European influence on our flappers. Gradually, due mostly to imported pictures, the vogue for 'pose' is fading.

"European actresses were the first to disregard personal appearance in emotional episodes. Disarranged hair—the wrong profile to the camera—were of no account during a scene. Their abandonment to emotion precluded all thought of beauty. Pola Negri[5] brought it to this country. It was adopted by some. But the flappers seem to have been a bit nervous as to the results. It was, perhaps, safer to be cute than character. This little White girl, however, appears to have a flair for this total lack of studied effect. She is the flapper impulsive—child of the moment—

3. Constance Talmadge (1898–   ) star of *Her Sister from Paris* (1925).
4. Alice White (?   ) star of *Gentlemen Prefer Blondes* (1928). It is not clear which film Scott Fitzgerald is referring to here.
5. Pola Negri (1897–   ) star of *Hotel Imperial* (1926).

wildly eager for every drop of life. She represents—not the American flapper—but the European.

"Joan Crawford[6] is doubtless the best example of the dramatic flapper. The girl you see at the smartest night clubs gowned to the apex of sophistication—toying iced glasses, with a remote, faintly bitter expression—dancing deliciously, laughing a great deal with wide, hurt eyes. It takes girls of actual talent to get away with this in real life. When they do perfect the thing, they have a lot of fun with it.

"Then, inevitably, there is the quality that is infallible in any era, any town, any time. Femininity, *ne plus ultra*. Unless it is a very definite part of a girl, it is insignificant, and she might as well take up exoticism. But sufficiently apparent, it is always irresistible. I suppose she isn't technically a flapper—but because she *is Femininity*, one really should cite Vilma Banky.[7] Soft and gentle and gracious and sweet—all the lacy adjectives apply to her. This type is reticent and unassuming—but just notice the quality of orchids on her shoulder as she precedes her reverential escort into the theater.

"It's rather futile to analyze flappers. They are just girls—all sorts of girls. Their one common trait being that they are young things with a splendid talent for life."

---

6. Joan Crawford (1904–   ) star of *The Taxi Dancer* (1927), *Mildred Pierce* (1945), *Trog* (1970), etc.
7. Vilma Banky (1903–   ), co-starred with Valentino in *The Eagle* (1925) and *Son of the Sheik* (1926).

H. L. Mencken

Appendix from Moronia

Valentino

By one of the chances that relieve the dullness of life and make
it instructive, I had the honor of dining with this celebrated
gentleman in New York, a week or so before his fatal illness. I
had never met him before, nor seen him on the screen; the
meeting was at his instance, and, when it was proposed, vaguely
puzzled me. But soon its purpose became clear enough. Valentino was in trouble, and wanted advice. More, he wanted advice
from an elder and disinterested man, wholly removed from the
movies and all their works. Something that I had written, falling
under his eye, had given him the notion that I was a judicious
fellow. So he requested one of his colleagues, a lady of the films,
to ask me to dinner at her hotel.

The night being infernally warm, we stripped off our coats,
and came to terms at once. I recall that he wore suspenders of
extraordinary width and thickness—suspenders almost strong
enough to hold up the pantaloons of Chief Justice Taft. On so
slim a young man they seemed somehow absurd, especially on a
hot summer night. We perspired horribly for an hour, mopping
our faces with our handkerchiefs, the table napkins, the corners
of the table-cloth, and a couple of towels brought in by the

From *Prejudices:* Sixth Series, by H. L. Mencken. Copyright 1927 by Alfred
A. Knopf, Inc. and renewed 1955 by H. L. Mencken. Reprinted by permission
of the publisher.

humane waiter. Then there came a thunder-storm, and we began to breathe. The hostess, a woman as tactful as she is charming, disappeared mysteriously and left us to commune.

The trouble that was agitating Valentino turned out to be very simple. The ribald New York papers were full of it, and that was what was agitating him. Some time before, out in Chicago, a wandering reporter had discovered, in the men's wash-room of a gaudy hotel, a slot-machine selling talcum-powder. That, of course, was not unusual, but the color of the talcum-powder was. It was pink. The news made the town giggle for a day, and inspired an editorial writer on the eminent Chicago *Tribune* to compose a hot weather editorial. In it he protested humorously against the effeminization of the American man, and laid it light-heartedly to the influence of Valentino and his sheik movies. Well, it so happened that Valentino, passing through Chicago that day on his way east from the Coast, ran full tilt into the editorial, and into a gang of reporters who wanted to know what he had to say about it. What he had to say was full of fire. Throwing off his 100% Americanism and reverting to the *mores* of his fatherland, he challenged the editorial writer to a duel, and, when no answer came, to a fist fight. His masculine honor, it appeared, had been outraged. To the hint that he was less than he, even to the extent of one half of one per cent., there could be no answer save a bath of blood.

Unluckily, all this took place in the United States, where the word honor, save when it is applied to the structural integrity of women, has only a comic significance. One hears of the honor of politicians, of bankers, of lawyers, even of the honor of the United States itself. Everyone naturally laughs. So New York laughed at Valentino. More, it ascribed his high dudgeon to mere publicity-seeking: he seemed a vulgar movie ham seeking space. The poor fellow, thus doubly beset, rose to dudgeons higher still. His Italian mind was simply unequal to the situation. So he sought counsel from the neutral, aloof and aged. Unluckily, I could only name the disease, and confess frankly that there was no remedy—none, that is, known to any therapeutics within my ken. He should have passed over the gibe of the Chicago journalist, I suggested, with a lofty snort—perhaps, better still, with a counter gibe. He should have kept away from the reporters in New York. But now, alas, the mischief was done. He was both insulted and ridiculous, but there was nothing to do about it. I advised him to let the dreadful farce roll along to exhaustion. He protested that it was infamous. Infamous? Nothing, I argued, is infamous that is not true. A man still has his inner integrity. Can he still look into the shaving-glass of a morning? Then he is still on his two legs in this world, and ready even for the Devil. We sweated a great deal, discussing these lofty matters. We seemed to get nowhere.

Suddenly it dawned upon me—I was too dull or it was too hot for me to see it sooner—that what we were talking about was really not what we were talking about at all. I began to observe Valentino more closely. A curiously naïve and boyish young fellow, certainly not much beyond thirty, and with a disarming air of inexperience. To my eye, at least, not handsome, but nevertheless rather attractive. There was an obvious fineness in him; even his clothes were not precisely those of his horrible trade. He began talking of his home, his people, his early youth. His words were simple and yet somehow very eloquent. I could still see the mime before me, but now and then, briefly and darkly, there was a flash of something else. That something else, I concluded, was what is commonly called, for want of a better name, a gentleman. In brief, Valentino's agony was the agony of a man of relatively civilized feelings thrown into a situation of intolerable vulgarity, destructive alike to his peace and to his dignity—nay, into a whole series of such situations. It was not that trifling Chicago episode that was riding him; it was the whole grotesque futility of his life. Had he achieved, out of nothing, a vast and dizzy success? Then that success was hollow as well as vast—a colossal and preposterous nothing. Was he acclaimed by yelling multitudes? Then every time the multitudes yelled he felt himself blushing inside. The old story of Diego Valdez once more, but with a new poignancy in it. Valdez, at all events, was High Admiral of Spain. But Valentino, with his touch of fineness in him—he had his commonness, too, but there was that touch of fineness—Valentino was only the hero of the rabble. Imbeciles surrounded him in a dense herd. He was pursued by women—but what women! (Consider the sordid comedy of his two marriages—the brummagem, star-spangled passion that invaded his very death-bed!) The thing, at the start, must have only bewildered him. But in those last days, unless I am a worse psychologist than even the professors of psychology, it was revolting him. Worse, it was making him afraid.

I incline to think that the inscrutable gods, in taking him off so soon and at a moment of fiery revolt, were very kind to him. Living, he would have tried inevitably to change his fame—if such it is to be called—into something closer to his heart's desire. That is to say, he would have gone the way of many another actor—the way of increasing pretension, of solemn artiness, of hollow hocus-pocus, deceptive only to himself. I believe he would have failed, for there was little sign of the genuine artist in him. He was essentially a highly respectable young man, which is the sort that never metamorphoses into an artist. But suppose he had succeeded? Then his tragedy, I believe, would have only become the more acrid and intolerable. For he would have discovered, after vast heavings and yearnings, that what he had come to was indistinguishable from what he had left. Was the fame of Beethoven any more caressing and splendid than the fame of Valentino? To you and me, of course, the question seems to answer itself. But what of Beethoven? He was heard upon the subject, *viva voce,* while he lived, and his answer survives, in all the freshness of its profane eloquence, in his music. Beethoven, too, knew what it meant to be applauded. Walking with Goethe, he heard something that was not unlike the murmur that reached Valentino through his hospital window. Beethoven walked away briskly. Valentino turned his face to the wall.

Here, after all, is the chiefest joke of the gods: that man must remain alone and lonely in this world, even with crowds surging about him. Does he crave approbation, with a sort of furious, instinctive lust? Then it is only to discover, when it comes, that it is somehow disconcerting—that its springs and motives offer an affront to his dignity. But do I sentimentalize the perhaps transparent story of a simple mummer? Then substitute Coolidge, or Mussolini, or any other poor devil that you can think of. Substitute Shakespeare, or Lincoln, or Goethe, or Beethoven, as I have. Sentimental or not, I confess that the predicament of poor Valentino touched me. It provided grist for my mill, but I couldn't quite enjoy it. Here was a young man who was living daily the dream of millions of other young men. Here was one who was catnip to women. Here was one who had wealth and fame. And here was one who was very unhappy.

John Dos Passos

Adagio Dancer

The nineteenyearold son of a veterinary in Castellaneta in the south of Italy was shipped off to America like a lot of other unmanageable young Italians when his parents gave up trying to handle him, to sink or swim and maybe send a few lire home by international postal moneyorder. The family was through with him. But Rodolfo Guglielmi wanted to make good.

He got a job as assistant gardener in Central Park but that kind of work was the last thing he wanted to do; he wanted to make good in the brightlights; money burned his pockets.

He hung around cabarets doing odd jobs, sweeping out for the waiters, washing cars; he was lazy handsome wellbuilt slender goodtempered and vain; he was a born tangodancer.

Lovehungry women thought he was a darling. He began to get engagements dancing the tango in ballrooms and cabarets; he teamed up with a girl named Jean Acker on a vaudeville tour and took the name of Rudolph Valentino.

Stranded on the Coast he headed for Hollywood, worked for a long time as an extra for five dollars a day; directors began to notice he photographed well.

He got his chance in *The Four Horsemen* and became the gigolo of every woman's dreams.

Excerpted from *U.S.A.* by John Dos Passos. Copyright by H. Marston Smith and Elizabeth H. Dos Passos, executors of the estate of John R. Dos Passos. By permission of Elizabeth H. Dos Passos.

Valentino spent his life in the colorless glare of klieg lights, in stucco villas obstructed with bricabrac oriental rugs tigerskins, in the bridalsuites of hotels, in silk bathrobes in private cars.

He was always getting into limousines or getting out of limousines,

or patting the necks of fine horses.

Wherever he went the sirens of the motorcyclecops screeched ahead of him

flashlights flared,

the streets were jumbled with hysterical faces, waving hands, crazy eyes; they stuck out their autographbooks, yanked his buttons off, cut a tail off his admirablytailored dress suit; they stole his hat and pulled at his necktie; his valets removed young women from under his bed; all night in nightclubs and cabarets actresses leching for stardom made sheepseyes at him under their mascaraed lashes.

He wanted to make good under the glare of the million-dollar searchlights

of El Dorado:

the Shcik, the Son of the Sheik;

personal appearances.

He married his old vaudeville partner, divorced her, married the adopted daughter of a millionaire, went into lawsuits with the producers who were debasing the art of the screen, spent a million dollars on one European trip;

he wanted to make good in the brightlights.

When the Chicago *Tribune* called him a pink powderpuff

and everybody started wagging their heads over a slave-bracelet he wore that he said his wife had given him and his taste for mushy verse of which he published a small volume called *Daydreams* and the whispers grew about the testimony in his divorce case that he and his first wife had never slept together, it broke his heart.

He tried to challenge the Chicago *Tribune* to a duel;

he wanted to make good

in heman twofisted broncobusting pokerplaying stockjuggling America. (He was a fair boxer and had a good seat on a horse, he loved the desert like the sheik and was tanned from the sun of Palm Springs.) He broke down in his suite in the Hotel Ambassador in New York: gastric ulcer.

When the doctors cut into his elegantlymolded body they found that peritonitis had begun; the abdominal cavity contained a large amount of fluid and food particles; the viscera were coated with a greenishgrey film; a round hole a centimeter in diameter was seen in the anterior wall of the stomach; the tissue of the stomach for one and onehalf centimeters immediately surrounding the perforation was necrotic. The appendix was inflamed and twisted against the small intestine.

When he came to from the ether the first thing he said was, "Well, did I behave like a pink powderpuff?"

His expensively massaged actor's body fought peritonitis for six days.

The switchboard at the hospital was swamped with calls, all the corridors were piled with flowers, crowds filled the street outside, filmstars who claimed they were his betrothed entrained for New York.

Late in the afternoon a limousine drew up at the hospital door (where the grimyfingered newspapermen and photographers stood around bored tired hoteyed smoking too many cigarettes making trips to the nearest speak exchanging wisecracks and deep dope waiting for him to die in time to make the evening papers) *and a woman, who said she was a maid employed by a dancer who was Valentino's first wife, alighted. She delivered to an attendant an envelope addressed to the filmstar and in-*

scribed from Jean, and a package. The package contained a white counterpane with lace ruffles and the word Rudy embroidered in the four corners. This was accompanied by a pillowcover to match over a blue silk scented cushion.

Rudolph Valentino was only thirtyone when he died.

His managers planned to make a big thing of his highly-publicized funeral but the people in the streets were too crazy.

While he lay in state in a casket covered with a cloth of gold, tens of thousands of men, women, and children packed the streets outside. Hundreds were trampled, had their feet hurt by policehorses. In the muggy rain the cops lost control. Jammed masses stampeded under the clubs and the rearing hoofs of the horses. The funeral chapel was gutted, men and women fought over a flower, a piece of wallpaper, a picce of the broken plateglass window. Showwindows were burst in. Parked cars were overturned and smashed. When finally the mounted police after repeated charges beat the crowd off Broadway, where traffic was tied up for two hours, they picked up twenty-eight separate shoes, a truckload of umbrellas, papers, hats, torn-off sleeves. All the ambulances in that part of the city were busy carting off women who'd fainted, girls who'd been stepped on. Epileptics threw fits. Cops collected little groups of abandoned children.

The fascisti sent a guard of honor and the antifascists drove them off. More rioting, cracked skulls, trampled feet. When the public was barred from the undertaking parlors hundreds of women groggy with headlines got in to view the poor body

claiming to be exdancingpartners, old playmates, relatives from the old country, filmstars; every few minutes a girl fainted in front of the bier and was revived by the newspapermen who put down her name and address and claim to notice in the public prints. Frank E. Campbell's undertakers and pallbearers, dignified wearers of black broadcloth and tackersup of crape, were on the verge of a nervous breakdown. Even the boss had his fill of publicity that time.

It was two days before the cops could clear the streets enough to let the flowerpieces from Hollywood be brought in and described in the evening papers.

The church service was more of a success. The police-commissioner barred the public for four blocks round.

Many notables attended.

America's Sweetheart sobbing bitterly in a small black straw with a black band and a black bow behind, in black georgette over black with a white lace collar and white lace cuffs followed the coffin that was

covered by a blanket of pink roses

sent by a filmstar who appeared at the funeral heavily veiled and swooned and had to be taken back to her suite at the Hotel Ambassador after she had shown the reporters a message allegedly written by one of the doctors alleging that Rudolph Valentino had spoken of her at the end

as his bridetobe.

A young woman committed suicide in London.

Relatives arriving from Europe were met by police reserves and Italian flags draped with crape. Exchamp Jim Jeffries said, "Well, he made good." The champion himself allowed himself to be quoted that the boy was fond of boxing and a great admirer of the champion.

The funeral train left for Hollywood.

In Chicago a few more people were hurt trying to see the coffin, but only made the inside pages.

The funeral train arrived in Hollywood on page 23 of the New York *Times*.

Ernest Hemingway

A Tribute to Mamma from Papa Hemingway

The following comments on Marlene [Dietrich] were written specially for LIFE *by novelist Ernest Hemingway. Like all his other friends, she calls him "Papa." He calls her sometimes "Mamma" and sometimes "Kraut."*

She is brave, beautiful, loyal, kind and generous. She is never boring and is as lovely looking in the morning in a GI shirt, pants and combat boots as she is at night on the screen. She has an honesty and a comic and tragic sense of life that never let her be truly happy unless she loves. When she loves she can joke about it; but it is gallows humor.

If she had nothing more than her voice she could break your heart with it. But she has that beautiful body and the timeless loveliness of her face. It makes no difference how she breaks your heart if she is there to mend it.

She cannot be cruel nor unjust but she can be angry and fools bore her and she shows it unless the fool is in bad trouble. Anyone who is in serious enough trouble has her sympathy.

If this makes her sound too perfect, you should know that she can destroy any competing woman without even noticing her. She does it sometimes for fun and then tosses the man

From "A Tribute to Mamma" by Ernest Hemingway, *Life* Magazine, August 18, 1952, © 1952 Time Inc. By permission of *Life*.

back where he belongs. She has a strange, for these times, code that will not let her take a man away from another woman if the woman wants him.

We know each other very well and are very fond of each other. When we meet we tell each other everything that has happened in between times and I don't think we ever lie to each other unless it is very necessary on a temporary basis.

All the wonderful stories I could tell you about Marlene are not for *Life*. She would not mind and I would not mind. But many people would. Marlene makes her own rules in this life but the standards of conduct and of decency in human relationships that she imposes on herself are no less strict than the original ten.

That is probably what makes her mysterious: that anyone so beautiful and talented and able to do what she wants should only do what she believes to be absolutely right and to have had the intelligence and the courage to make the rules she follows.

She loves writing and is an intelligent and scrupulous critic and the happiest time I have is when I have written something that I am sure is good and she reads it and likes it. Since she knows about the things I write about which are people, country, life and death and problems of honor and of conduct, I value her opinion more than that of many critics. Since she knows about love, and knows that it is a thing which exists or does not exist, I value her opinion there more than that of the professors. For I think she knows more about love than anyone.

My wife Mary admires Marlene and thinks she is one of the finest women in the world. She knows some fine and wonderful stories too. But she said she would rather put it that way.

I know that everytime I have seen Marlene Dietrich ever, it has done something to my heart and made me happy. If this makes her mysterious then it is a fine mystery. It is a mystery we have known about for a long time.

James Baldwin

Sidney Poitier

The first time I met Sidney, I walked up to him at an airport. He didn't know me, but I admired him very much, and I told him so. I've never done that with anyone, before or since, and Sidney looked at me as though he thought I was crazy, but he was very nice about it. Some years later, I really met him. We were both in Philadelphia. He was doing *A Raisin in the Sun,* and I was working with Kazan in *Sweet Bird of Youth,* and we hit it off.[1]

Then, of course, years passed. Things happened to Sidney; things happened to me. All artists who are friends have a strange relationship to each other; each knows what the other is going through, even though you may see each other only briefly, at functions, at benefits, at airports; and this is especially true, I think, for black artists in this country, and especially over the last several years. It's ironical indeed, but it's only the black artists in this country—and it's only beginning to change now— who have been called upon to fulfill their responsibilities as artists and, at the same time, insist on their responsibilities as citizens. As Ruby Dee once said to me, when we were working on the Christmas boycott campaign following the murder of the four little girls in Birmingham, "Soon, there won't be enough

From *Look* magazine, July 23, 1968. Reprinted by permission of Lantz-Donadio Literary Agency. Copyright © 1968/ by James Baldwin.

1. *A Raisin in the Sun:* the play by Lorraine Hansberry. *Sweet Bird of Youth:* the play by Tennessee Williams.

colored people to go around." She wasn't joking—I might add that that statement has, today, a rather sinister ring.

As the years passed, and given the system in which all American artists, and especially all American actors, work, I began to tremble for Sidney. I must state candidly that I think most Hollywood movies are a thunderous waste of time, talent and money, and I rarely see them. For example, I didn't think *Blackboard Jungle* was much of a movie—I know much more than *that* about the public-school system of New York—but I thought that Sidney was beautiful, vivid and truthful in it. He somehow escaped the film's framework, so much so that until today, his is the only performance I remember. Nor was I overwhelmed by *Cry, the Beloved Country*,[2] but Sidney's portrait, brief as it was, of the young priest, was a moving miracle of indignation. That was the young Sidney, and I sensed that I was going to miss him, in exactly the same way I will always miss the young Marlon of *Truckline Cafe* and *Streetcar Named Desire*. But then, I miss the young Jimmy Baldwin too.

All careers, if they are real careers—and there are not as many of these occurring as one might like to think—are stormy and dangerous, with turning points as swift and dizzying as hair-breadth curves on mountain roads. And I think that America may be the most dangerous country in the world for artists—whatever creative form they may choose. That would be all right if it were also exhilarating, but most of the time, it isn't. It's mostly sweat and terror. This is because the nature of the society isolates its artists so severely for their vision; penalizes them so mercilessly for their vision and endeavor; and the American form of recognition, fame and money, can be the most devastating penalty of all. This is not the artist's fault, though I think that the artist will have to take the lead in changing this state of affairs.

2. *Blackboard Jungle* (1955), directed by Richard Brooks. *Cry, the Beloved Country* (1951), directed by Zoltan Korda.

The isolation that menaces all American artists is multiplied a thousand times, and becomes absolutely crucial and dangerous for all black artists. "Know whence you came," Sidney once said to me, and Sidney, his detractors to the contrary, *does* know whence he came. But it can become very difficult to remain in touch with all that nourishes you when you have arrived at Sidney's eminence and are in the interesting, delicate and terrifying position of being part of a system that you know you have to change.

Let me put it another way: I wish that both Marlon and Sidney would return to the stage, but I can certainly see why they don't. Broadway is almost as expensive as Hollywood, is even more hazardous, is at least as incompetent, and the scripts, God knows, aren't any better. Yet I can't but feel that this is a great loss, both for the actor and the audience.

I will always remember seeing Sidney in *A Raisin in the Sun.* It says a great deal about Sidney, and it also says, negatively, a great deal about the regime under which American artists work, that that play would almost certainly never have been done if Sidney had not agreed to appear in it. Sidney has a fantastic presence on the stage, a dangerous electricity that is rare indeed and lights up everything for miles around. It was a tremendous thing to watch and to be made a part of. And one of the things that made it so tremendous was the audience. Not since I was a kid in Harlem, in the days of the Lafayette Theatre, had I seen so many black people in the theater. And they were there because the life on that stage said something to them concerning their own lives. The communion between the actors and the audience was a real thing; they nourished and recreated each other. This hardly ever happens in the American theater. And this is a much more sinister fact than we would like to think. For one thing, the reaction of that audience to Sidney and to that play says a great deal about the continuing and accumulating despair of the black people in this country, who find nowhere any faint reflection of the lives they actually lead. And it is for this reason that every Negro celebrity is regarded with some distrust by black people, who have every reason in the world to feel themselves abandoned.

I ought to add, for this also affects any estimate of any black star, that the popular culture certainly does not reflect the truth concerning the lives led by white people either; but white Americans appear to be under the compulsion to dream, whereas black Americans are under the compulsion to awaken. And this fact is also sinister.

I am not a television fan either, and I very much doubt that future generations will be vastly edified by what goes on on the American television screen. TV commercials drive me up the wall. And yet, as long as there is *that screen* and there are *those commercials,* it is important to hip the American people to the fact that black people also brush their teeth and shave and drink beer and smoke cigarettes—though it may take a little more time for the American people to recognize that we also shampoo our hair. It is of the utmost importance that a black child see on that screen *someone who looks like him.* Our children have been suffering from the lack of identifiable images for as long as our children have been born.

Yet, there's a difficulty, there's a rub, and it's precisely the nature of this difficulty that has brought Sidney under attack. The industry is compelled, given the way it is built, to present to the American people a self-perpetuating fantasy of American life. It considers that its job is to entertain the American people. Their concept of entertainment is difficult to distinguish from the use of narcotics, and to watch the TV screen for any length of time is to learn some really frightening things about the American sense of reality. *And the black face, truthfully reflected, is not only no part of this dream, it is antithetical to it.* And this puts the black performer in a rather grim bind. He knows, on the one hand, that if the reality of a black man's life were on that screen, it would destroy the fantasy totally. And on the other hand, he really has no right *not* to appear, not only because he must work, but also for all those people who need to see him. By the use of his own person, he must smuggle in a reality that he knows is not in the script. A celebrated black TV actor once told me that he did an entire show for the sake of *one line*. He felt that he could convey something very important with that *one line*. Actors don't write their scripts, and they don't direct them. Black people have no power in this industry at all. Furthermore, the actor may be offered dozens of scripts before anything even remotely viable comes along.

Sidney is now a superstar. This must baffle a great many people, as, indeed, it must baffle Sidney. He is an extraordinary actor, as even his detractors must admit, but he's been that for a long time, and that doesn't really explain his eminence. He's also extraordinarily attractive and winning and virile, but that could just as easily have worked against him. It's something of a puzzle. Speaking now of the image and not of the man, it has to do with a quality of pain and danger and some fundamental impulse to decency that both titillates and reassures the white audience. For example, I'm glad I didn't write *The Defiant Ones,*[3] but I liked Sidney in it very much. And I suppose that his performance has something to do with what I mean by smuggling in reality. I remember one short scene, in close-up, when he's talking about his wife, who wants him to "be nice." Sidney's face, when he says, "She say, 'Be nice. Be nice,' " conveys a sorrow and humiliation rarely to be seen on our screen. But white people took that film far more seriously than black people did. When Sidney jumps off the train at the end because he doesn't want to leave his buddy, the white liberal people downtown were much relieved and joyful. But when black people saw him jump off the train, they yelled, "Get back on the

---

3. *The Defiant Ones* (1958) directed by Stanley Kramer; Sidney Poitier co-starred with Tony Curtis.

train, you fool!" That didn't mean that they hated Sidney: They just weren't going for the okey-doke. And if I point out that they were right, it doesn't mean that Sidney was wrong. That film was made to say something to white people. There was really nothing it *could* say to black people—except for the authority of Sidney's performance.

Black people have been robbed of everything in this country, and they don't want to be robbed of their artists. Black people particularly disliked *Guess Who's Coming to Dinner*,[4] which I made a point of seeing, because they felt that Sidney was, in effect, being used against them. I'm now on very delicate ground, and I know it, but I can't really duck this issue—because it's been raised so often. I can't pretend that the movie meant anything to me. It seemed a glib, good-natured comedy in which a lot of able people were being wasted. But, I told myself, this movie wasn't made for *you*. And I really don't know the people for whom it *was* made. I moved out of their world, insofar as this is ever possible, a long time ago. I remember the cheerful English lady in a wineshop in London who had seen this movie and adored it and adored the star. She was a nice lady, and certainly not a racist, and it would simply have been an unjust waste of time to get angry with her for knowing so little about black people. The hard fact is that most people, of whatever color, don't know much about each other because they don't care much about each other. Would the image projected by Sidney cause that English lady to be friendly to the next West Indian who walked into her shop? Would it cause her to *think*, in any real way, of the *reality*, the presence, the simple human *fact* of black people? Or was Sidney's black face simply, now, a part of a fantasy—the fantasy of her life, precisely—which she would never understand? This is a question posed by the com-

4. *Guess Who's Coming to Dinner* (1967) directed by Stanley Kramer.

munications media of the 20th century, and it is not a question anyone can answer with authority. One is gambling on the human potential of an inarticulate and unknown consciousness— that of the people. This consciousness has never been of such crucial importance in the world before. But one knows that the work of the world gets itself done in very strange ways, by means of very strange instruments, and takes a very long time. And I also thought that *Guess Who's Coming to Dinner* may prove, in some bizarre way, to be a milestone, because it is really quite impossible to go any further in that particular direction. The next time, the kissing will have to start.

I thought of something else, something very difficult to convey. I remember a night in London, when Diana Sands was starring in *The Owl and the Pussycat*. There were about four or five of us, walking to some discotheque, and with us was a very angry, young, black cat. Across the street from us was Sidney's name in lights in some movie I've not seen. Now, I understand the angry, young, black cat, and he was right to be angry. He was not angry at Sidney, but at the world. But I knew there was no point in saying that at the time I was born, the success of a Sidney Poitier or a Diana Sands was not to be imagined. I don't mean to congratulate the American people on what they like to call progress, because it certainly isn't. The careers of all black artists in this country prove that. Time passes and phenomena occur in time. The *presence* of Sidney, the precedent set, is of tremendous importance for people coming afterward. And perhaps that's what it's really all about—just that.

Sidney, as a black artist, and a man, is also up against the infantile, furtive sexuality of this country. Both he and Harry Belafonte, for example, are sex symbols, though no one dares admit that, still less to use them as any of the Hollywood he-men are used. In spite of the fabulous myths proliferating in this country concerning the sexuality of black people, black men are still used, in the popular culture, as though they had no sexual equipment at all. This is what black men, and black women, too, deeply resent.

I think it's important to remember, in spite of the fact we've been around so long, that Sidney is younger than I, and I'm not an old man yet. It takes a long time in this business, if you survive in it at all, to reach the eminence that will give you the power to change things. Sidney has that power now, to the limited extent that *anyone* in this business has. It will be very interesting to see what he does with it. In my mind, there's no limit to what he might become.

But Sidney, like all of us, is caught in a storm. Let me tell you one thing about him, which has to do with how black artists particularly need each other. Sidney had read *Another Country* before it came out. He liked it, and he knew how frightened I was about the book's reception. I'd been in Europe, and I came back for the publication because I didn't want anyone to think I was afraid to be here. My publisher gave a party at Big Wilt's Smalls Paradise in Harlem. Sidney came very early. I was ready to meet the mob, but I was scared to death, and Sidney knew it, and he walked me around the block and talked to me and helped me get myself together. And then he walked me back, and the party was starting. And when he realized that I was all right, he split. And I realized for the first time that he had only come for that. He hadn't come for the party at all.

And the following may also make a small, malicious point. There's speculation that the central figure of my new novel, who is a black actor, is based on Sidney. Nothing could be further from the truth, but people naturally think that, because when they look around them, Sidney's the only black actor they see. Well, that fact says a great deal more about this country than it says about black actors, or Sidney, or me.

Notes on Authors

Louis Aragon (1897–   ), French poet, novelist and essayist. Author of numerous volumes of poetry, many social problem novels, and *Holy Week* (1958), an epic about Louis XVIII.

James Baldwin (1924–   ), American novelist and essayist. Author of *The Fire Next Time* (1963).

Bertolt Brecht (1898–1956), German dramatist. Author of *Mother Courage and her Children* (1939).

Truman Capote (1924–   ), American novelist. Author of *In Cold Blood* (1965).

G. K. Chesterton (1874–1936), British novelist, essayist, biographer, poet, journalist. Author of *The Man Who Was Thursday* (1908).

Jean Cocteau (1889–1963), French poet, dramatist, novelist, film-maker. Author of *Les Enfants Terribles* (1930); director of *Orphée* (1949).

Gabriele D'Annunzio (1863–1938), Italian poet, dramatist, novelist, soldier and man of action. Author of *Il Fuoco* (1900).

John Dos Passos (1896–1970), American novelist. Author of the trilogy *U.S.A.* (1938).

Theodore Dreiser (1871–1945), American novelist. Author of *An American Tragedy* (1925).

T. S. Eliot (1888–1965), American-born, naturalized British poet, dramatist, critic. Author of *The Waste Land* (1922) and *Murder in the Cathedral* (1935).

James T. Farrell (1904–   ), American novelist. Author of the *Studs Lonigan* trilogy.

William Faulkner (1897–1962), American novelist. Author of *The Sound and the Fury* (1929).

F. Scott Fitzgerald (1896–1940), American novelist. Author of *The Great Gatsby* (1925).

E. M. Forster (1879–1970), British novelist and essayist. Author of *A Passage to India* (1924).

ANDRE GIDE (1869–1951), French novelist, poet, editor. Author of *The Immoralist* (1902).

MAXIM GORKY (1868–1936), Russian novelist and dramatist. Author of *The Lower Depths* (1902).

GRAHAM GREENE (1904–1948), British novelist. Author of *The Heart of the Matter* (1948).

ERNEST HEMINGWAY (1899–1961), American novelist. Author of *For Whom the Bell Tolls* (1940).

W. D. HOWELLS (1837–1920), American novelist, critic, poet, editor. Author of *The Rise of Silas Lapham* (1885).

ALDOUS HUXLEY (1894–1963), British novelist, essayist and poet. Author of *Brave New World* (1932).

HENRY ARTHUR JONES (1851–1929), British dramatist. Author of *Michael and his Lost Angel* (1896).

JACK KEROUAC (1922–1969), American novelist and poet of the Beat Generation. Author of *On the Road* (1957).

JACK LONDON (1876–1916), American novelist. Author of *The Sea-Wolf* (1904).

HEINRICH MANN (1871–1950), German novelist, brother of Thomas Mann. Author of *Professor Unrat* (1905) on which the film *The Blue Angel* was based.

THOMAS MANN (1875–1955), German novelist. Author of *The Magic Mountain* (1924).

W. SOMERSET MAUGHAM (1874–1965), British novelist and dramatist. Author of the novel *Of Human Bondage* (1915).

H. L. MENCKEN (1880–1956), American essayist, critic, editor, and co-founder with George Jean Nathan of *The American Mercury*. Author of *The American Language* (1919–1948).

FRANK NORRIS (1870–1902), American novelist. Author of *McTeague* (1899).

CARL SANDBURG (1878–1967), American poet, historian, folklorist. Author of *Abraham Lincoln* (1926–1939).

JEAN-PAUL SARTRE (1905–   ), French philosopher, novelist, dramatist. Author of *L'Etre et le Néant* (1943).

G. BERNARD SHAW (1856–1950), Irish dramatist, novelist, critic, social reformer. Author of *Man and Superman* (1903).

Upton Sinclair (1878–1968), American novelist and muckraking journalist. Author of *The Jungle* (1906).

Leo Tolstoy (1828–1910), Russian novelist and dramatist. Author of *War and Peace* (1864–1869).

H. G. Wells (1866–1946), British novelist. Author of *The Time Machine* (1895) and *Tono-Bungay* (1909).

Virginia Woolf (1882–1941), British novelist, essayist, and critic. Author of *The Waves* (1931).

Index